AIRCRAFT

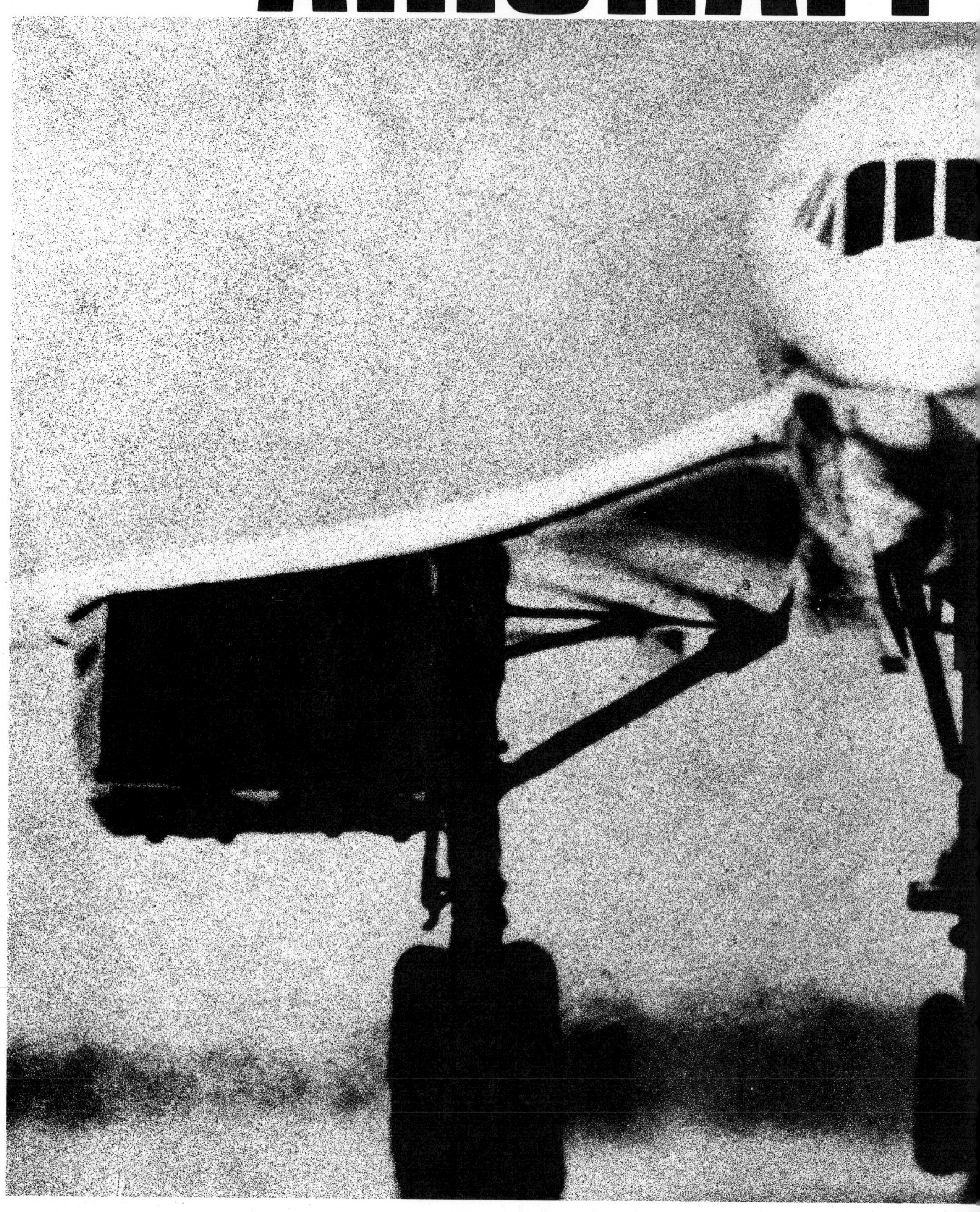

& AIRPORTS

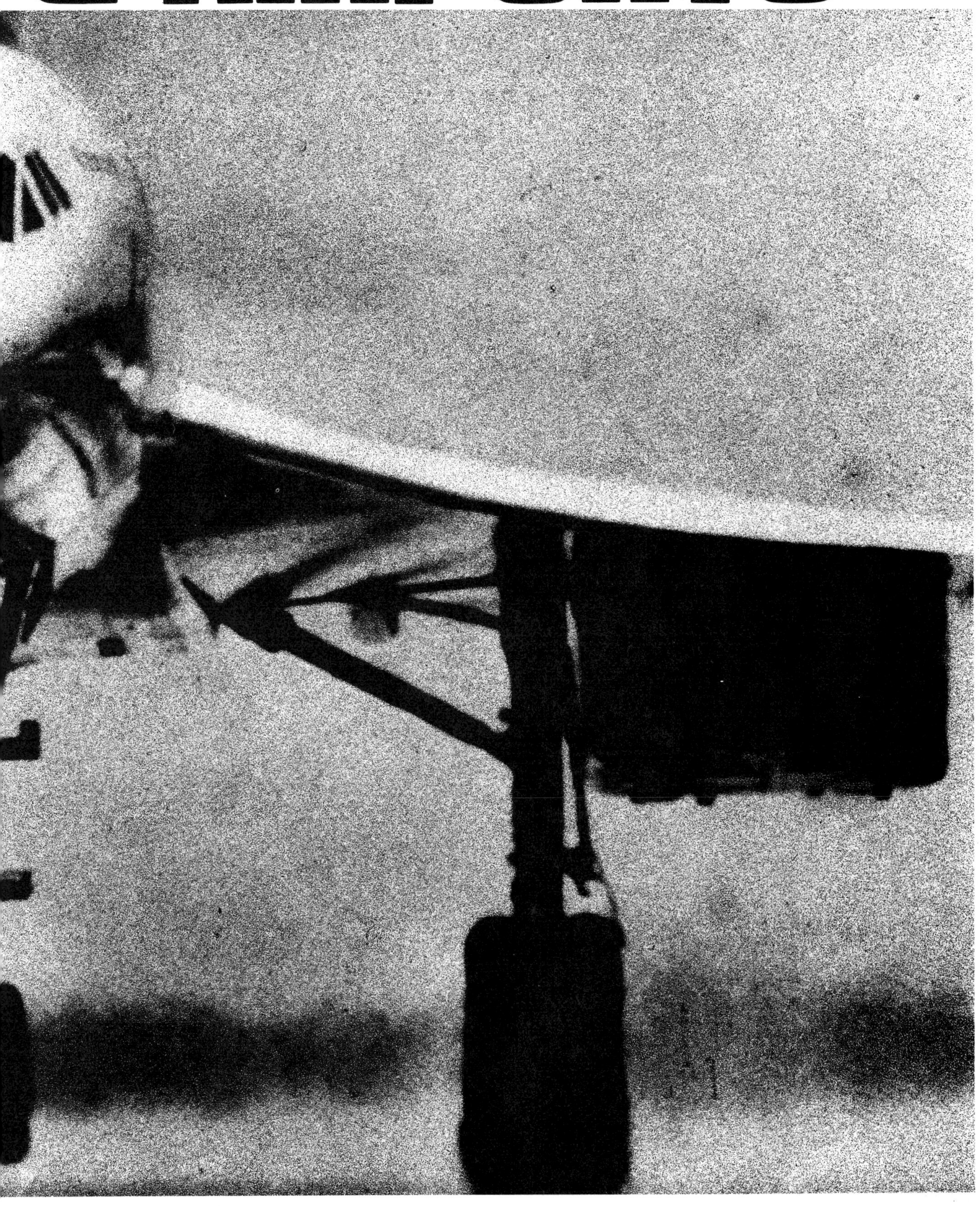

Marshall Cavendish London & New York

Edited by Donald Clarke
Published by Marshall Cavendish Books Limited
58 Old Compton Street, London W1V 5PA

Printed in Great Britain

ISBN 0 85685 430 1

This material has previously appeared in the publication *How It Works*

INTRODUCTION

It is not very often in the history of technology that an achievement can be precisely credited, but there is no doubt that Wilbur and Orville Wright were the first to fly a powered heavier-than-air craft. Balloons, airships and gliders had contributed to the pool of knowledge of flight; Hiram Maxim's steam-powered flying machine actually lifted itself off the rails in 1894, but the rails themselves were designed to prevent free flight. It was not until Kitty Hawk in 1903 that Man was finally able to imitate the birds.

For it was only with the combination of aerodynamic design and a suitable powerplant that the practical experience of flight could begin to be collated. Only six years later, Bleriot flew across the English Channel. Only 24 years after Kitty Hawk, Lindbergh flew alone across the Atlantic. And less than 45 years after the success of the Wright Brothers, men could fly faster than the speed of sound. Since the ancient dream of flight became a reality, its development has been astonishingly rapid.

Aircraft and Airports tells the whole exciting story: from the Montgolfier balloon of 1783 through Otto Lilienthal's successful glider experiments to the Concorde, and even the aerodynamic aspects of the proposed space-shuttle craft. The technology is explained with the help of diagrams and cut-away views; flight electronics, aerial photography and many other aspects are fully elucidated. The book is a concise, yet remarkably complete record of the most exciting chapter in the history of technology.

CONTENTS

MODERN AVIATION

A 1911 Blériot monoplane with a 50 hp Gnome engine in a garage in King Street, Brighton, England.

THE PIONEER PERIOD

BALLOONS AND AIRSHIPS

The first manned flight took place by means of a hot air balloon, on 21 November 1783. The balloon, made by the Montgolfier brothers Joseph and Etienne, paper manufacturers, was 75 ft (23 m) high by nearly 50 ft (15 m) in diameter—a frail affair of cloth backed with paper and heated by a furnace burning chopped straw. The pilots were Pilatre de Rozier and the Marquis d'Arlandes.

Only a few weeks later Jacques Charles, also French, made the first ascent in a hydrogen-filled balloon, and almost at once the gas balloon established itself as superior to the hot air version. Although it took longer to inflate it was quiet, easier to handle, lifted more, and above all could be used again. The hot air balloons had a tendency, not surprisingly, to set themselves alight or at least to finish their flights in a charred and brittle condition.

The use of hydrogen balloons grew unchecked until the development of airships. They proved useful in both research and war, in the latter particularly as military observation platforms, for which purpose they were used by both sides in the American Civil War and again in World War I. They were generally captive balloons, anchored to the ground by long cables. In sport, they reached their peak in the famous Gordon Bennett races which took place in Europe between 1906 and 1938, in which the greatest distance covered was 1368 miles (2191 km).

In 1955 the US Navy were operating blimps (small airships) for offshore patrols, and pilots were being trained on gas balloons. In an attempt to cut costs, the Navy sponsored a programme to develop hot air balloons and this culminated in a practical design being produced by a company in South Dakota in 1963. The Navy lost interest in the project, but the company decided to market the design as a sporting balloon, and the modern re-usable hot air balloon was born. Hot air balloons are now manufactured in varying sizes from 30,000 to 140,000 cu ft (850 to 3964 m^3) to carry from one to six people.

A balloon is a lighter-than-air unpowered aircraft. Unlike heavier-than-air machines, which stay airborne by moving through the air to create dynamic lift, a balloon obtains its lift by displacement, which is a static force and does not require movement through the air to create it. An airship is fitted with one or more engines and also with controls (rudder and elevators), but a balloon has no engine and cannot be steered: it merely drifts with the wind.

A balloon is in equilibrium, that is, balanced in the air and not moving up or down, when its total weight is the same as the weight of the volume of air it is occupying, or displacing. Since the fabric, basket, crew, and equipment are all heavier than air, they must be balanced by filling the envelope with some gas lighter than air. When the difference between the weight of the gas in the envelope and the outside air is the same as the weight of all the components making up the balloon, including the passengers, the balloon will be in equilibrium.

Gases which are lighter than air, and therefore suitable for filling a balloon, include hydrogen, helium, and ordinary air which has been heated. Some gases are lighter than air because the weight of their molecules is less than the average weight of the molecules in the air, that is, they have a lower density than air. Hot air is lighter than cold air because any gas expands when heated. The molecules are driven further apart and therefore a given volume will contain a lower weight of molecules. At sea level 1000 cu ft (28 m^3) of air at 212°F (100°C) will have a lifting capacity of 17.4 lb (7.9 kg) when the surrounding air is at 60°F (16°C). A similar amount of helium has a lifting capacity of 65 lb (29.5 kg), and for hydrogen the lift available is 70 lb (31.75 kg).

From the point of view of lift alone, it is obvious that the best thing to fill a balloon with is hydrogen and the worst is hot air. Ordinary coal gas can, and has been, used to fill balloons. Its disadvantage is that it varies considerably in purity, and the lift obtainable is therefore very unpredictable. The domestic gas of today weighs more than the gas available in the early days of ballooning. Gases are expensive, since they have to be extracted from the air and transported. It costs considerably more to inflate a hydrogen balloon than it does to inflate a hot air balloon. Hydrogen is highly in-

flammable, but helium, which is safer because it neither burns nor forms explosive mixtures with air, is much more expensive than hydrogen in most countries, except the USA.

These factors aside, there are other aspects of gas and hot air which have resulted in the development of two distinct types of balloon, different in design, performance, and to some extent in the manner in which they are controlled.

Gas balloons

Hydrogen easily penetrates most materials and the fabric of a hydrogen balloon envelope is therefore quite heavy, about half the total weight of the balloon, made from fabric impregnated with rubber or neoprene. The envelope is spherical, the most efficient shape to contain a given volume, and is contained in a string net which distributes the load evenly over the fabric. Below the envelope, the net is drawn together at a load ring, from which a basket to carry crew and equipment is suspended.

The envelope is not sealed: at the bottom is a long narrow open tube called the appendix. As the balloon rises, atmospheric pressure decreases and the gas in the balloon expands. The appendix allows gas to escape, thus preventing the balloon from bursting as a result of its internal pressure. When the balloon descends, the appendix closes (like a wet drinking straw if it is sucked too hard). This prevents air from getting into the balloon and forming an explosive mixture with the hydrogen.

To ascend in a hydrogen balloon it is necessary to reduce weight by discharging ballast in the form of sand, since lift cannot be increased. Similarly in order to descend it is necessary to reduce lift, since additional ballast cannot be obtained while airborne. This is done by opening a small valve in the top of the balloon; the valve is operated by a cord down to the basket and is held shut by springs or elastic. The height to which a balloon can rise is limited because the density of the atmosphere decreases (the air becomes thinner) as the height above sea level increases. Therefore, as the balloon rises, the air around it becomes less dense, until it reaches a height at which the atmospheric density is as low as the total density of the balloon. At this point, as the densities are equal, the balloon is in equilibrium with the air and will not rise any further.

The small valve and the ballast are the only forms of control in a gas balloon. Once the balloon is in equilibrium, they will not need to be used much unless the balloon is affected by outside factors, such as a general cooling or heating of the outside air, which will cause the lifting gas to contract or expand. Gas balloons, therefore, have very good endurance. On the other hand, every manoeuvre in a gas balloon is a 'wasting' process: even to descend it is necessary to get rid of gas.

Operationally, then, the main advantages of gas balloons are endurance and lifting power. The main disadvantages are the cost and inconvenience of inflating the balloon, a process which can take as long as two hours.

Hot air balloons

Modern hot air balloons are almost the only really significant design development to have taken place since balloons were invented. Despite their relatively poor lifting power and endurance, they have been responsible for a tremendous upsurge in the sport because of their low running costs, their simplicity, and their safety.

Structurally a hot air balloon is quite different from a gas balloon. Hot air cannot penetrate fabrics in the way that hydrogen can: the envelope is therefore made of very light material, usually rip-proof nylon treated with polyurethane to reduce porosity.

The profile of a hot air balloon is termed 'natural shape': wide at the top tapering towards the bottom in the shape naturally created by the internal pressure. Loads are carried on tubular nylon tapes sewn into and integral with the envelope. From these tapes, steel wires lead down to the burner, which is in the same position as the load ring on a gas balloon.

Left: an engraving of the first manned hydrogen balloon flight, in December 1783. The flight began at the Tuileries Palace in Paris and ended in a field near Nesle, a distance of 27 miles (43 km).

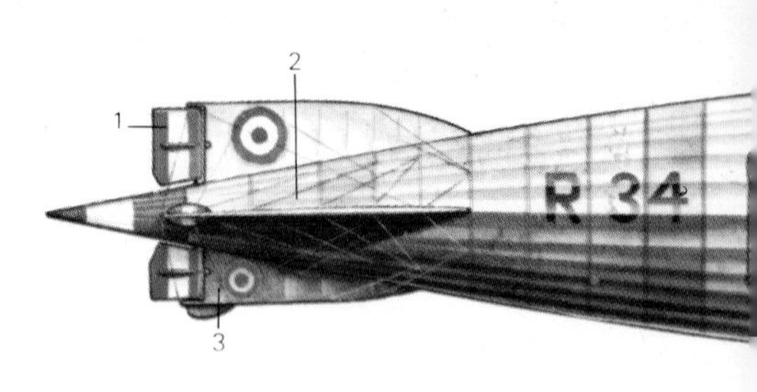

The basket is suspended from the burner by steel wires or a rigid structure, depending on the manufacturer. At the base of the balloon there is a large opening to allow heat from the burner to enter. A modern hot air balloon burner uses propane, which is fed under its own bottle pressure to the burner jets. The heat generated may be anything from 3 to 5 million Btu per hour, much more than many industrial space heaters.

Hot air balloons are fundamentally different from gas balloons in that it is possible to increase or decrease the lift simply by heating the air or allowing it to cool. Ballast and valve are therefore not strictly necessary. When flying a hot air balloon the pilot simply turns on the burner if he wants to ascend, and leaves it off and allows the air to cool if he wants to descend. The air in fact takes some time to cool, and the burner can be left off for quite long periods before the balloon starts to lose height. Inflation can be accomplished in a matter of minutes and this compensates for the relatively poor endurance of hot air balloons (up to about five hours depending on the load), since several flights can be made in a single day.

One control is common to both types of balloon. This is the ripping panel, a panel in or near the top of the balloon which can be opened quickly on landing to deflate the balloon rapidly. Unless this panel is opened the balloon acts like a sail and can drag the basket and its occupants a considerable distance. In the early days before the ripping panel was invented (in 1839), balloonists were on occasions dragged literally miles over the countryside before being stopped by a tree or similar obstacle. Hot air balloon ripping panels are held closed with a self fastening material such as Velcro, and can be secured ready for flight in minutes. Gas balloon panels have to be sewn and gummed to prevent leakage.

The airship

There are, or have been, three categories of airship: rigid, semi-rigid and non-rigid. The rigid types consisted of a light metal framework containing several gasbags slung inside under nets, and with a separate outer cover. The German Zeppelins and most airships of the 1920s and 1930s were this type. The metals used were aluminium alloys, the outer skin was of cotton, and the gasbags were cotton lined with 'goldbeater's skin', a thin membrane taken from the intestines of cows.

The other types, semi-rigid and non-rigid, are known as pressure airships since their shape is maintained mostly by the internal pressure. The semi-rigid types had a metal keel along the length of the envelope. The *Norge*, an Italian airship which flew from Rome to Alaska over the North Pole in 1926, was a semi-rigid craft. (Airships were also called

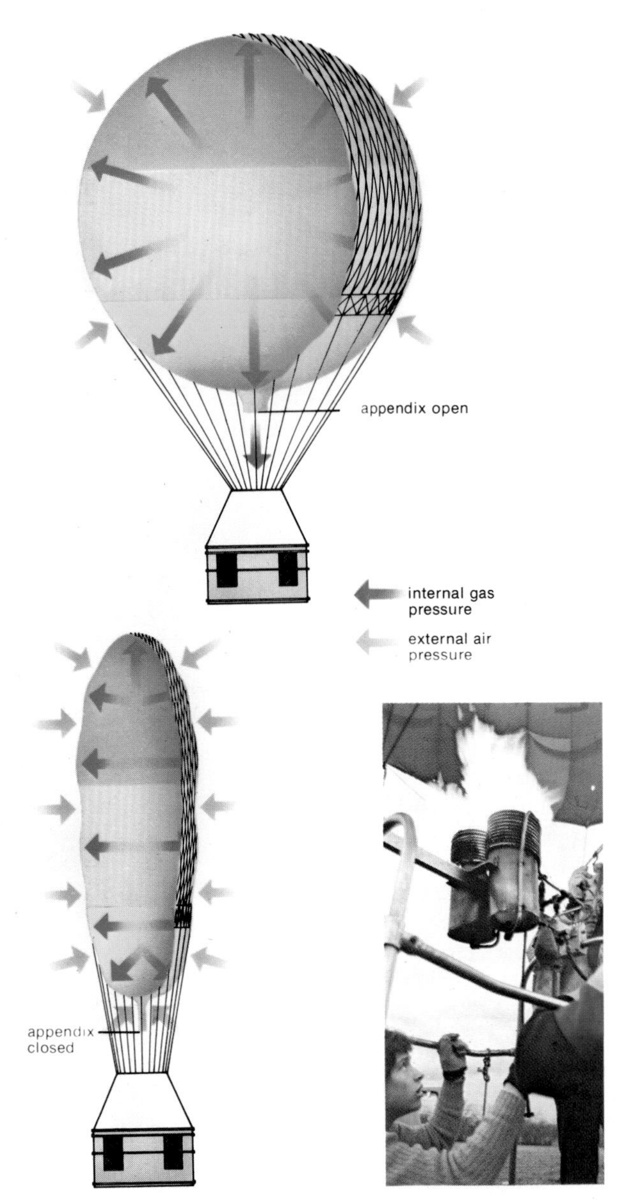

Left top: Most hydrogen balloons have an opening called an appendix to allow gas to escape if the pressure gets too high. The pressure inside the balloon goes up as it ascends because the air pressure outside it is going down. When the two pressures are equal the appendix automatically closes. Balloons intended to go very high are under-inflated.
Left: inflating a hot-air balloon.

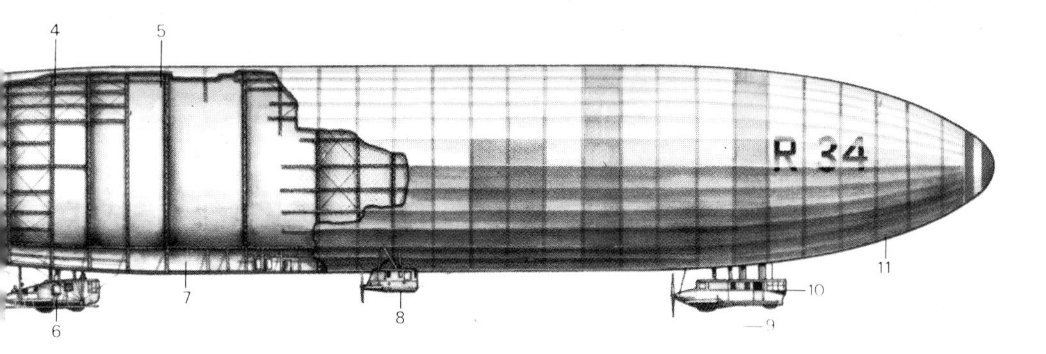

Left: *the British airship R34 made the first double crossing of the Atlantic by air in July 1919, taking about 11 days. Her length was 643 feet (196m) and diameter was 79 feet (24m). Top speed was about 55 mph (88 kph).*
Below: a Goodyear blimp over New York.

1 vertical stabilizer
2 horizontal stabilizer
3 landing skid
4 aluminium alloy framework
5 gasbags
6 rear car
7 corridor inside framework connecting front and rear cars and crew accommodation (not shown)
8 starboard power car (port car not shown)
9 radio aerial
10 front power car and control cabin
11 fabric outer skin
12 propeller
13 compressed air landing bag
14 engine oil cooler
15 handling rail
16 access ladder

dirigibles, because they were balloons which could be steered, from the Latin verb *dirigere;* to direct.)

The only type still used today is the non-rigid or blimp, which has no internal framework. Modern airships are made in this way of a synthetic fibre, Dacron, coated with neoprene, a man-made rubber. Aluminium paint on the outside reflects the sun's light and heat, reducing the extent to which the interior is heated. Battens on the nose prevent the wind pressure from flattening it when the craft is moving.

Early airships used to control lift by releasing gas and replacing it with air, a wasteful method that caused a gradual reduction of lift as more and more gas was lost. This could be compensated for by carrying water ballast, which could be released to lighten the airship. But later airships replaced the system with ballonets, collapsible air bags inside the gasbag but connected to the outside air. By varying the amount of air in these with pumps, the volume of the gas in the rest of the bag can be changed. There are usually two ballonets, to the forward and rear of the gasbag, so that the balance of the ship can be adjusted.

The tailfins operate just like those on an aircraft, and are the control surfaces by which the ship is steered. Conventional elevators are used to change the altitude of the craft when it is moving; the change of atmospheric pressure with altitude is compensated for automatically by varying the amount of air in the ballonets.

The lightest gas is hydrogen, which is comparatively cheap to manufacture. But its extreme flammability has resulted in the much more expensive, slightly less effective, but completely safe helium being used in all modern airships. Helium is found in small amounts with natural gas in the United States, but is otherwise very expensive to produce in large quantities.

In the beginning it was France that led the way. After the invention of the balloon in 1783, ways were sought of making it independent of the direction of the wind. The problem was to produce a suitably light yet powerful means of propulsion, and it was Henri Giffard who first produced a 3 hp engine weighing 350 lb (160 kg). His 70,500 cu ft (2000 m^3) hydrogen-filled craft ascended from the Hippodrome in Paris in 1852, and flew at 6 mile/h (9 km/h). There was an improvement on this in 1884 when the French built another airship, *La France*, which achieved a top speed of 15 mile/h (24 km/h) by means of a 9 hp electric motor.

Germany came into the picture in 1895 with the first rigid airship, built by David Schwarz. It was braced internally by a system of steel wires. Five years later, Count Zeppelin carried this idea further in his much bigger design, built at Friedrichshafen. This had an aluminium frame consisting of 16 hoops connected and kept rigid by wire stays longitudinally and diagonally. The design proved a success and although one was lost, more than 20 airships of the same type were built. On the power of two 15 hp Daimler engines, it made a speed of about 26 mile/h (42 km/h). In 1912, the latest of this class carried 23 passengers on a cruise of seven and a half hours. The Germans were thus well prepared to use airships for military purposes when war broke out in 1914.

The heyday of the giant rigid airships was in the late 20s and the 30s. The USA decided to use only helium in its airships, and banned its export. This meant that the large British and German craft had to rely upon hydrogen. The flammability of the gas and the lack of manoeuvrability of the ships often had appalling consequences. Many of the largest airships met with disaster, notably the British *R101* in 1930, the American *Akron* and *Macon* in 1933 and 1935, and the Zeppelin *Hindenburg* in 1937.

The heavy loss of life in these crashes swung opinion against the use of airships, and they were no longer used for carrying passengers. But later, during the Second World War, the USA used large numbers of non-rigid airships without a single loss for sea patrolling. Their ability to operate for long period of time at low speed and low altitude made them invaluable for detecting minefields and escorting convoys.

More recently, Goodyear have built four non-rigid airships, which are often used as vibration-free airborne platforms for television sports coverage.

Count F. von Zeppelin

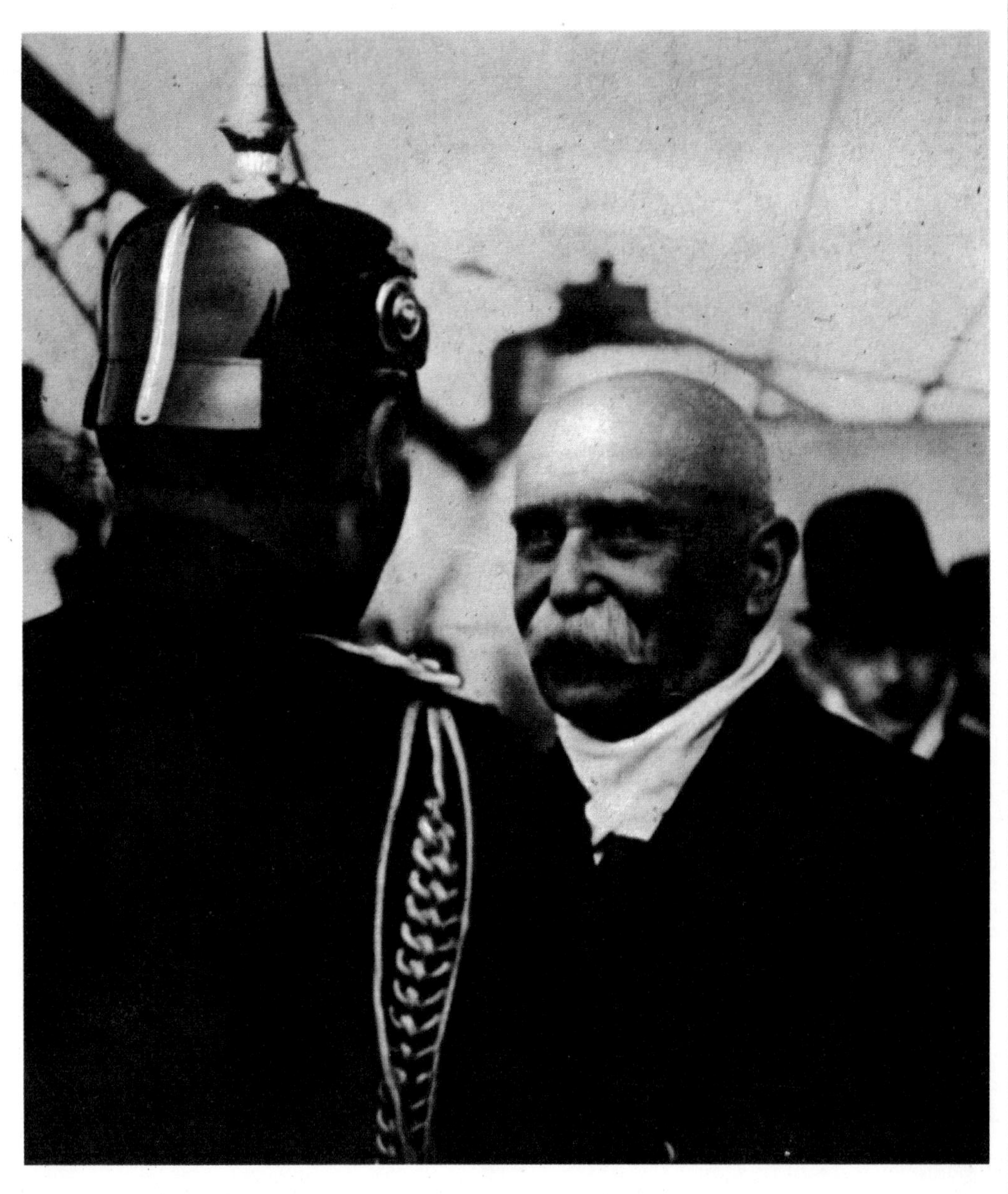

The name Zeppelin is known world wide as a highly successful range of German airships but less well known is the man after whom the airships were named. Ferdinand was born on 8 July 1838 at Constance in Germany, the son of Count Frederick von Zeppelin. As was the custom in Germany, he joined the army as a volunteer in the American Civil War. On reaching the rank of lieutenant-general he left the army and started a new career in aviation.

For several years Zeppelin and his staff worked on the design of a rigid airship, but they received little support. Most of the airships built previously had been of the non-rigid type which consisted of a sausage-shaped balloon with a cabin suspended below containing the crew, engines and control surfaces. These non-rigid airships became rather unwieldy when their size was increased—some were 290 ft (88 m) long—and Zeppelin was convinced that the answer was to house separate gas-bags inside a rigid framework. The framework was to be made up of a lightweight metal structure covered with fabric.

Zeppelin formed a company and built a huge floating shed on Lake Constance. Then he built his first airship, the LZ1, which was 420 ft (128 m) long and powered by two Daimler engines of only 16 hp each. On 2 July 1900 the LZ1 made its first flight, which was neither a failure nor a success. The method of control, using a rudder and moving weights, was not adequate and modifications were made before the next flight in October. The improvements were still not sufficient, and a new Zeppelin, LZ2, was planned with two 85 hp engines. After a poor first flight, LZ2 took off in January 1906 with the Count at the controls. She was flying reasonably well when both engines failed and a forced landing had to be made. LZ2 was moored for the night but a strong wind got up and she was wrecked. Zeppelin was determined to carry on. LZ3 followed in a few months and was a great success, and in 1908 the Count made a spectacular 12 hour flight over the Swiss Alps in LZ4.

The next great milestone in Count von Zeppelin's life was the founding of a new company to operate a passenger carrying service using Zeppelins. In 1909 this company, with the abbreviated name DELAG, was set up by Zeppelin, backed by the rich Colsman family. The first airship to be delivered was LZ7, *Deutschland*, and in June 1910 the service began with flights from Dusseldorf. The network expanded and in four years DELAG carried over 34,000 passengers without a fatal accident—a remarkable achievement for these early days of aviation.

Count von Zeppelin was more interested in building military airships than running an airline, and he devoted much of his time to this end. After a long hard struggle he convinced both the German army and navy to operate Zeppelins. After two of his naval airships crashed in 1913 with heavy casualties the 75-year old Count took a less active part in the Zeppelin company's day-to-day operations. He did not actually retire, and even developed a new interest in large heavier-than-air craft. Zeppelin's airships were widely used to drop bombs during World War I, but by 1917 (the year of his death) the old Count is reputed to have said: 'Airships are an antiquated weapon. The aircraft will control the air'.

AERODYNAMICS

All heavier-than-air craft from a glider to a jet airliner rely on the application of mechanical energy to the air around to give an upward thrust, maintaining the craft in the air against gravitational forces. This idea is the same for autogyros, helicopters, vertical take off aircraft, and anything that might be described as an aircraft as opposed to an airship, which derives its lift by being lighter than the air it displaces.

In a glider, the energy is provided by a towing plane or a launching winch. The wings have a cross-sectional shape known as an aerofoil [airfoil] to derive lift from the forward motion, while a tailplane and fin give the machine added stability and let the pilot control the direction of flight. As soon as no further energy is supplied, the glider begins to sink, and must always come back to earth despite rising air currents—'thermals'—that might give temporary respite. To maintain a heavier-than-air craft aloft requires a continuous input of energy—some means of maintaining the forward motion against wind resistance.

An aerofoil is a body shaped to produce 'lift' as it travels through the air. The most common example of an aerofoil is an aircraft wing, but the same principle is used to provide the driving force of the blades of fans, propellers and helicopter rotors. On some racing cars, aerofoils are installed upside down to press the car down, holding it firmly to the road at speed.

Seen in cross section, the upper side of an aerofoil is curved, and the lower side more or less flat. As it moves through the air, its leading (front) edge splits the air it encounters into two streams, one of which passes over the aerofoil, and the other under it. The streams rejoin each other behind the trailing (rear) edge of the aerofoil.

The curved upper surface of the aerofoil is longer from front to back than the straight lower surface. The air stream that takes the longer, upper route must therefore move faster relative to the aerofoil than the stream that goes underneath in order to reach the trailing edge at the same time.

The faster a fluid (such as a liquid or gas) moves, the lower its pressure—this is known as Bernoulli's principle after the 18th-century Swiss scientist Daniel Bernoulli, who discovered it. The fast air stream over the top of the aerofoil has a lower pressure than the slower one under it, and this pressure difference forces the aerofoil up from underneath.

Tilting an aerofoil so that its leading edge is higher than its trailing edge increases the distance travelled by the upper air stream, and so increases the 'lift'. The angle of tilt of an aircraft wing is called the angle of attack. The slower an aircraft flies, the greater the angle of attack its wings must have to create enough lift to keep it in the air. The increased 'nose-up' attitude of an airliner as it comes in slowly to land is quite noticeable.

The angle of attack cannot be increased indefinitely, however. This is due to the phenomenon of laminar flow. The friction between the wing and the air flowing over it causes the layer of air next to the wing (called the boundary layer) to move more slowly relative to the wing than the air further away. The same effect can be seen in rivers, where

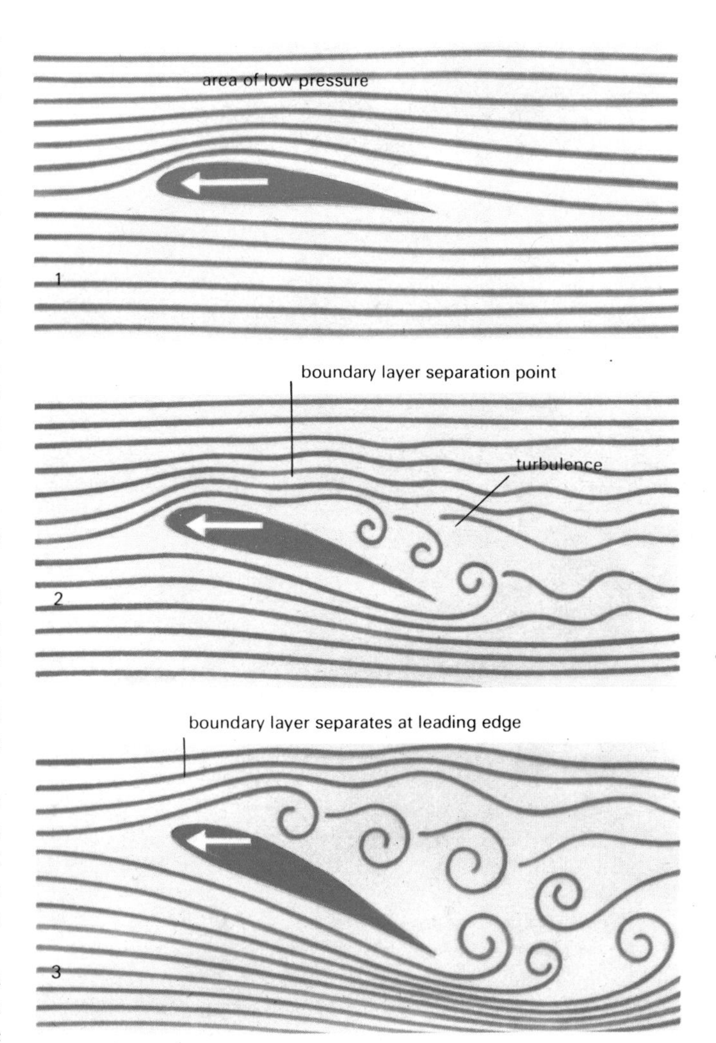

Above: a level aerofoil creates little turbulence (1) but as a plane slows its nose rises, and the boundary layer begins to separate from the top (2). Finally it separates the whole way along so that there is no more lift, and the aircraft stalls.

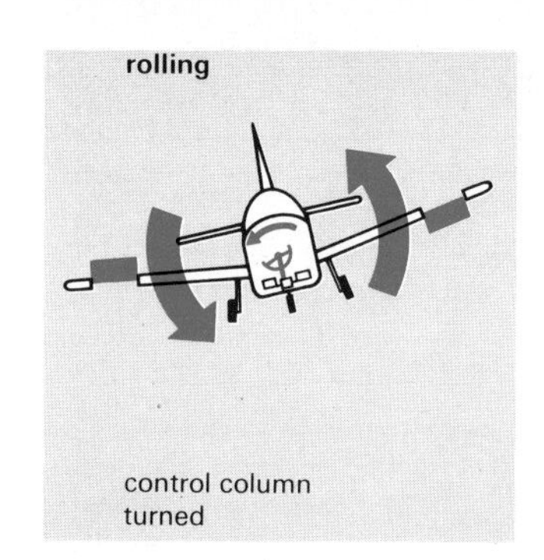

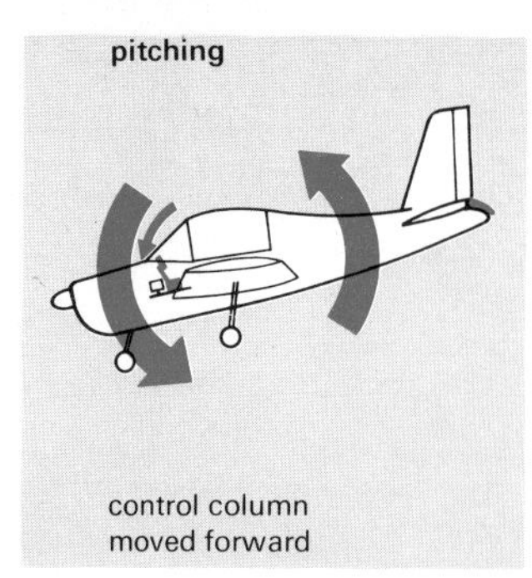

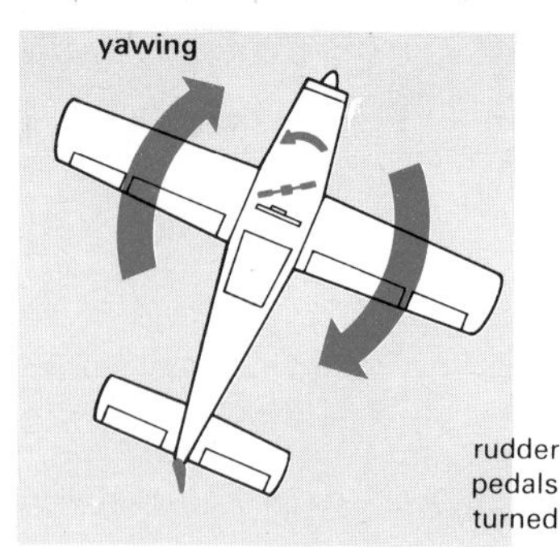

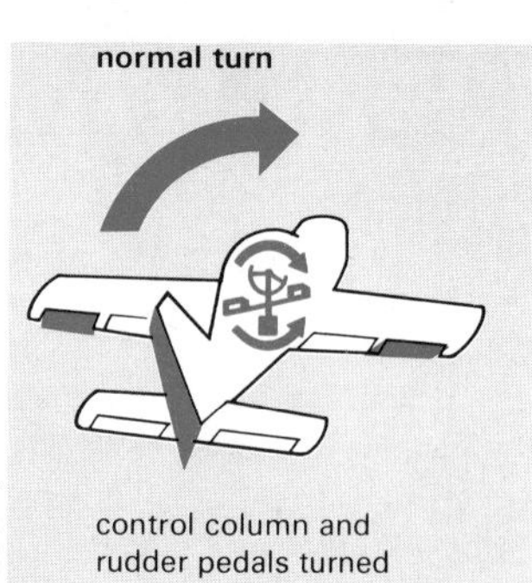

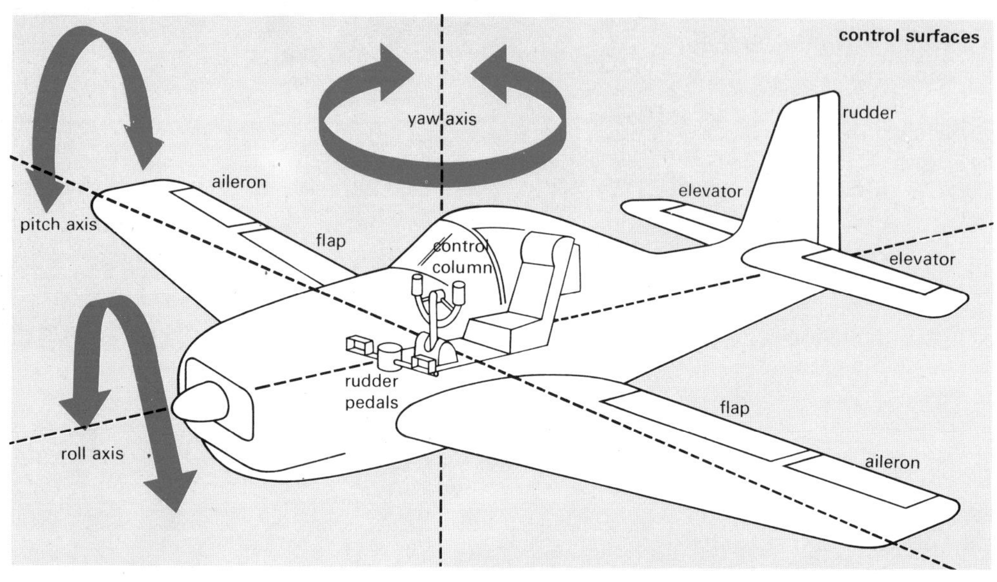

An aircraft has three sets of control surfaces to tilt it about three axes. The ailerons, operated by twisting the control column, cause it to roll. The elevators, operated by moving the column back and forth, cause it to pitch and thus to dive or climb. The rudder, worked by pedals, causes it to yaw, or swivel. A normal turn is executed by yawing and rolling toward the inside of the turn.

the flow near the banks is slower than in the middle.

As long as the flow over the wing remains smoothly laminar, it lifts well. But if the angle of attack is too great, the pressure above the trailing edge of the wing becomes so low that the boundary layer separates from it and the air flow becomes turbulent. As the angle increases, the point at which the boundary layer separates moves nearer the leading edge, and less and less of the wing produces lift. Finally, so little of the wing is functioning that the aicraft 'stalls' and goes into an uncontrollable dive until it regains normal flying speed.

Usually the wing will not form a continuous horizontal line, but will be divided in the middle with the tips raised by a small amount relative to the centre to give what is known as dihedral. Without this there would be nothing to keep the main axis of the wing horizontal during normal flight. As it is, dihedral results in greater lift from the lower wing when the aircraft tilts, thus producing a tendency to restore the wing to a horizontal mode.

The actual lift produced by a wing will vary with the speed of the plane. The faster it goes, the more lift will be produced; this is why aircraft have to attain a considerable speed on the ground before they acquire enough lift for take off.

At the same time higher speeds involve more wind resistance—more drag—so jets and other high-speed aircraft have thin wings to reduce drag. If a plane slows down to below what is known as stalling speed, it literally falls out of the sky, the lift being insufficient to keep it horizontal. With thin wings the stalling speed tends to be higher than with thick wings, so jet aircraft require higher take off and landing speeds.

It would be difficult to control a plane if these factors could not be varied. Jet aircraft would need enormously long runways because of their high minimum speeds, while if these factors were taken care of through thicker wings, their maximum speeds would be severely cut.

Thus a device known as the flap has been developed to modify the wing section so that lift can be changed by the pilot. Part of the trailing edge of the wing, and sometimes the leading edge as well, is hinged downwards to exaggerate the aerofoil section and give more lift at lower speeds. The hinge is often arranged to open a slot between wing and flap through which air can flow to reduce turbulence. Fully extended flaps considerably increase drag, slowing the aircraft. This effect can be increased on some aircraft by opening out transverse flaps in the tops of the wings or elsewhere called air brakes.

Once an aircraft is in the air, it has to be capable of moving in three ways: in pitch—up and down; in yaw—side-to-side; and in roll.

Pitch is controlled by hinged surfaces on the trailing edge of the tailplane known as elevators. Moving these upwards curves the tailplane into an inverted aerofoil section, resulting in downward pressure on the tailplane and hence a tendency for the aircraft to adopt a nose-up or climbing attitude. Turning the elevators downwards has the opposite effect.

Yaw is controlled by a flap on the tail fin known as the rudder. If the rudder alone is used the aircraft slews sideways, but this way of turning is inexact and badly controlled. There is no counteracting horizontal force to prevent the aircraft continuing to turn regardless of the pilot's wishes. Additionally, the horizontal centrifugal forces would throw passengers and crew towards the outside of the turn.

By moving the ailerons, control surfaces at the wing tips, the aircraft can be made to bank or roll inwards at the same time as the rudder turns it, so that the aircraft tilts towards

the centre of the turn like a bicycle. This is a more stable and comfortable way of turning.

In early aircraft the control surfaces—ailerons, elevators and rudder—were moved by the unaided exertion of the pilot through control wires. With today's high speed aircraft, the forces on the control surfaces are much too great for this, and so they are now generally moved by hydraulic cylinders, operated by the pilot through servo mechanisms. The arrangement works in a similar way to the power steering on a large car. This power assistance makes the controls of a modern aircraft very light, yet they are set to resist the pilot's action just enough to give him an indication that the surfaces are responding properly.

To move the elevators, he moves his control column backwards and forwards; to move the ailerons, he turns the control column. The rudder is activated by two pedals, leaving the hands free to operate the other control surfaces at the same time for banked turns.

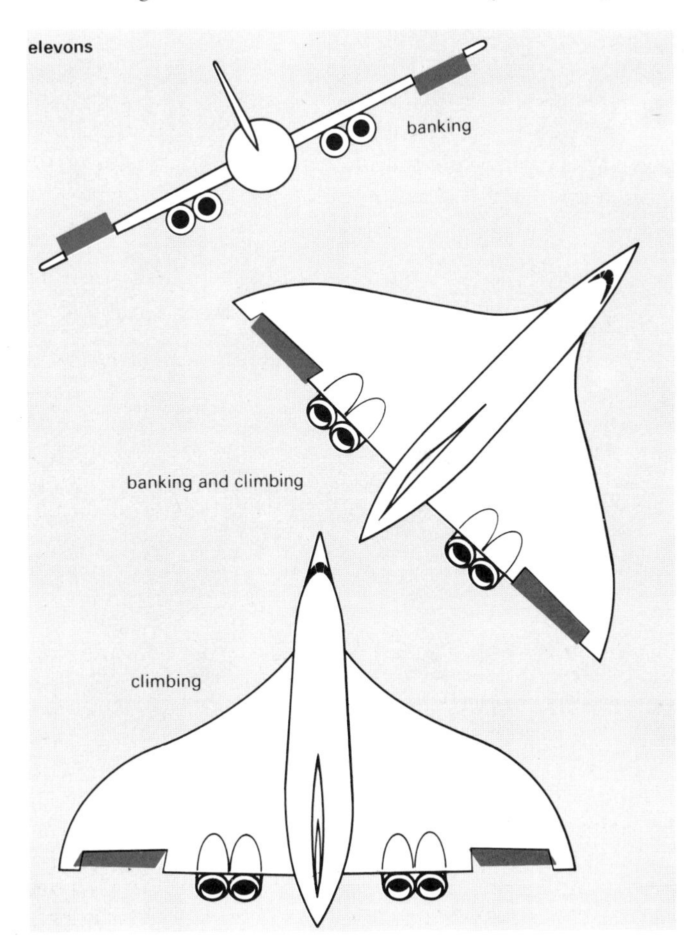

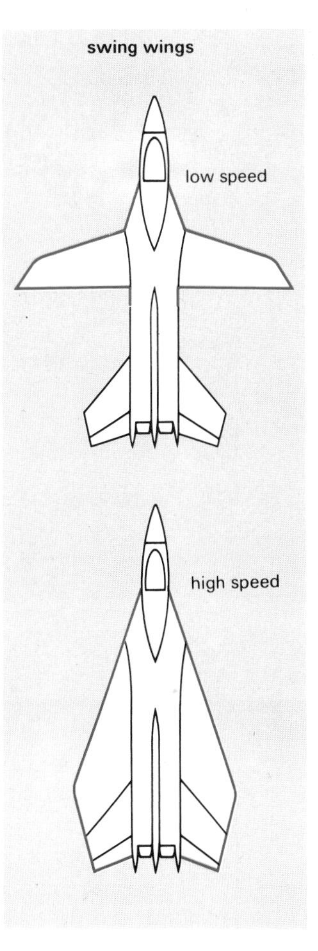

Above: as an aircraft is designed, wind tunnel tests are conducted using models to determine aerodynamic characteristics.
Far left: a delta-winged aircraft, having no separate tailplane, has elevons to serve as both elevators and ailerons. To roll the plane, one elevon is raised and the other lowered. For a climbing turn, one is raised and the other remains level. and the rudder is also used.
Left: variable geometry or 'swing-wings' are found on some supersonic planes. At low speeds, as for take-off and landing, when maximum lift is needed, the wings are extended; at high speeds they are folded back for minimum drag. There are elevons on the tailplane.

Otto Lilienthal

Otto Lilienthal was one of the leading figures in aviation pioneering, as well as being an engineer and inventor. During the course of his life he made many hundreds of heavier than air unpowered flights, and although accounts vary as to the distances he covered in his gliders it seems fairly well established that during the 1890s he achieved flights of at least 750 feet (229 m).

He was born in Anklam, Prussia on 23 May 1848 and trained in engineering at Potsdam Technical School, after which he studied at the Berlin Technical Academy from 1867 to 1870. As boys he and his brother Gustav used to study the flight of birds, in particular that of the stork, from which he established the fact than an arched surface wing was the most suitable design for heavier than air flight, and also the importance of rising air currents for soaring. In 1889 he published a book called *Der Vogel flug als Grundlage der Fliegekunst*, about bird flight, and this, together with his essays on flying machines in 1894, were acknowledged to be the basic works on aeronautics.

In 1880, after serving in the Franco-Prussian War, he founded his own engineering factory which produced marine signals, light steam motors, steel pulleys and sirens, many of which were his own inventions. During this time he carried on his aviation research and after much exhaustive experimentation with gliders and flying models with flapping wings he eventually built his first man carrying glider in 1891. This consisted of two curved, fabric covered wings to which he attached himself by his arms using his hanging body for balance. He launched himself from a running start and in fact even built an artificial hill 50 feet (15 m) high from which he was able to take off regardless of the direction of the wind. About this time he wrote 'The feat of launching by running down a slope into the wind until sufficient velocity is reached to lift the operator and his 40 pound wings requires practice. In the beginning the height should be moderate and the wings not too large or the wind will soon show that it is not to be trifled with. To those who from a modest beginning, and with gradually increased extent and elevation of flight, have gained full control of the apparatus, it is not in the least dangerous to cross deep and broad ravines.'

By 1893 the size of his glider had reached a 7 m (23 feet) span, with an overall plane surface of 14 m^2 (16.7 sq yd) and a weight of approximately 20 kg (44 lb). He continued his work on gliders until 1896 when he introduced a biplane powered by a small motor which flapped the wings. Before he could progress with this innovation, however, he was killed when his glider crashed in the hills near Rhinow on 9 August 1896.

His work, which directly inspired such other aviators as the Wright Brothers and Octave Chanute, was continued after his death by his brother Gustav. Otto Lilienthal is commemorated by the Lilienthal Medal, one of the highest awards for soaring.

AIRCRAFT HISTORY

The aircraft had a long period of gestation. Apart from its lack of a suitable engine, progress was hampered in the beginning by too much attention to bird flight. This led to a great deal of wasted effort on flapping-wing machines, known as ornithopters, although as early as 1804, Sir George Cayley had flown a model glider and, before he died in 1857, had flown at least two full-sized gliders with someone on board. Many of the early experimenters also made the mistake of concentrating on inherent stability in their aircraft instead of on controllability. Even Otto Lilienthal, who made gliding flights of 300 to 750 feet (90-230 m) in the 1890s, exercised control simply by moving his body, and only at the time of his death as the result of a flying accident in 1896 was engaged on the design of a body harness linked to a rear elevator on his latest glider.

Above: Lilienthal's manned gliders consisted of a set of wings with padded armrests. The crossbar controlled the craft.

During the second half of the 19th century a great effort went into achieving flight in England, France, the United States and Germany but it was diffused and fumbling. Little was known by one designer of what others were doing until Octave Chanute decided to collect and disseminate proved facts and other information to all who would listen to him. From 1896 onwards, he was engaged in building and flying his own gliders in the United States, and in spreading particulars about the principles involved in flight with fixed wings. In 1903 he visited Europe and lectured in Paris. Before that, he had given valuable help along the same lines to the Wright Brothers.

Some of these principles had been laid down by Cayley in 1809. He had outlined the forces of thrust, drag and lift, and had pointed out the value of the cambered, or arched, aerofoil wing shape in preference to the flat plate. As early as 1868, M P W Boulton in England had invented and patented the aileron. The Wrights' first glider of 1899 had wings that could be warped, or twisted, by cables for lateral control. Thus, by the time the Wrights made their first flight at the end of 1903, most of the devices for controlled flying were known and yet S P Langley in the United States and a string of pioneers in France and England were still meeting with little success. Even the Wrights in 1903 had not fully resolved the control situation; they found that wing-warping by itself was not enough. Their bright idea of linking the wing-warping with rudder movement was generously given away by Chanute to the Europeans, but too many of these still aimed at inherent stability through giving their wing tips a dihedral or upward-tilted angle.

There were many ambitious projects before real powered flight was accomplished by the Wrights. The biggest of them was the design by W S Henson in 1842 for an 'Aerial Steam Carriage'. It had a tail-piece to provide control and stability, box-kite wings, and a three-wheeled undercarriage for take off and landing. It was to have a wing-span of 150 ft (46 m) with wings properly constructed using spars and ribs, and it was to be propelled by two six-bladed airscrews. It was never built. Hiram Maxim staged an elaborate experiment to prove lift in 1894 with a device that weighed 3½ tons and applied 360 hp through two steam engines. It was not intended to fly but it did lift off its rails, and there the project ended. In 1895-6 the Englishman Pilcher, a disciple of Otto Lilienthal, made several successful glider flights on the banks of the Clyde. In France, people like du Temple de la Croix, Penaud and Ader worked hard with model aircraft driven by steam, twisted rubber and clockwork. In England, H F Phillips came back to Cayley's cambered wing and further showed the distribution of pressure and lift between the upper and lower surfaces of a wing.

This incoherent jumble of effort was given fresh interpretation by the Wright Brothers. Having learned all they could about the research and development up to their time, they proceeded to put the most promising ideas to the test. At the same time, they worked out their own calculations

Left: poster for the first aviation fair, in France in 1909.
Below: the Wrights' Flyer *had a tail-first design. Wing warping would tilt but not steer the plane.*

concerning not only the relation of thrust to lift and of the efficiency of propellers but also stresses and methods of construction. By their third glider they had developed a satisfactory airframe and began looking to the newly-arrived automobile engine for their power. Failing in their attempt to get from the new industry an engine of a suitable power to weight ratio, they set to work to build their own engine, and on 17 December 1903 the first flight was made. Two months earlier S P Langley's latest aircraft had fouled the launching mechanism and plunged into the Potomac. The triumph of Wilbur and Orville Wright was complete and exclusive. Orville, who made that first flight, was in the air only 12 seconds and travelled a distance of 120 ft (37 m). Three more flights were made that day and the last covered 852 ft (260 m). After that they went home to Dayton, Ohio from their flying ground at Kill Devil Hills in North Carolina and in 1904 built their second aircraft, again a biplane, with reduced wing camber and a more powerful engine.

Little attention was paid to them and their achievements by the rest of the world but they continued their experiments in control and in 1905 they produced their third aircraft. This was extremely successful and before the year ended, a flight of 24 miles (38 km) had been made at an

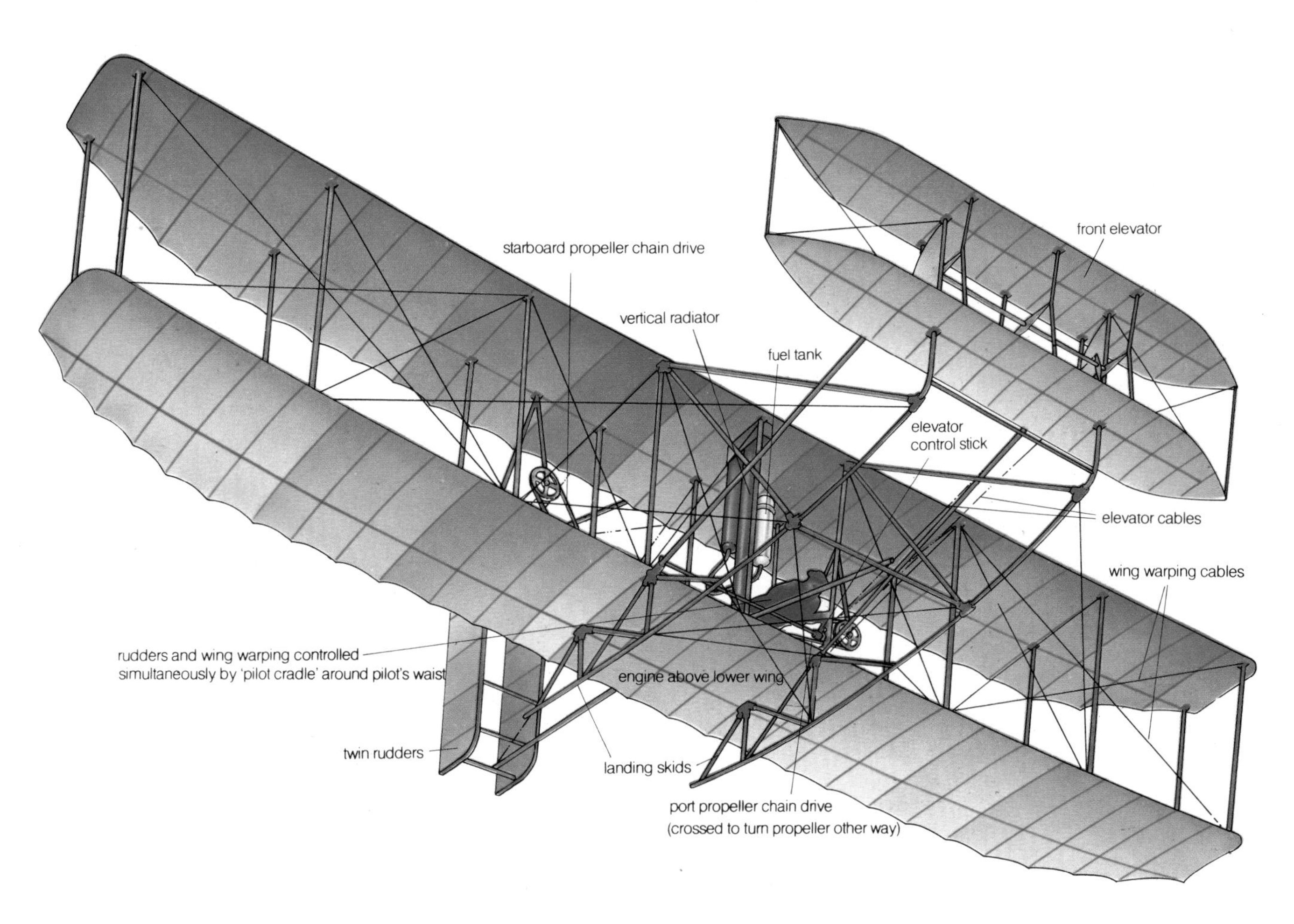

Orville & Wilbur Wright

The Wright brothers are now generally accepted as the first men to fly in an aircraft, but recognition of their achievement was not universally accepted for many years—even in their home country, the United States. One reason for this lack of recognition was perhaps due to the Wright brothers' reluctance to let anyone see their early flights in case an unscrupulous inventor should steal their ideas. A further problem was the definition of what constituted a 'flight'; several people claimed to have made a flight before the Wrights, but these 'flights' were really short uncontrolled hops. There is no doubt that the Wright brothers made the world's first practical powered aircraft.

Wilbur and Orville Wright were the sons of a minister of the United Brethren Church and the family moved from place to place. The boys were interested in mechanical devices, and their father gave them a model helicopter which convinced them that this was not the way to fly. Later their father became a bishop, but the boys went into the newspaper and printing business before turning to the booming bicycle trade, first selling, then manufacturing bicycles of their own design.

The Wright brothers were interested in the gliding experiments carried out in Germany by Otto Lilienthal, and his death due to a gliding accident in 1896 seems to have started them thinking seriously about the problems of flight. Wilbur was then 28 years old and Orville just 25. They had a thriving bicycle business in Dayton, Ohio, and could afford to finance their experiments themselves. Throughout these experiments thoroughness was the key to their success, for they approached the problem of flight methodically stage by stage. They studied the work of their predecessors, especially their fellow American Octave Chanute, and learned from their mistakes. For instance Lilienthal controlled his glider by shifting his body to change the weight distribution, but the Wrights decided this was no way to control an aeroplane. They studied bird flight more closely and noticed that the buzzard twisted its wing tips to retain its balance. By twisting the wings of an aircraft the same effect could be achieved, and wing warping was a major step towards controlled flight.

The Wright brothers decided to start with a glider and they favoured a biplane—as had Chanute. Before venturing into the air, however, they tested their glider by flying it tethered like a huge box kite at Kitty Hawk, North Carolina. In October 1900 they made several manned flights but the results were disappointing and they realised that much of the existing information they had used was wrong, so they decided to carry out their own research. They built a wind tunnel to test new wing sections and made many other experiments. By October 1902 they had produced a glider which was readily controlled: the next stage was a powered aircraft.

The Wrights decided that a petrol [gasoline] engine was the most suitable source of power, but existing examples did not meet their requirements, so they designed and built their own. They then had to design a suitable propeller. During the summer of 1903 the Wrights built their first aircraft, the *Flyer*, and transported it to Kill Devil Hills near Kitty Hawk. Wilbur won the toss and attempted a take off, but ploughed into the sand and damaged the *Flyer*. On 17 December they were ready again and it was Orville's turn—he flew for 12 seconds. A further three flights were made including one of 59 seconds covering 852 feet (260 m).

A new *Flyer* was built in 1904 and this made about 80 flights, including simple manoeuvres and a complete circuit of the field. The longest flight achieved was 5 minutes 4 seconds. During the following year *Flyer No* 3 made several long flights, including one lasting over 38 minutes. The Wright brothers had produced a practicable aircraft.

For a period of 2½ years the Wrights did no flying, but instead concentrated on building improved aircraft and engines. In 1908 they were ready to fly again and *Flyer No 3* reappeared with several improvements. A passenger was carried for the first time. It was not until April 1908 that their nearest rival exceeded 5 minutes, so when Wilbur demonstrated their new model A in France, observers were astonished by its performance—one flight lasted 2 hours 20 minutes. Considerable numbers of the model A were built and this was followed by the model B and the model R racer.

From about 1910 the Wright brothers' influence on aviation began to decline, and Wilbur died of typhoid fever in 1912. Orville retained an interest in aviation and lived until the age of 77 in 1948.

Above: Orville Wright.
Below: Wilbur at the controls in 1911. He was seated rather than prone; controls were improved.

Below: Orville takes off in December 1903. Wilbur has just let go of the wing. The plane took off from a wooden rail and is flying away from the camera.

average speed of 38 mph (61 km/h). For the next two and a half years, they did no flying. Futile negotiations with the US and British Governments and anxiety about the risk of having their secrets pried into were at the bottom of this inactivity. In 1908, Wilbur visited Europe in search of business while Orville stayed at home, preparing for the military trials to which the American authorities had at last consented.

Meanwhile, Europe had been moved to fresh effort by gliding pioneer Chanute's encouragement. In France this was led by Esnault-Pelterie, later to be a prominent figure, and yet the first copies of the Wright glider were failures. In England, S F Cody had worked forward from man-lifting kites to a relatively inefficient glider. Slightly earlier, in France, Leon Levavasseur had built a monoplane with bird-like wings. It was a failure, but this pioneer, together with Louis Blériot, was to give monoplanes a place in competition with the currently favoured biplanes.

The first aircraft factory was set up in 1905 at Billancourt, France, by the Voisin brothers, who had already built two float gliders towed by motor boats. They built for themselves and other designers, but the fashion in Europe was still to aim at stability rather than control. Soon the Brazilian pioneer aviator Santos-Dumont had turned away from airships to experiment with monoplanes and biplanes and also with tractor (front mounted) airscrews. In 1906, he flew 720 ft (220 m) in a tail first pusher biplane. In 1909, A V Roe in England produced a tractor biplane and J W Dunne built the world's first swept-wing aircraft, again a biplane, and again aimed at inherent stability. A year later, F W Lanchester did for aerodynamics what Newton and Bernoulli had done for hydrodynamics, when he put forward his theory (never disputed) of the circulation of air over the wing surfaces.

By 1909, the Wrights had made flights in public on both sides of the Atlantic, and the cause was given a healthy impetus. In the United States, Glenn Curtiss came to the fore as a designer of both aircraft and engine in the *June Bug*, which had wingtip ailerons for lateral control. European designers, with the exception originally of Henri Farman, followed the Wrights in aiming at good control either by wing-warping or by the fitting of ailerons. A string of new types now appeared and at the Rheims aviation week in August 1909, more than 30 aircraft were on show, six of them built to the Wright specification. A Curtiss successor to the *June Bug* won the speed contest at 47.85 mile/h (77 km/h), an Antoinette won the height award at 508 ft (155 m) and a Farman the distance at 112 miles (180 km). The same year Blériot had staggered across the English Channel in his underpowered monoplane and the aircraft had ceased to be regarded as an erratic and essentially dangerous toy. Its progress was helped by the development of more powerful engines.

The Wright aircraft types remained popular, but by 1910 the influence of the Wrights on development had virtually

An early airport often turned out to be the nearest muddy field. The appearance of an aircraft was a magnet for the curious, especially small boys, some of whom grew up to be the daring barnstormers of the next generation. The planes in this picture appear to be Blériot's, or of a very similar design, still using wing warping. The craft in which he crossed the channel in 1909 had a tail wheel rather than a skid, as in this picture.

ceased and a vigorous independent line was being pursued by designers in various countries. The best performers continued to be biplanes though a good deal of work was done on monoplanes, and the germ of the cantilever wing, supported only by the fuselage instead of a system of wires, was contained in a patent registered by Junkers in Germany as early as 1910, A year later, another improvement appeared in a German device for raising the undercarriage legs on hinges to lie flush with the fuselage in flight. At the same time an oleo undercarriage leg (a telescopic leg incorporating an oil-filled shock absorber) was designed at the Royal Aircraft Factory at Farnborough, England. All these advances marked the movement from the wood-and-wire structure to the use of metal in aircraft. They also accompanied the increasing popularity of the tractor airscrew and the universal adoption of a tube-shaped fuselage to connect the wings, tail and landing gear, and to provide a less exposed position for pilot, passengers and power plants.

Louis Blériot

The French aviator Louis Blériot was the first man to make a sea crossing by air when he made his historic flight in July 1909 across the English Channel in a small monoplane. Born in Cambrai, France, Blériot became a wealthy man by making motor accessories, particularly car headlamps, before turning his interest to flight. Around 1899 he built a model aircraft with wings that flapped like a bird (an ornithopter), and then in 1905 he collaborated with the French aviation pioneer Gabriel Voisin in the building of a glider constructed like a box-kite. It was fitted with floats and towed by boat to launch it from the river Seine. Blériot experimented with powered biplanes during 1906 but soon turned to the monoplane design which was to influence European aircraft development strongly.

Of the early Blériot monoplanes, the most successful was airborne for 20 minutes but lacked manoeuvrability. This was a common failing in European aircraft at that time because they were not usually as carefully thought out as the Wright brothers' pioneer aircraft. In contrast to some of the weird arrangements of the time, the seventh Blériot design introduced a layout for light aircraft that is still used today; monoplane, enclosed fuselage tapering to the tail, front-mounted engine and propeller, rear tailplane and rudder, two-wheel main undercarriage and a small tail wheel. Blériot's eighth plane made a pioneer cross country flight of 17 miles (27 km) in 1908. But it was his number XI design that proved to be his greatest success.

The London *Daily Mail* newspaper had put up a prize of £1000 for the first person to cross the English Channel. The initial attempt was made on 19 July 1909 by the Englishman, Hubert Latham, incidentally the first man to successfully roll and light a cigarette in an open cockpit. But Latham's plane suffered engine failure and came down in the sea. While he struggled to build a replacement, on July 25 Louis Blériot took off from near Calais at 4.41 AM and landed at Dover 37 minutes later, where he was soon greeted by a customs officer. Blériot's monoplane was powered by a three cylinder Anzani engine of only 25 horsepower. It was controlled by a simple joystick which warped the wings to provide control, as ailerons were not then in general use.

In World War I Blériot set up a successful aircraft factory that built 10,000 military planes for the French government, including the famous SPAD fighter. He was awarded the first flying licence of the International Aeronautical Federation, and set up flying schools at Pau, France, and in Hendon, England. In a Blériot monoplane, the chief instructor at the Hendon school made the first non-stop flight from London to Paris on 12 April 1911—fifty years to the day before the first manned space flight. Louis Blériot died in Paris on 2 August 1936, following a heart attack.

Top of page: Blériot and his wife at Dover after his historic cross-channel flight in 1909.
Above: Blériot the same day. He was 37 years old. The money he had made as a French industrialist enabled him to experiment in aviation.
Right: the 25 hp monoplane itself, now in a museum.

THE AIRCRAFT ENGINE

When the Wright brothers came to search for an engine to put into their glider in 1903, they thought they could manage to fly with one of only 8 horsepower, provided it was not too heavy. They approached, without success, half-a-dozen makers of car engines. Eventually, they built their own engine and got 12 hp from it, but it was still relatively heavy at 15 lb (7 kg) to the horsepower. Thirty years later, engine designers were aiming at a ratio of 1 hp per pound of engine weight (2.2 hp per kg). In the years leading up to World War I, the French led the field in aircraft engine design, producing several 50 hp and two 100 hp engines by 1908. But the best of these still only had a power to weight ratio of 3.7 lb to the hp.

Early engines were water cooled, with the cylinders arranged in line or in a V formation as in a car. But in 1907 a new and highly successful type was introduced: the rotary engine. In this, the crankcase and cylinders revolved in one piece around a stationary crankshaft. The pistons were connected to a single pivot mounted off-centre, so that they moved in and out as they revolved with their cylinders. The propeller was connected directly to the front of the crankcase and turned with it. The rotary engine had fewer parts than a conventional engine, and since the cylinders moved rapidly around, they could be air cooled by fins mounted so as to take advantage of the draught. Both factors contributed to make it light. Rotary engines always

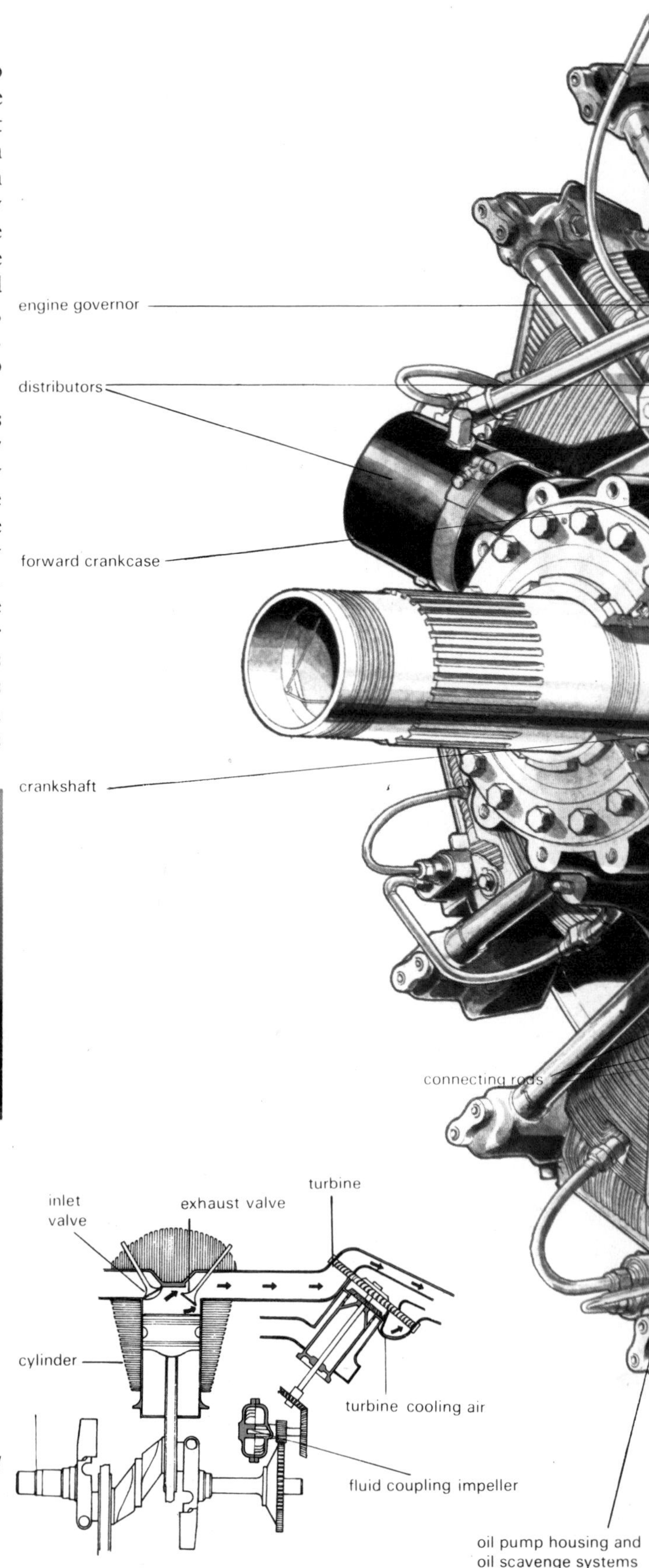

Above: the Wright's engine, which they built themselves. It had a poor power-to-weight ratio, even for the time. Right: the TC18 (Turbo-Compound) R3350EA engine, as fitted in the DC-7. It produces 3400 hp at take-off for a dry weight of 3645 lb (1653 kg). It is supercharged and has three 'blown-down' power recovery turbines spaced around the rear, as seen in the small drawing.

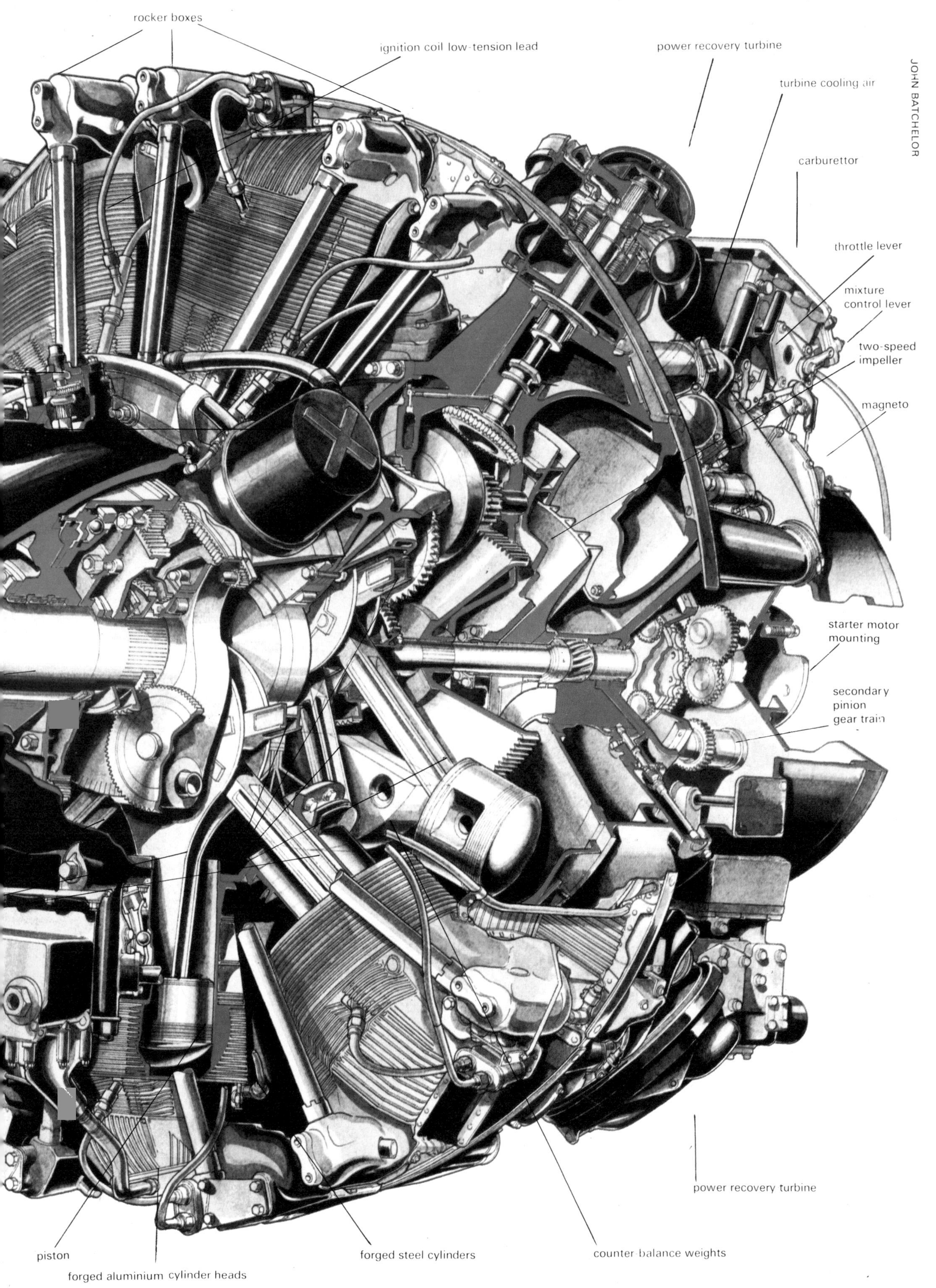
rocker boxes
ignition coil low-tension lead
power recovery turbine
turbine cooling air
JOHN BATCHELOR
carburettor
throttle lever
mixture
control lever
two-speed
impeller
magneto
starter motor
mounting
secondary
pinion
gear train
power recovery turbine
piston
forged aluminium cylinder heads
forged steel cylinders
counter-balance weights

Above: the famous Rolls-Royce Merlin engine. This example is in the Science Museum in London. The Merlin is a good example of the Rolls-Royce design philosophy of successive modifications, which means starting with a good design in the first place.

had an odd number of cylinders. This reduced vibration, since there were never two pistons moving in exactly the same direction at the same time. The original 1907 Gnome engine had seven, and later types nine.

Other types of engine produced at the time included the Spanish Hispano-Suiza, a design well ahead of its time with eight steel cylinders arranged in a V and screwed into an aluminium block. In the later years of the war this engine yielded, in successive versions, 150, 220 and 300 hp. The Rolls-Royce Eagle, a V12 engine with a broadly similar layout adapted from an original Mercedes design, produced 360 hp in its Mark 8 version of 1917. This was the engine that carried Alcock and Brown across the Atlantic in 1919.

Both the Rolls and the Hispano engines had conventional water cooling. This often gave trouble, since vibration and the shock of landing caused the plumbing to break. It was to overcome this problem that a third type of engine was introduced: the air-cooled radial engine, in which static cylinders were arranged in a circle and cooled by the backlash of the propeller.

Proper cooling is one of the most critical points of aircraft engine design. Such engines have always produced far more power for their size than automobile engines of the same date, and consequently have generated much higher temperatures. These problems led to great rivalry between the designers of air and water-cooled engines. Their object was to produce engines that were adequately cooled with the lightest possible system—thus improving the vital power to weight ratio—and at the same time were utterly reliable.

As far as reliability went, the water-cooled engine seemed to have all the advantages. Any capacity of radiator could be used to produce the desired temperature. The temperature of the engine was kept within safe limits by the boiling point of the cooling water, since it could rise no higher than this until the water boiled away completely. Some engines used this feature in evaporative cooling systems, where the water was allowed to boil at the engine. The steam was ducted off, re-condensed into water and returned to the engine. The system had been used as early as 1907 in the French Antoinette engine. In other engines, ethylene glycol (anti-freeze) was used as a coolant, raising the boiling point to 140°C (284°F) to provide an additional safety margin.

The principal trouble with this type of engine was the weight and complexity of the cooling system—it was one more thing to go wrong. Air-cooled engines did not suffer from this problem, since their system had no moving parts. Their cylinders were always arranged radially in one or more circular rows. This placed them just behind the propeller, an ideal position for cooling. They were also spaced quite wide apart, so that the outside could be covered with large fins to increase the surface areas and thus improve heat dissipation.

Early radial engines had their cylinders completely exposed to the air, but in the early 1930s a shaped ring cowling was added around the engine to improve air flow around the cylinders and reduce the drag caused by the wide, flat-fronted engine. The main trouble with the air cooled radial was that there was no fixed upper limit on its temperature, so it would overheat very quickly if over-extended. This problem, however, led to the production of high quality heat resistant alloys which made the development of the jet engine possible later on.

The engine designers of the 1920s and 1930s managed to produce reliable engines with ingenious new features by sheer good design and workmanship. One of the best of these improvements was the sleeve valve, which replaces the complex valve gear of a conventional engine with a single tube sliding up and between the piston and the cylinder—it completely encircles the piston. It has ports, or holes, in its upper end. These slide past matching ports in the cylinder head which are connected to the fuel-supply and exhaust systems, thus opening and closing them at the correct time. This greatly reduces the number of moving parts in the engine, particularly as the sleeve can be moved by quite simple machinery set around the inner edge of the ring of cylinders instead of the conventional long train of rods and levers reaching to the outside. The alloy of which the sleeve is made is vital, because of its expansion as it heats up. If it expands too much it jams against the cylinder; too little and it jams against the piston.

Many engines had superchargers—compressors to force extra fuel and air into the cylinders and thus improve the engine's performance. These had been used as early as 1910, but were never entirely satisfactory because the compressor needed power to drive it, thus wasting some of the extra power it gave. Several attempts were made to build a turbo-charger powered by a turbine driven by the exhaust gases, but there was no alloy that would withstand the high temperature. This was found later.

By the mid-1930s, engines were producing so much power that the propeller was being driven at an excessive speed. The tips of the blades broke the sound barriers and created shock waves that reduced the propeller's efficiency. The difficulty was overcome by gearing the propeller down. The more advanced American engines had variable gearing. By the end of the 1930s most propellers also had variable pitch (blade angle) so that they could run efficiently at different speeds.

There was always an incentive for designers to produce more and more powerful engines. During the 1920s and 1930s it was the glamorous (and lucrative) Schneider Trophy; later it was the desperate need to build fast aircraft in the Second World War. Rolls-Royce produced a V-12 water-cooled engine for the Schneider Trophy which gave 2600 hp, though it could only maintain this for one hour. This was all that was needed for two successive races, but the basic design of the short-lived engine was used for the famous Rolls-Royce Merlin, which powered the Spitfire, Hurricane and Mustang in the Second World War. The original 1934 Merlin produced only 790 hp, but by the end of the war this had been increased to well over 2000 by successive modifications.

Left: early Mustangs, photographed in 1944 over Burma. These P-51As were still powered by the Allison engine; the plane did not achieve its potential until fitted with the Merlin.

DEVELOPMENT:

TWO WORLD WARS

WORLD WAR ONE

Before the First World War there was little to differentiate civil from military aircraft. Yet although 'stick and string' or 'birdcage' designs were still evident in the early months of the war, progress had been made in design, particularly in the area of improving performance by means of streamlining. Notable in this respect were the French Deperdussin 'Monocoque' and the British Sopwith 'Tabloid' and Royal Aircraft Factory SE 2 and 4. All were capable of speeds exceeding 100 mph (160 kph) at a time when speed rarely rose above 75 mph. The Deperdussin, with its faired undercarriage and single wing, was actually a precursor of the 1920s, while the two British biplanes foreshadowed the high-performance types to be developed during 1914-1918.

Fighters

The major task envisaged for aircraft in World War I was reconnaissance, and it soon became apparent that it would be useful to prevent the enemy from obtaining information in a similar way. A few adventurous pilots took potshots at each other with small arms, but this was not very effective. What was needed was a forward-firing machine gun which could be aimed and fired by the pilot.

The legendary French airman Roland Garros came up with the first useful solution: in the spring of 1915 a machine gun was fitted to the forward fuselage of his Morane-Saulnier scout, and wedge-shaped deflector plates of steel were fixed to the rear side of each propeller blade where any bullets might strike them. The fighter plane had been invented, and German reconnaissance aircraft began to mysteriously disappear. Garros' plane, however, was forced down behind enemy lines by engine trouble, and the game was up. The Germans called on their talented Dutch designer, Anthony Fokker, to produce a similar design.

Fokker was born in Java. His family returned home in 1897, but the boy did not like school very much; his tinkering with electric and mechanical devices took precedence, and finally resulted in a hand-to-mouth existence as a performer in air shows. He built his own aircraft, frequently using parts salvaged from crashes, having a flair for improvising as he went along.

During the first few weeks of the war, Fokker sold everything in his shop at any price he cared to name, to the very military officials who had refused to be impressed until the war surprised everybody. Fokker was a neutral businessman, as well as a cynic, and everyone thought the war would be over in a few months anyway. The same German military wanted Fokker to copy Garros' idea of deflector plates: this blinkered conservatism was not confined to the Germans. The first American military pilots were required to wear spurs in their cockpits.

Above: the Fokker E IV was a successor of the E III which carried three machine guns. Pilot was the famous Max Immelmann.
Left: Fokker with one of his designs.
Next page top left: a French Morane-Saulnier 'Bullet' of 1914, with deflector blades.
Right: Hauptmann Ritter von Tutscher (27 victories) ready to take off, in March 1918.
Next page centre: Bristol F.2B. This two-seater was slower than German fighters in level flight, but could often escape by out-diving a pursuer.

Fokker, however, immediately saw that a better design was needed, and fitted an interrupter gear which prevented the gun from firing when the propeller was in the way. The otherwise unremarkable Fokker Eindekker comprised what was called in Britain the 'Fokker scourge' which began to cleanse the skies of Allied aircraft. The Allies used pusher types, such as the Airco de Havilland DH 2, which could fire forward with no fear of hitting the propeller, but the aerodynamic deficiencies of this design could not be tolerated, and a hydraulic synchronizing gear was designed which was more flexible than the German device. From the middle of 1916 it was fitted to the Sopwith 1½-Strutter and the Pup. The Germans countered with the two-gun Albatros D I in the spring of 1917, and the race was on.

The early Fokker designs were inherently stable; quality control was never his strong point—other factories turned out 'better' aircraft—but his genius as a designer was instinctive. He soon realized that stability was no longer a problem; design solutions and more powerful engines had taken care of that. The E-type Fokkers went through several modifications, but in the meantime the Albatros did also, and the Allied aircraft were also improving.

The excellent Sopwith Camel was powered by a succession of Bentley rotaries up to 180 hp. It had ailerons on both wings, a strong airframe and twin Vickers machine guns which were belt-fed, rather than drum-fed, so that they did not need re-loading by the pilot. More than 5000 Camels were built, and they shot down nearly 1300 enemy aircraft. The Camel was fast and heavy, and in the hands of an expert there was little it could not do.

The French Nieuport was lightly built; if it pulled at all steeply out of a dive, the wing fabric was likely to rip off, a frightening thing that once happened to Eddie Rickenbacker, who only survived by landing the plane at full throttle. The SPAD, however, was another story. Rickenbacker himself regarded it as the ultimate fighter aircraft. (The Americans never built a plane fit for use in that war.) SPAD was a French aircraft company led by Deperdussin; after a financial scandal, Louis Bleriot was put in charge of the *Societé pour Aviation et ses Derives*.

The rotary engine was the engine in which the crankshaft was stationary; it pumped itself around the crankshaft with the propeller fastened to the engine itself. This had advantages with its air-cooling and so forth, but as the technology of military aircraft improved by leaps and bounds, the rotary became impossible: the larger the engine the more it wanted to behave like a gyroscope, making the handling of the aircraft difficult and dangerous. This is why

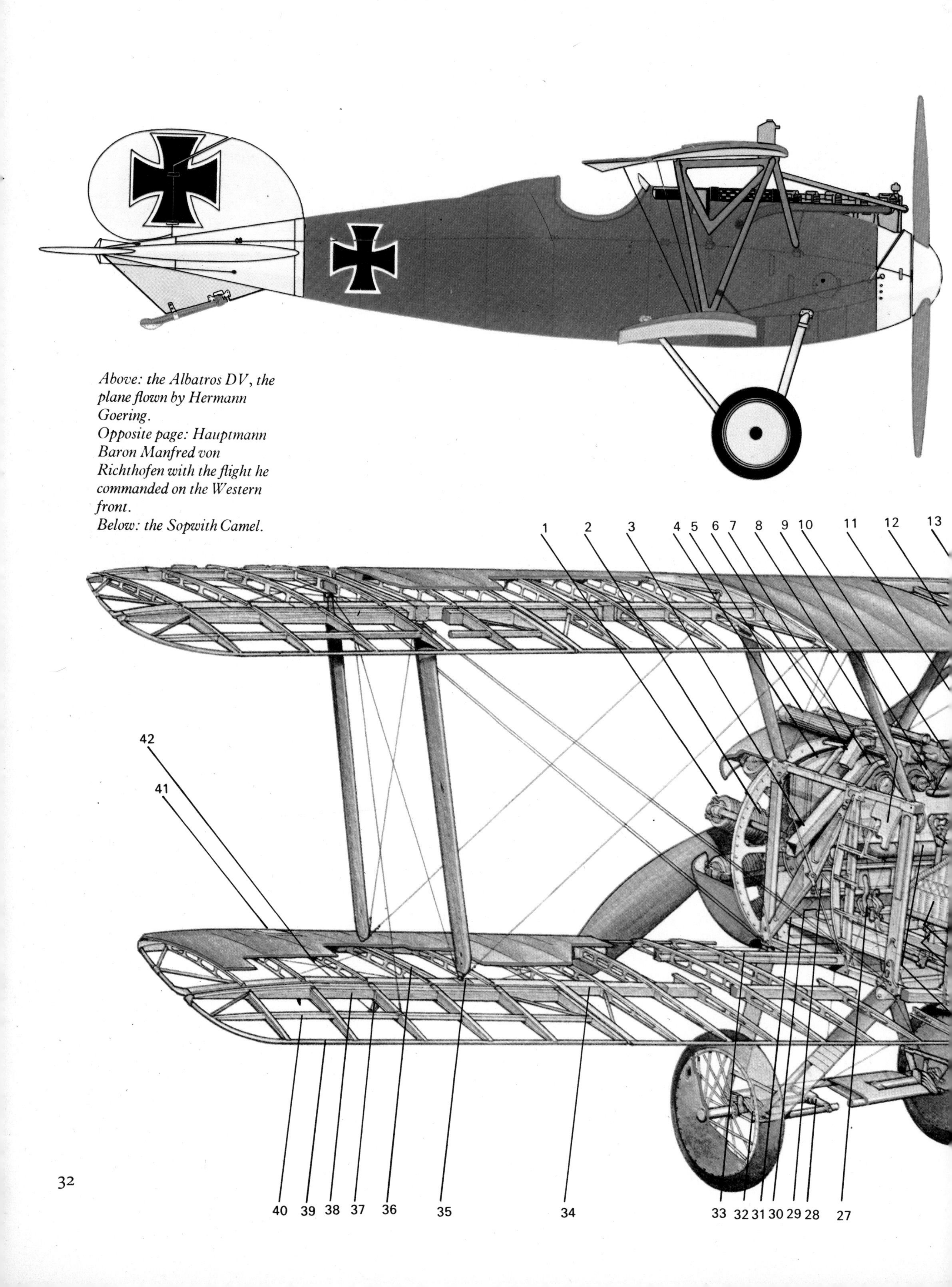

Above: the Albatros DV, the plane flown by Hermann Goering.
Opposite page: Hauptmann Baron Manfred von Richthofen with the flight he commanded on the Western front.
Below: the Sopwith Camel.

Sopwith Camel F1
1. Bentley BR1 150hp motor
2. Firewall (not shown)
3. Cartridge disposal chute
4. Castor-oil tank
5. Twin .303in Vickers air-cooled MGs
6. Link chute
7. Mount for MGs
8. Plywood decking
9. Cocking handles for twin MGs
10. Instrument panel
11. Auxiliary fuel tank
12. Main fuel tank
13. Open centre-section
14. Control column
15. Intermediate formers
16. Rubber shock cord
17. Steerable ash tail-skid
18. Steel tube outline/nose ribs
19. Fairleads
20. Ash longerons
21. Control cables
22. Tank bearer
23. Turn-buckles
24. Wicker seat
25. Seat bearer
26. Carburettor air intake
27. Throttle quadrant
28. Undercarriage axle hinge point
29. Rear engine mount
30. Rudder bar
31. Foot-board
32. Bungee shock-absorber straps
33. Ash front spar (routed)
34. Solid ash rear spar on lower wing only
35. Mild steel fittings
36. Compression strut
37 Aileron control horn
38 Spruce aileron spar
39 Steel tubing round wing edge
40 Spruce sub-spar
41. Inspection window
42. Wire drag bracings

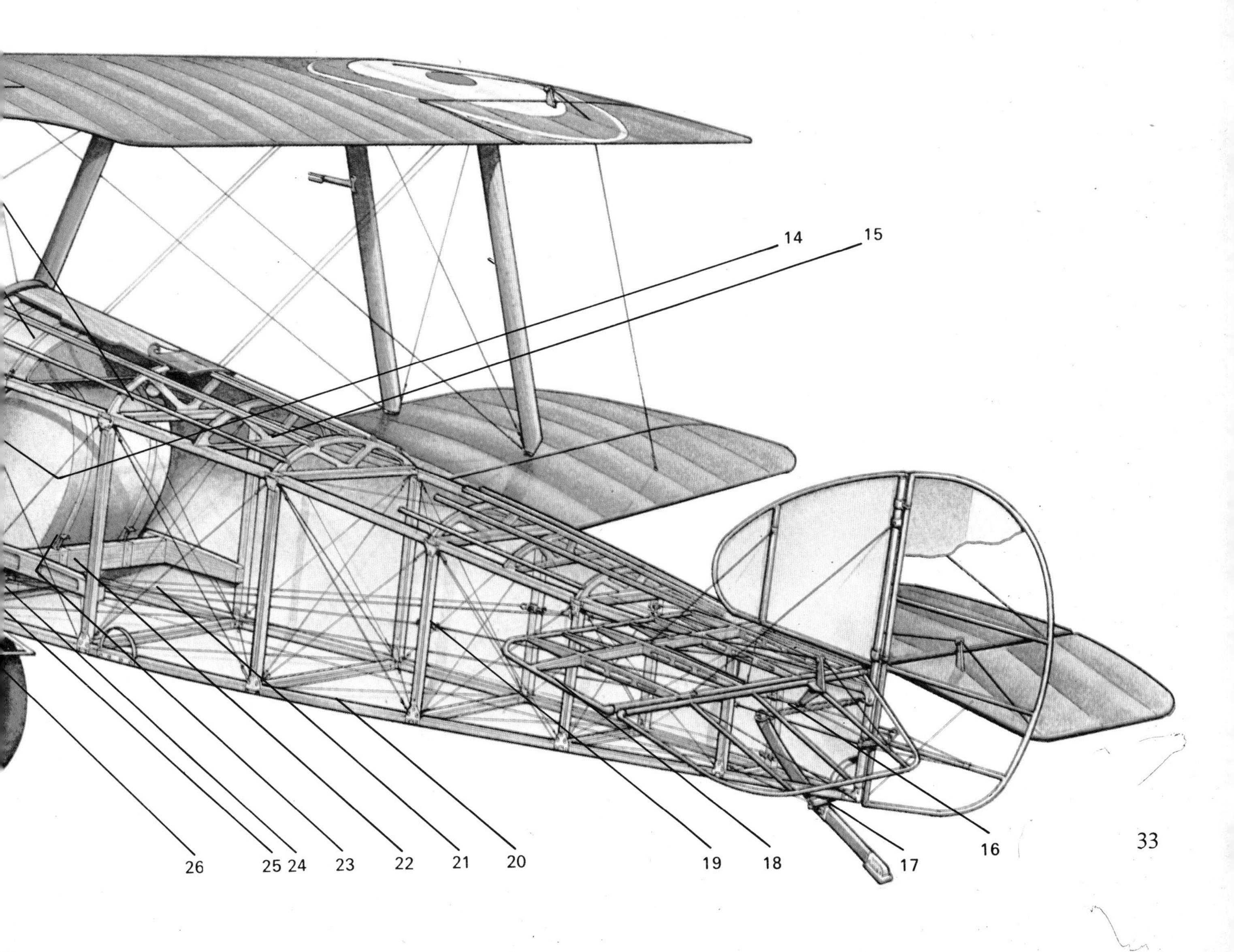

Right: American ace Eddie Rickenbacker in his Spad XIII. The slotted bar between the machine guns enabled the convergence point of the bullets to be checked. Note the heat guards at the muzzles. Below: the Spad XIII, with markings of the 22nd Aero Squadron. Its 200 hp Hispano-Suiza engine gave it 130 mph (209 kph) at 6500 feet. Nearly 8500 were made and it was used until 1923.

the Camel needed an expert pilot. By 1915 many designers were coming to realize that stationary engines were the engines of the future.

The SPAD used a water-cooled V-8 automobile engine built by the Spanish Hispano-Suiza company. French ace Georges Guynemer actually had a 37 mm Hotchkiss installed between the V of the engine, firing through the hollow center of the gear-driven propeller, making the airplane a flying cannon. The engine had overhead cams, dual ignition, forced lubrication and other features which are still modern today. The wings were very thin, so that there was not much lift at low speeds, and it had to be landed at speed. The SPAD was not as manoeuvrable as some other planes, but it was that aim of a fighter designer, a stable gun platform: it was fast, either climbing or on the level, and it would stay together no matter what the pilot forced it to do. The aces loved it. The French Stork Squadron shot down more than two hundred enemy aircraft in the first six months after they had SPADs. Eventually more than 14,000 were built, including a few with 300 horsepower engines.

Meanwhile, Fokker was stuck with the Oberursel rotary engine. There was a water-cooled in-line Mercedes he wanted to use, but the Albatros factory had sewn up the Mercedes output; Fokker couldn't get one. Greater power was out for the moment, so Fokker's next design—in the end, his most famous—was the triplane, designed for rate of climb and manoeuvrability. The triplane was not a new idea; a Canadian squadron equipped with Tommy Sopwith's triplane shot down 87 Germans in three months during 1917. Three wings instead of two meant that the fuselage and the wingspan could be shorter, which was important for manoeuvrability, especially rate of turn; they meant better visibility, because the upper and lower wings were far from the line of sight, and the centre wing in line with it, so not obscuring vision very much.

Fokker's design had a phenomenal rate of climb and could reach 115 mph in level flight. It had excellent handling qualities at low speeds; although ground loops were common on landing, this was true of World War I planes in general. The aircraft was very strong and could absorb many bullet holes; one of its qualities was an absence of bracing wires which could be shot away. It was the favourite aircraft of the most famous ace of all, Baron von Richthofen.

But Fokker still wanted one of those Mercedes engines. So he organized a competition of aircraft factories, with the backing of the mutual admiration of Fokker and the fighter pilots themselves, and with the stipulation that in fairness all the new designs should use the same engine: the Mercedes. The competition took place in January 1918. Fokker brought several designs, and the first one tested (by

the Bloody Baron himself) had a fuselage which was almost the standard triplane design, but with longer biplane wings. As a result the craft was directionally unstable and had a bad stall behaviour. So Fokker and his workmen dragged it into a hanger and welded a two-foot section into the fuselage, as well as enlarging the fin. The result was an order for four hundred of the new model, which other factories had to build, including Albatros, paying Fokker royalties.

The new model was called the D-VII. About a thousand of them were eventually built; the US military used them after the war, and the Dutch were flying them until 1939. It had thick wings, and seemed to be able to stand still in mid-air, or hang from its propeller at 45 degrees, still under control and still spraying bullets around the sky.

The Fokker D-VII was the only German aircraft named by the Armistice terms as booty, but Fokker managed to smuggle the entire contents of his factories across the border into neutral Holland, by means of bribes.

Above: the famous Fokker 'Tripe'. Von Richthofen's first all-red plane was an Albatros. The red colour was supposed to be reserved for aces, but later, when Richthofen's squadron was flying triplanes, they all painted their planes red because they were worried about the conspicuousness of their leader's craft.
Left: the DVIII parasol monoplane was Fokker's last contribution to the war effort, in 1918. Its clean lines minimized slipstream drag, but only a few reached combat.

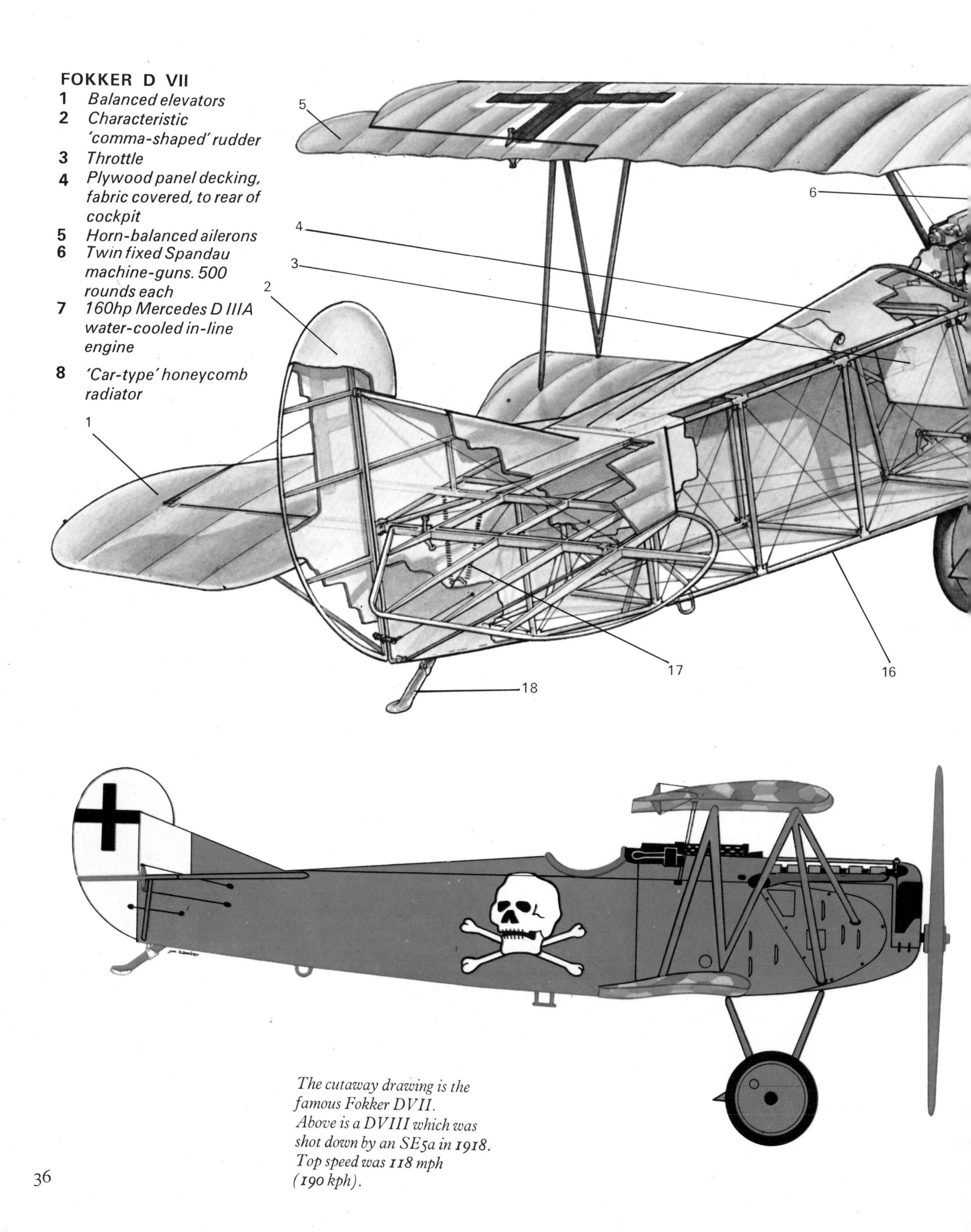

The cutaway drawing is the famous Fokker DVII. Above is a DVIII which was shot down by an SE5a in 1918. Top speed was 118 mph (190 kph).

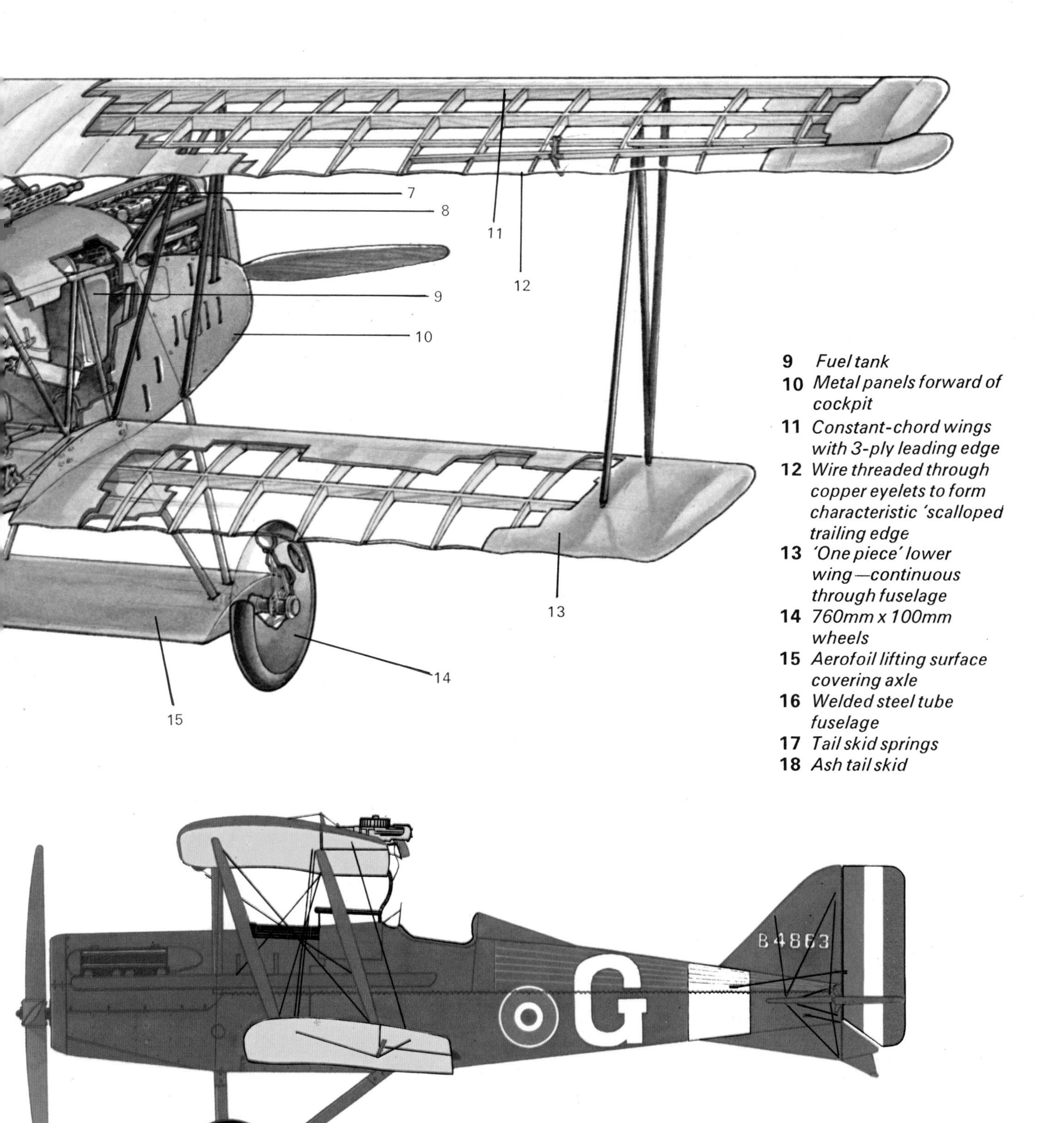

The SE5a was the workhorse of the RAC, and had a good combat record. The plane in this drawing is that piloted by James McCudden, who won the Victoria Cross in it.

Bombers

The use of bombs in war preceded that of machine guns, the first bombing raid being made in November 1911 by an Italian against Turkish positions in Libya. In the course of the two-year war fought by Italy to gain possession of Libya a fair amount of aerial work was undertaken, a factor that is often ignored by air historians. Thus by the outbreak of World War I some real progress had been made towards the development of true bombing aircraft. The most notable of these were the series of multi-engined aircraft that were built by the Italian pioneer Caproni, and the world's first four-engined bomber, the Russian Sikorsky Ilya Muromets, as it was renamed after the beginning of the war. In France, bombing was the special province of the Voisin series of aircraft, all ungainly pusher biplanes, but capable of carrying an acceptable load of bombs.

From its earliest days bombing fell into two categories, heavy and light. The Germans and British were quick to follow the Italians and the Russians, the former with their Gotha, AEG and *Riesen* (giant) aircraft, and the British with three biplanes from the Handley Page drawing boards.

The two main German twin-engined bombers were the AEG G IV and the Gotha G V, both of which had bomb loads in the order of 1,000 lbs (455 kg), speeds of 100 mph (160 kph) and ranges of 500 miles (1,600 km). Both types appeared in the autumn of 1916, and the Gotha in particular played an important part in the German bombing of England, which led directly to the formation of a unified and independent Royal Air Force by the amalgamation of the Royal Flying Corps and Royal Naval Air Service in April 1918. Most remarkable of Germany's bombers, however, was the series of R aircraft, vast multi-engined bombers that were not to be exceeded in size by production aircraft until after World War II. The best of these aircraft was the Zeppelin-Staaken R VI, which could carry a 4,000 lb (1,800 kg) bomb load over 700 miles (1,125 km) at a speed of 80 mph (130 kph). Wing span was 138 feet 5½ inches (42.2 m), and the whole series typified by the R VI was a *tour de force* in aeronautical engineering unequalled in World War I.

Britain's answers to these aircraft were the Handley Page 0/100, 0/400 and V/1500. The 0/100 and 0/400 were basically the same aircraft with different engines, and constituted Britain's main bombing force from 1916 to 1918. Bomb load was 2,000 lb (900 kg). Just entering service as the war ended was the V/1500, a four-engined machine intended to bomb industrial targets in Germany. Its maximum speed was almost 100 mph (160 kph) and range 1,200 miles (1,930 km), and the payload a very useful 7,500 lb (3,410 kg). This last would have made the V/1500 the world's first true strategic bomber had it been available in large numbers in 1918.

In the field of light bombing, the British and French fared

Above: an RAF air gunner is fitting the nose cap, which armed the weapon and had vanes to rotate it, to a Cooper 25 lb (11 kg) bomb, which was dropped by hand at the crew's discretion.

Far left: ground crew servicing the Handley Page V/1500. Wing span was 126 feet (38.4 m), length 64 feet (19.5 m).
Left: a Gotha GV being loaded with bombs. It could carry a bombload of over 1000 lb (455 kg).

better than the Germans, as exemplified by the two best single-engined bombers of the war: the Airco de Havilland DH 4 and up-engined 9A, and the Breguet 14. Both types were as fast as contemporary fighters, had an excellent defensive armament and could carry 500 to 600 lb (230 to 270 kg) of bombs. Operating in the tactical role, these two aircraft fulfilled a useful but not vital part in the final Allied victory.

The Germans did not make much use of the light bomber as such, concentrating on the ground-attack type. This class of machine was intended to be a manoeuvrable, two-seater but single-engined biplane capable of supporting the men on the ground from low altitude with bombs and machine gun fire. Best of these were the Halberstadt CL IV, the Hannover CL IIIa, and the Junkers CL I and J I. The two Junkers aircraft pioneered the use of metal in aircraft, the corrugated metal covering contributing considerably to the strength so needed in this type of aircraft. (The CL I was in fact a monoplane). These ground-support planes, as we would now designate them, proved very useful machines, and paved the way for the type of close-support work by aircraft that became so important in World War II.

The British, who used fighters to support their ground forces with machine gun fire and light bombs, also developed special low-level attack aircraft, the operations of fighters having shown the need for heavier armament and armour protection. The best example of this type of British aircraft was the Sopwith Trench Fighter (TF) 2, which appeared in limited numbers in 1918. Derived from the Snipe fighter, the Salamander had 2,000 rounds of ammunition for each gun, compared with the fighter's average of about 200, and had 650 lb (295 kg) of armour protection. Ammunition capacity and armour protection were to be factors that became vitally important in close-support aircraft in World War II.

Reconnaissance

At first reconnaissance was a simple matter: the observer merely peered over the side of his cockpit to see what was below the aircraft, and jotted down any relevant thing he saw. Despite the distinct lack of trained observers, such reconnaissance swiftly proved itself of use, and soon afterwards the first fighters appeared to try to prevent it. Thus there emerged a need for reconnaissance machines to defend themselves. The solution appeared easy: just arm the observer with a 'flexible' light machine gun of the Lewis type to beat off any attacker. Immediate problems were encountered here, however, for the observer in the commonest types such as the British BE-2 and German Albatros B I normally sat in the front cockpit, between the wings and surrounded by a 'birdcage' of rigging and bracing wires. It was hardly the ideal position from which to pour defensive fire, for there was every likelihood that the observer would shoot away a vital part of his own aircraft. The solution was simple, but took some time to implement: exchange the positions of the pilot and observer, thus giving the latter a clear field of fire over most of the upper hemisphere of his field of vision, as well as downwards on each side of the aircraft.

Better performance was also desirable, and so the new generation of reconnaissance machines were considerably more powerful than their predecessors. But although it was possible to increase performance in matters such as speed, designers had a very tricky job with such aircraft in other respects. In order to make the task of the crew as easy as

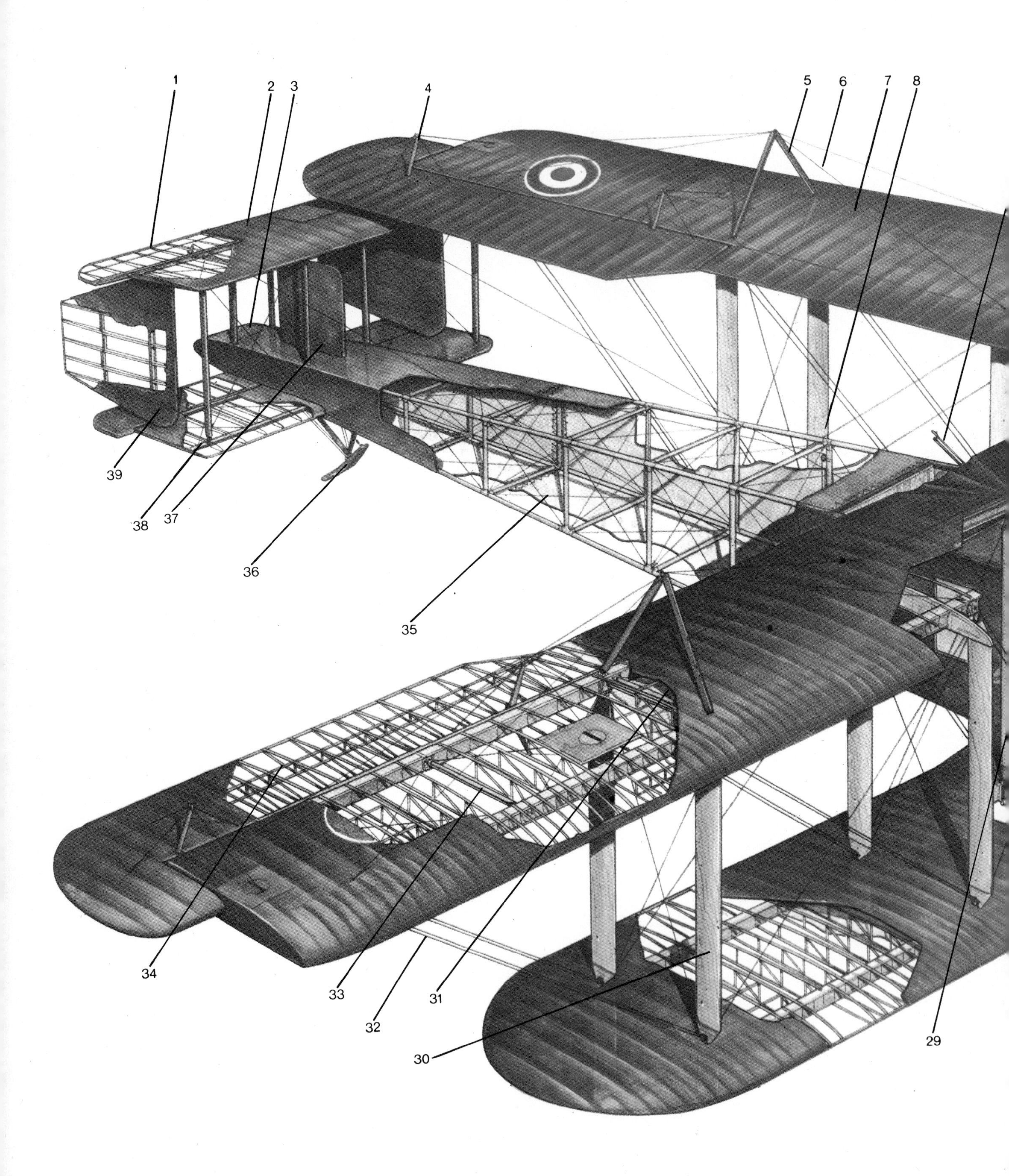
1
2
3
4
5
6
7
8
39
38
37
36
35
34
33
32
31
30
29

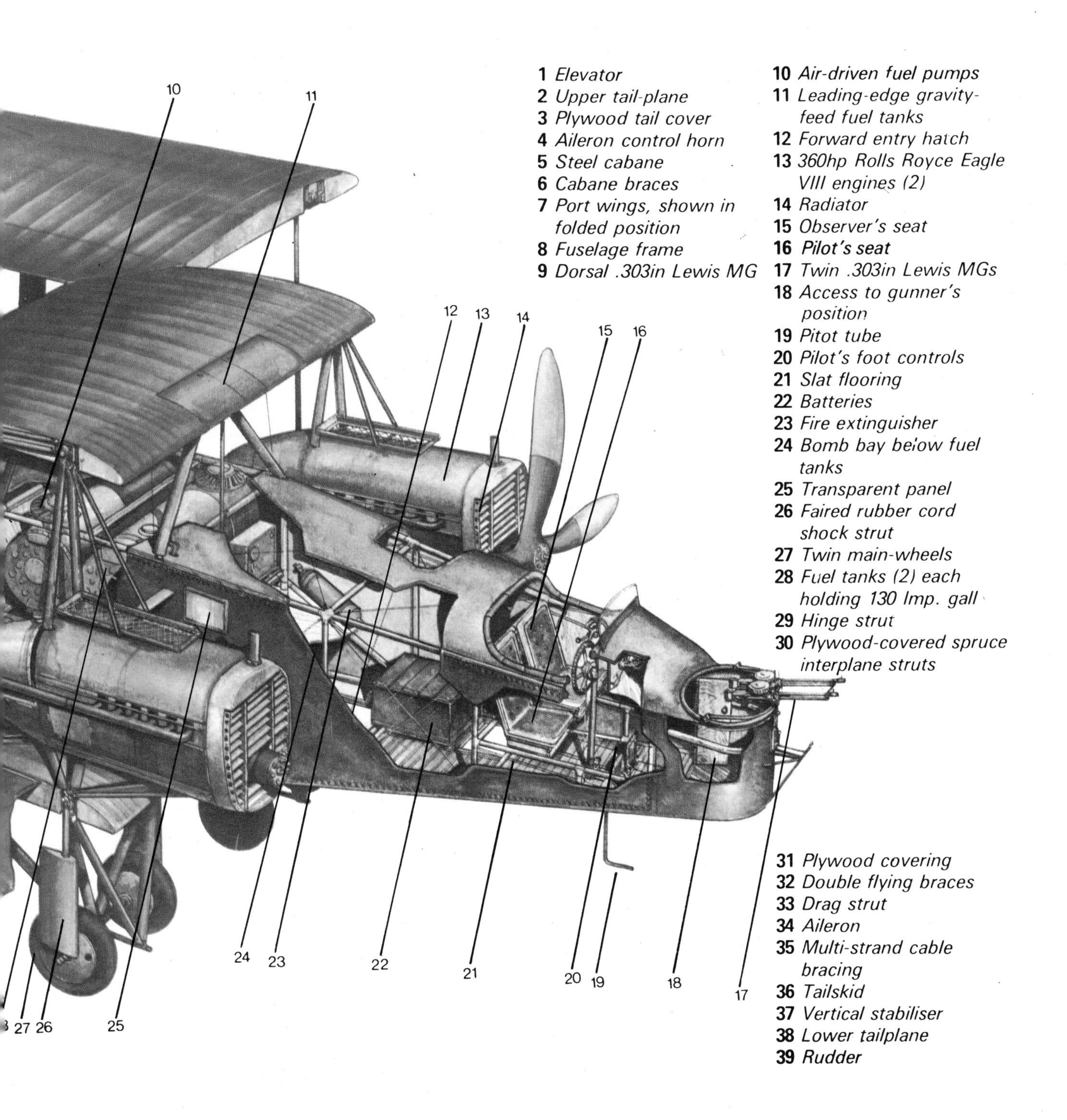

The Handley Page HP 0/400 had two Rolls-Royce V-8 engines of 350 hp each. There were 3 to 5 crew members. Wing span was 100 feet (30.5 m) (upper) and 70 feet (21 m) (lower). Length was 62 feet 10¼ inches (about 19 m). She could carry a bombload of about 2000 lbs (907 kg), more than any other Allied aircraft of the period, as well as some Cooper bombs.

66

Above left: a Sopwith 1½-strutter takes off from a platform mounted on a gun turret.
Left: a Short 166 seaplane flying past Ark Royal, *hastily converted in 1913. She carried 10 planes.*
Above top: the Furious *went through several conversions beginning in 1913. This picture shows Sopwith Camels on the flying-off deck.*
Above: a towed lighter as a one-plane carrier was a dead-end experiment.

possible for the primary task of reconnaissance, a certain amount of inherent stability was desirable. Yet in air-to-air combat any measure of inherent stability was a liability. How was the designer to balance these two conflicting requirements? The answer, particularly on the British side, was that he could not: the Royal Aircraft Factory RE-8, which entered widespread service in 1917, was in many respects too stable to protect itself adequately in combat. Yet when given protection by fighters, it proved an admirable reconnaissance and artillery spotting aircraft, and showed itself to be one of the best and most successful types flown by Britain during World War I. The RE-8 was not fast but its endurance was good, armament of one fixed gun for the pilot and one or two flexible guns for the observer was adequate, and the payload good, the type being able to carry 260 lb (120 kg) of bombs or one of the clumsy radio sets needed for the essential work of artillery spotting. The Armstrong Whitworth FK-8 fulfilled a similar function at about the same time.

Germany operated a plethora of reconnaissance types, and these served the army exceptionally well. From the Albatros B I, Aviatik B I and LVG B I, all unarmed biplanes in service at the beginning of the war, the Germans quickly moved on to the armed C-class machines, exemplified by the Albatros C I, III and VI (1915-6), the DFW C IV (1916), and the LFG (Roland) C II (1916). These were adequate machines with good armament and range, and in the case of the Roland C II, excellent performance. In the closing stages of World War I the Germans continued to produce first-class reconnaissance machines, all engined with powerful and reliable Mercedes or Benz inline motors.

Although their appearance was often very similar to that of single-engined fighters, these reconnaissance machines were somewhat larger than the fighters, for apart from an extra crewman, they all had to carry radio for artillery spotting or cameras for the photographic reconnaissance roles. Both these items had been reduced in weight and size very considerably by the end of the war, but were still bulky, heavy articles that required a considerable area of wing to provide lift.

Maritime aircraft

Land-based maritime aircraft were for the most part obsolete aircraft from other theatres fitted out to carry a few small bombs and used as patrol aircraft against submarines, operating in conjunction with small non-rigid airships. Towards the end of the war there emerged the aircraft-carrier, and a few modern types were adapted to fly from the decks of such vessels. The most interesting 'landplane' for maritime use developed during the war, however, was the Sopwith Cuckoo. This was the first torpedo-bomber to be designed for use from a carrier, but few were delivered before the armistice. Nevertheless, it pointed the way to what was to be the carrier's most potent weapon in the next war.

The classic flying-boats of the war were undoubtedly the Curtiss America series, the Franco-British Aviation Type H, the Felixstowe F 2A and the Macchi M5. The first three were fairly substantial patrol flying-boats, but the last was an interesting and quite high-performance fighter for use in the Adriatic. Because of their need to operate from water, all these craft were solidly built, and this stood their crews in good stead in combat, in which small calibre machine gun fire frequently failed to shoot down the larger flying-boats.

The aeronautical technology developed during the First World War is not to be sneered at. Later engines were more reliable, but their power-to-weight ratio was not that much better; given the materials the designers had to work with, today's designers could not have done much better.

THE INTER-WAR YEARS

The first fifteen years after the end of World War I are usually considered sterile ones for military aviation. Admittedly, money was in short supply and therefore air force authorities all over the world had to be parsimonious when it came to ordering new types. No enormous orders were placed, but small orders for a variety of fighting types helped air forces to keep up a steady, if slow, progress.

The important factor was that all the elements needed to make the rapid progress of the middle and late 1930s possible were being developed in a variety of otherwise unremarkable aircraft. Structures, for example, had been mostly of wood, braced with wires, during World War I. There had been exceptions, such as the Fokker welded tubular steel construction pioneered by Reinhold Platz, and the Junkers corrugated iron covering, which so strengthened structures that no bracing wires were needed. Shortly after the end of the war, Short Brothers produced a monocoque aircraft covered in metal, the Silver Streak, which was to prove the true progenitor of later stressed-skin metal monocoque aircraft. Throughout the 1920s a number of builders on both sides of the Atlantic experimented with metal construction and skinning, paving the way for the designers of the 1930s.

Careful attention also became the norm in the field of streamlining. A few pre-World War I aircraft had shown what might be achieved in this field, and during the war the later Albatros fighters and reconnaissance machines had achieved a fair level of streamlining. But after the war it was the Americans, particularly the Curtiss company, that began to make great strides. The performance of Curtiss aircraft, with their beautifully cowled engines, impressed the Europeans, and the British and Italians soon began to overtake the Americans. Streamlining entered the military field with aircraft such as the Fairey Fox, but the greatest strides were made in racing aircraft such as the Supermarine and Macchi series of floatplane racers for the Schneider trophy. The culmination of streamlining on the post-war type of fighter was on the British Hawker Hart.

Right: the Supermarine S6, with a Vickers airframe and a Rolls-Royce engine, won the Schneider Trophy in 1929 and boosted the world airspeed record to over 400 mph (644 kph). The airframe was the predecessor of the Spitfire, and the engine was developed to become the Merlin.

During the late 1920s, several companies in several countries built tri-motor transport planes. The Fokker tri-motor was even built under licence in America. In June 1927, a month after Lindbergh's solo flight, Richard Byrd and three friends flew the Atlantic non-stop from New York to Normandy in a Fokker tri-motor. (A year later, in another Fokker, Amelia Earhart became the first woman to fly the Atlantic.) The most famous tri-motor of all was undoubtedly the Ford, affectionately nick-named the 'tin goose'. This was the first aircraft to fly over the South Pole, in November 1929, again carrying Richard Byrd.

The tri-motors made an important contribution to civil aircraft because of their reliability; beginning in 1932, more than 4,800 German Junkers tri-motors were built in at least 30 different versions, some of them seaplanes. The 'barn-storming' adolescence of aviation was over, and aircraft were safe enough to carry paying passengers. The Boeing Monomail was a low-wing monoplane built in 1931 especially for postal service; it was the first American transport aircraft with retractable landing gear. In 1932 the Boeing 247, a twin-engined low-wing monoplane with retractable landing gear, was the first really modern passenger airliner. Exclusively available to United Airlines, it made a success of that company, and forced TWA to commission a similar airplane from Douglas.

The result of that commission, the DC-1, became the DC-2 when it went into production, and more than 200 were built. Its successor, the DC-3, first flew in late 1935, and became the most prestigious aircraft in the world. Just before the Second World War, four-fifths of the aircraft used by American transport carriers were DC-3s. During the war itself, the DC-3 was known as the C-53 Skytrooper, the C-47 Skytrain, the RAF Dakota, and in general as the work-horse of World War II. More than 13,000 were built, of which about 1,000 are still in use today: not a bad record for a design more than forty years old. By the late 1930s American transport aircraft were being exported; the United States had made up for lost time and become leaders.

Above centre: the famous Ford Tri-motor, called the 'tin goose'. The aircraft had an excellent reputation for reliability. Several nations built aircraft with three engines.
Left: a United Airlines DC-3. This forty-year-old design set the standard for the world's passenger airliners; many hundreds of them are still in service around the world.

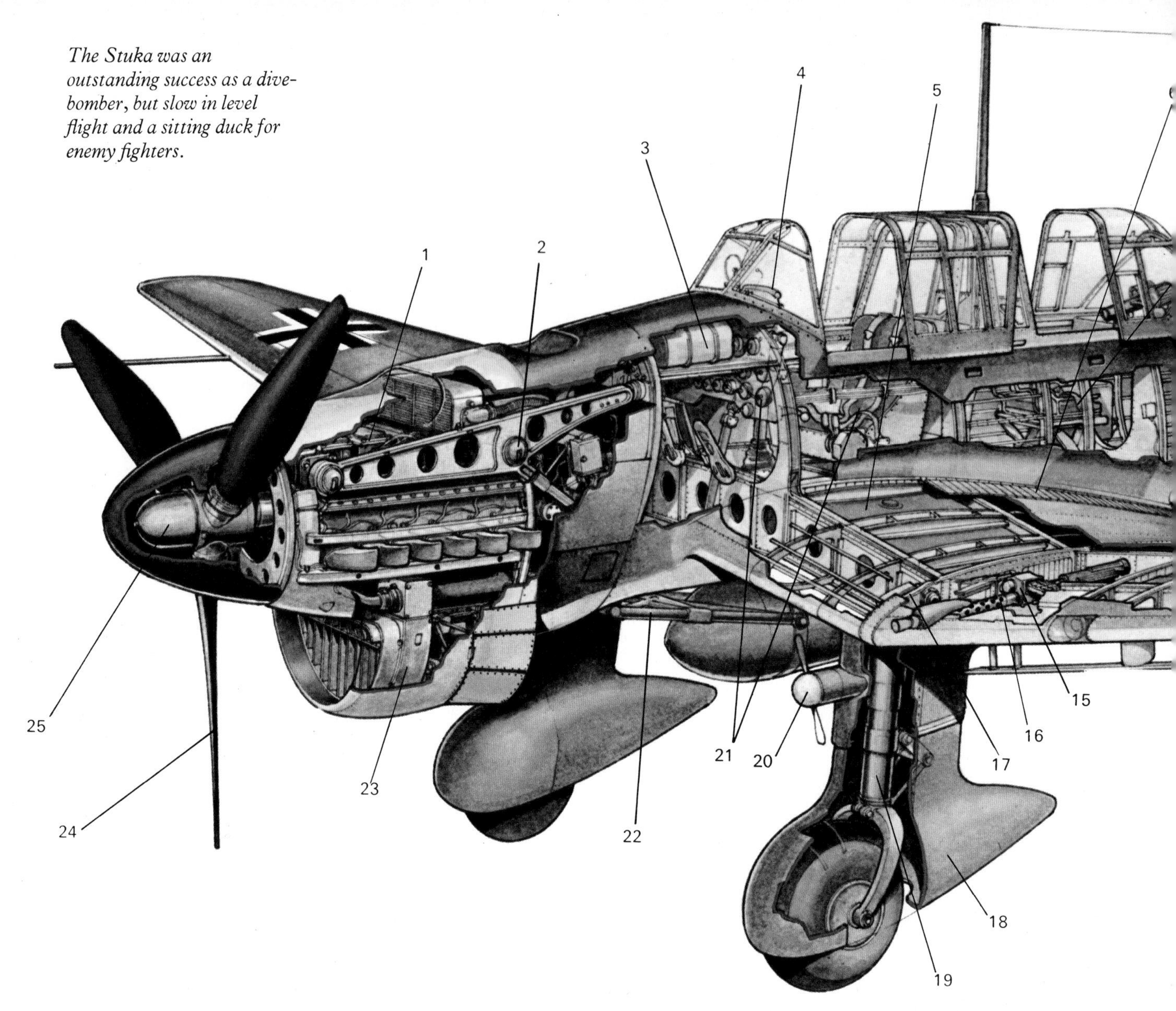

The Stuka was an outstanding success as a dive-bomber, but slow in level flight and a sitting duck for enemy fighters.

At the same time, the Americans made great strides in developing modern twin-engined bombers, first with the Boeing YB-9 in the early 1930s and then with the Martin B-10, which was fast enough at 215 mph (345 kph) to outfly contemporary fighters.

The wind tunnel, pioneered by the Wright brothers among others, became an important design tool in the 1930s. Apart from acceptance of the necessity for streamlining and retractable landing gear, wind tunnel tests resulted in the British Handley Page automatic slot, an air-pressure operated device mounted on the leading edge of the wing to warn of an approaching stall, and actually delay the stall by inducing an extra flow of air through the slot to smooth the air flow. At the trailing edge, moveable flaps were attached to increase lift at low forward speeds by increasing the wing and accentuating camber.

Curtiss had undertaken much development work with the dive-bombing notion in the 1920s, with emphasis on its application to naval aircraft, and by the end of the 1930s the US Navy was well advanced in the theory of dive-bombing, and had some interesting types in service or being designed. The Germans, however, saw the dive-bomber as 'flying artillery' to support their rapidly moving ground forces, spearheaded by armoured formations with which conventional artillery units would not be able to keep up. This type of tactics was experimented with and proved in the Spanish Civil War, in which the Germans and Italians helped the Nationalists under General Franco. The basic German dive-bomber was the Junkers Ju 87 Stuka.

Russia had considered strategic bombing by four-engined aircraft late in the 1920s, and the Tupolev design bureau had produced a series of large aircraft, culminating in the great ANT-6 early in the 1930s. But then came a change of policy in favour of tactical use of Russian air-power, and this early lead in heavy bombing was discarded. The United States was also interested in this type of bombing, and designs by Boeing, Consolidated and Douglas materialized in the late 1930s. The designs of the first two companies went into production as the Boeing B-17 Flying Fortress and the Consolidated B-24 Liberator, powerful four-engined aircraft capable of carrying some 8,000 lb (3,635 kg) of bombs over great ranges.

The B-17 first flew in 1935, but only a few were delivered in time for the war, and most of these were destroyed by the Japanese in December 1941. That same month, however, the remaining B17s carried out the first offensive of the war by American aircraft, bombing some Japanese ships. Eventually more than 12,700 were built. The slightly less famous B-24 Liberator was designed in 1939. It was a versatile aircraft, used as a troop transport, for reconnais-

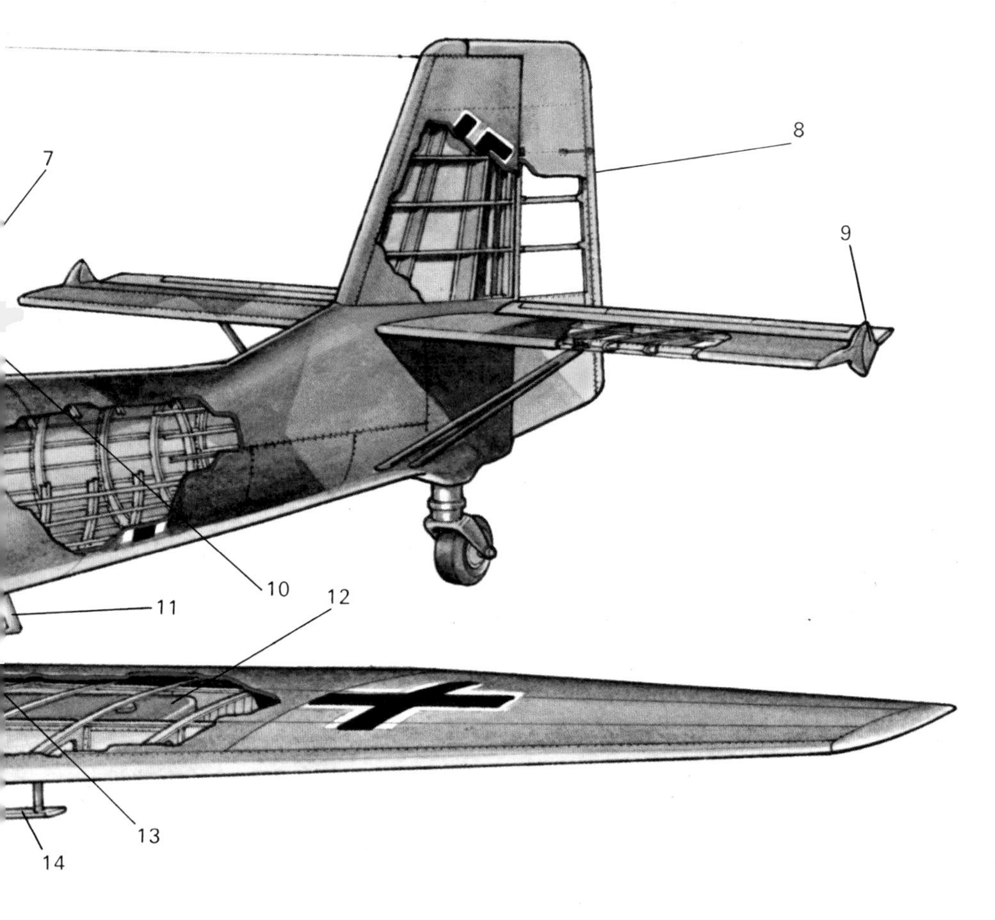

1 Junkers Jumo 211 12-cylinder inverted-Vee
2 Anti-vibration mounts
3 Oil tank
4 Crash-protection padding
5 Self-sealing fuel tank
6 Non-slip walk-way
7 Radio operator's/ Gunner's folding seat
8 Rudder trim tab
9 Elevator mass balance
10 7.9mm MG 15
11 Crew entry step
12 Self sealing fuel tank
13 Inboard flap
14 Dive brake
15 Case and link container for MG 17
16 Port 7.9 MG 17
17 Front spar attachment
18 Wheel spat
19 Undercarriage oleo leg
20 Dive-bombing siren
21 Pilot's cockpit and instruments
22 Bomb sling
23 Radiator
24 Junkers 3-blade VS 11 constant-speed prop
25 Pitch change mechanism in propeller boss

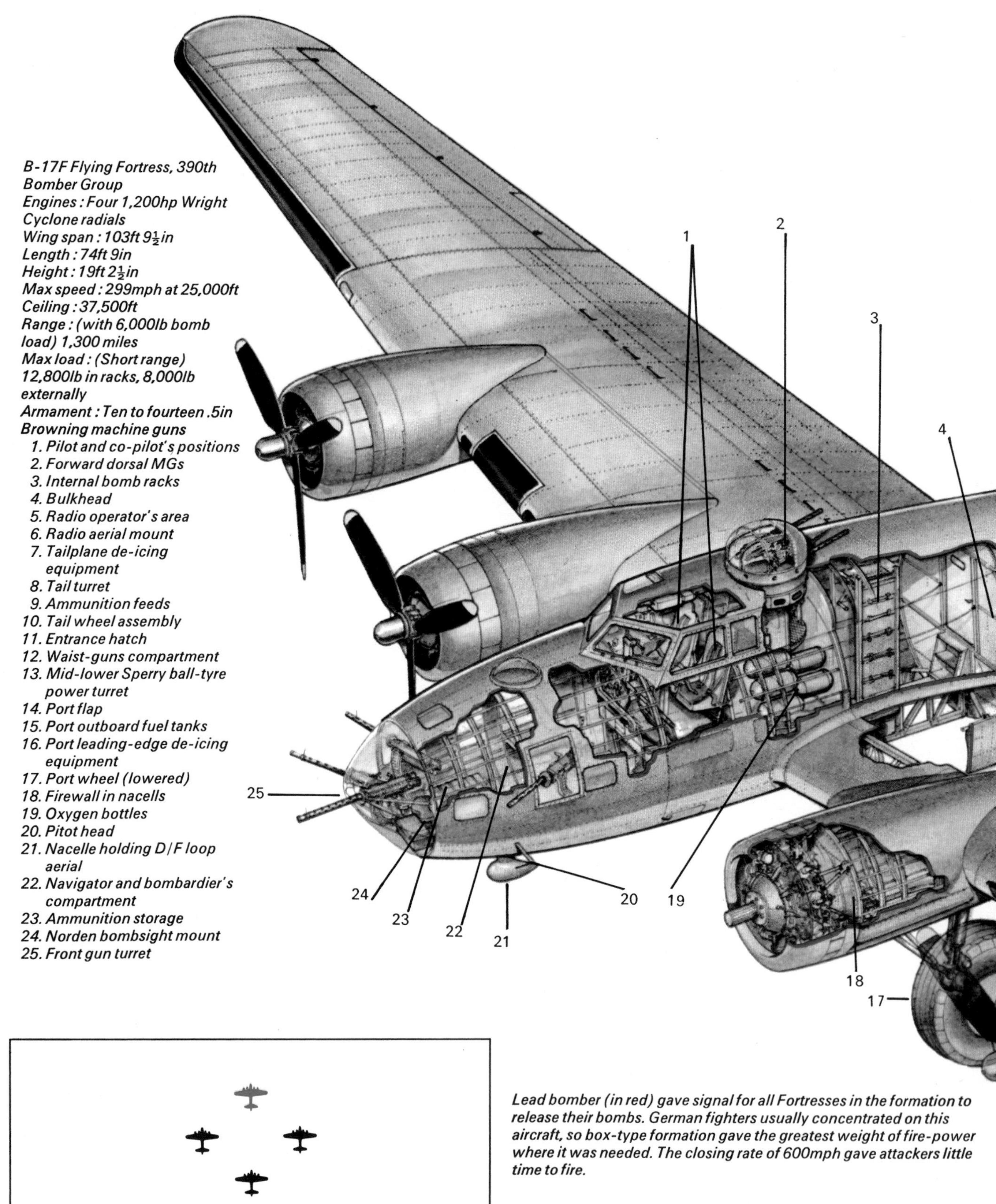

B-17F Flying Fortress, 390th Bomber Group
Engines: Four 1,200hp Wright Cyclone radials
Wing span: 103ft 9½in
Length: 74ft 9in
Height: 19ft 2½in
Max speed: 299mph at 25,000ft
Ceiling: 37,500ft
Range: (with 6,000lb bomb load) 1,300 miles
Max load: (Short range) 12,800lb in racks, 8,000lb externally
Armament: Ten to fourteen .5in Browning machine guns

1. *Pilot and co-pilot's positions*
2. *Forward dorsal MGs*
3. *Internal bomb racks*
4. *Bulkhead*
5. *Radio operator's area*
6. *Radio aerial mount*
7. *Tailplane de-icing equipment*
8. *Tail turret*
9. *Ammunition feeds*
10. *Tail wheel assembly*
11. *Entrance hatch*
12. *Waist-guns compartment*
13. *Mid-lower Sperry ball-tyre power turret*
14. *Port flap*
15. *Port outboard fuel tanks*
16. *Port leading-edge de-icing equipment*
17. *Port wheel (lowered)*
18. *Firewall in nacells*
19. *Oxygen bottles*
20. *Pitot head*
21. *Nacelle holding D/F loop aerial*
22. *Navigator and bombardier's compartment*
23. *Ammunition storage*
24. *Norden bombsight mount*
25. *Front gun turret*

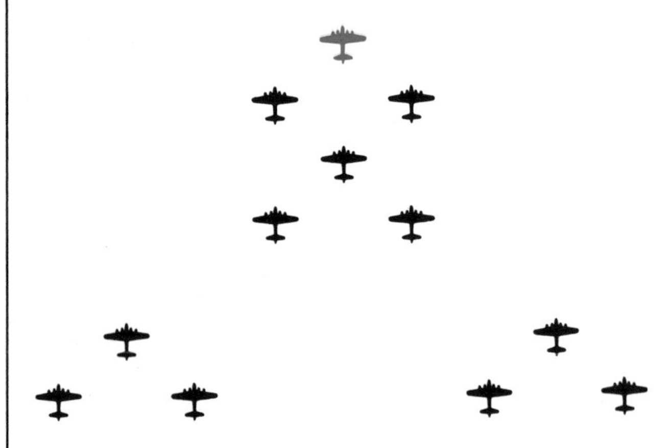

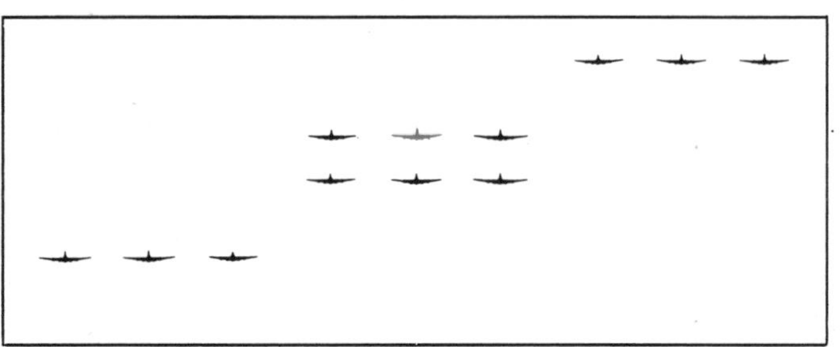

Lead bomber (in red) gave signal for all Fortresses in the formation to release their bombs. German fighters usually concentrated on this aircraft, so box-type formation gave the greatest weight of fire-power where it was needed. The closing rate of 600mph gave attackers little time to fire.

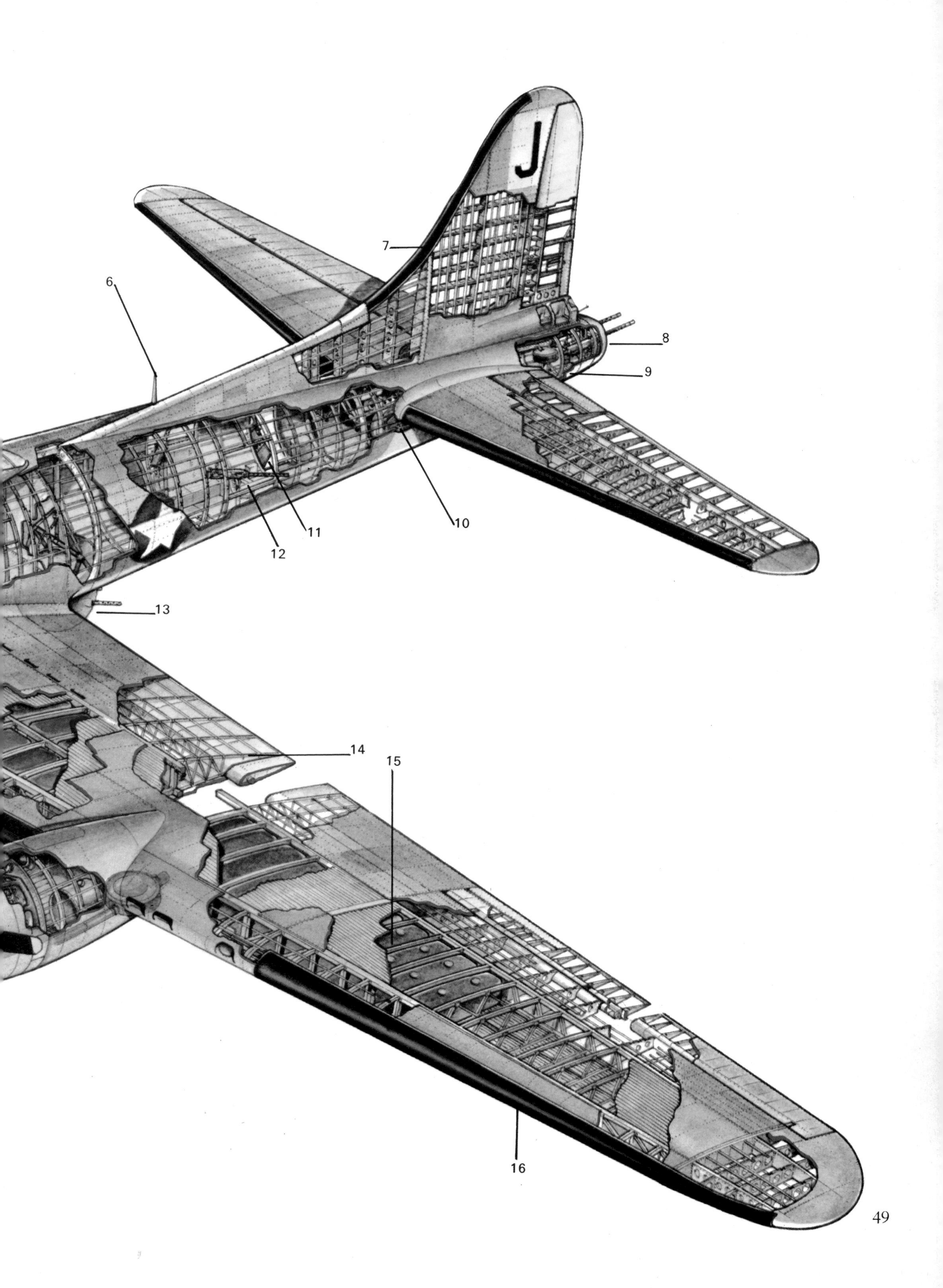
J
6
7
8
9
10
11
12
13
14
15
16

Above: Consolidated B-24 Liberator.
Below: Avro Lancaster.

sance and as a submarine killer as well as a bomber. It was the Liberator which bombed the Romanian oilfields at Ploesti from bases in Libya. More than 18,000 Liberators were built, more than any other American aircraft of the war.

At the same time great advances were made in the provision of adequate bomb-sights. Britain too was interested in heavy bombing, and a trio of four-engined bombers was under development in the late 1930s: the Short Stirling, the Handley Page Halifax and the Avro Lancaster, the last a four-engined version of the unsuccessful Avro Manchester twin-engined bomber.

In the field of fighters it was Russia that led the world in the early 1930s, with the introduction of a new type of fighter, the Polikarpov I-16. This was a small stubby aircraft which soon became obsolete, but for the first time on a production fighter it featured an enclosed cockpit, cantilever monoplane wings, a retractable undercarriage and an armament including provision for cannon and rockets. Both these weapons had been experimented with during World War I, principally by the French, but now they became an accepted feature on fighter aircraft.

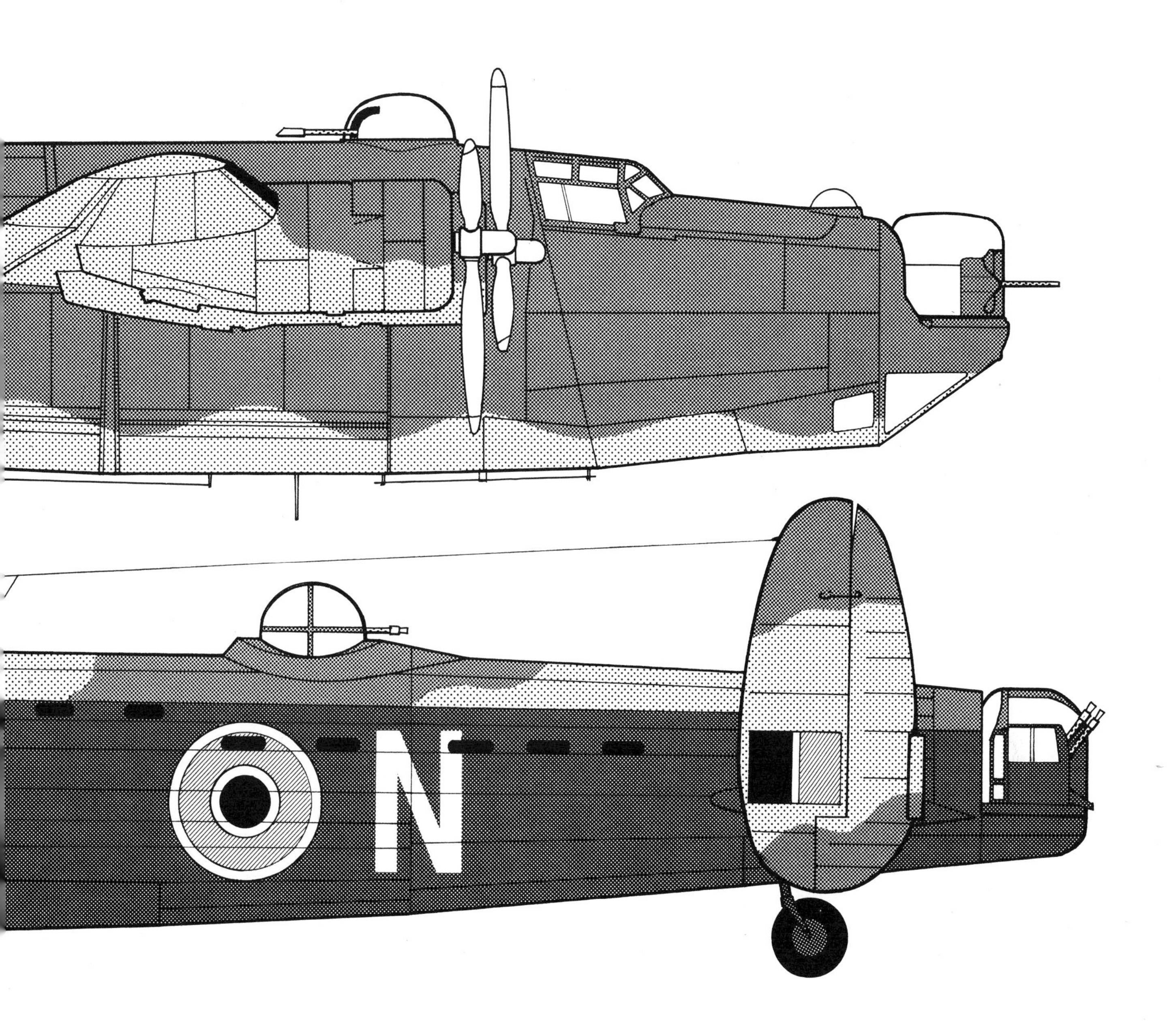

Other nations had already been designing such fighters, and the I-16 was soon followed by the German Messerschmitt Bf 109, the British Hawker Hurricane and Supermarine Spitfire, the French Morane-Saulnier MS 406 and Bloch 151, and the American Curtiss P-40 series. With the exception of the Bloch fighter, all these types were powered by in-line engines, whose high power combined with low frontal area recommended them for short-range aircraft. At this time radials found more favour as powerplants for heavier, long-range aircraft, as they were more economical in fuel than inlines.

The scene was thus set for World War II with aircraft that were of cantilever construction, with enclosed cockpits and retractable undercarriages, of metal construction for the most part, and with speeds in the 250 to 350 mph (400 to 565 kph) range. Armament on fighters comprised either a mixture of cannon and machine guns, as on French and German aircraft, or a large number of machine guns, as on British and American aircraft. In general, performance was radically improved, with ceilings now raised to about 35,000 ft (10,670 m) by the use of various types of engine supercharging developed in the 1920s and 1930s.

RETRACTABLE UNDERCARRIAGE

The benefits of streamlining have been recognized from the earliest days of flying. By smoothing the profiles of aircraft and removing as far as possible awkward protrusions, their speed could be increased and the range for a given quantity of fuel burned extended. An obvious candidate for this treatment is the undercarriage or landing gear, which is not only large but serves no purpose once the aircraft has left the ground. The undercarriage comprises the wheels, axles, brakes and the supporting structure, and is inevitably bulky since it has to be strong enough to absorb the stresses of take-off and landing. The drag of these units, that is their resistance to motion through the air, is great even at low speeds and increases sharply as the plane accelerates.

In 1908, only five years after the birth of powered flight, the first primitive mechanically operated retractable undercarriage appeared. It was fitted to an aircraft built by an American, Matthew Sellers, and was patented in the USA three years later.

In the surge of enthusiasm for aviation which appeared following the successes of aircraft in World War I it was the racing plane builders which made the first demands on technology. The Dayton-Wright monoplane which competed in France for the 1920 Gordon Bennett air race had the first really modern retractable landing gear, and it was

Above: Stirling landing gear partly retracted for servicing. Large planes of this vintage sometimes had gear which did not fully retract, leaving a bit of tyre showing.

followed in 1922 by a British aircraft, the Bristol Monoplane racer. The US aircraft had wheels which retracted into circular recesses in the fuselage after a fashion which was to characterize American single-engined fighters for many years afterwards. Those of the British racer folded into circular wells in the underside of the wing.

For some years after the war technical developments in aviation stagnated. In particular little headway was made in engine design, so cruising speeds remained low and there was little justification for the general adoption of expensive innovations where the benefits were relatively small. Quite significant improvements could be made by the very simple expedient of enclosing the landing gear in streamlined fairings known as spats, which were cheap and light. Those retractable wheel systems which did appear were to be found on amphibious aircraft, since fixed wheels could not be used in operation from water. In such cases the need was simply to prevent the wheels from dragging in the water, and little thought was given to refining their installation so as to improve cruising performance.

But in America the ability of the aircraft to conquer vast distances with speed was beginning to be recognized and in 1930 Boeing brought out a very clean design, called the

Below left: the scissor-type hydraulic mechanism on this modern nose-wheel gear is designed to tilt up the nose of the aircraft during take-off.
Bottom of page: this BAC-Sepecat Jaguar is an example of a modern aircraft where the wheels must be tucked away into the fuselage because the wings are too thin to accomodate them.

Monomail, for the US postal services; it was the first utility aircraft to boast a retractable undercarriage. Two years later the same company flew its Model 247, the world's first modern transport aircraft, which in addition to many other technical advances, could fold its wheels away. The introduction of variable-pitch propellers, which permitted higher cruising speeds to be attained without sacrificing the low-speed efficiency required for good landing and take-off performance, was a technical break-through which justified greater efforts in drag-reduction.

By the late 1930s most of the new commercial and military types coming into service or projected employed retractable landing gear, made possible by developments in the technology of high-pressure hydraulic mechanisms. The undercarriages of even the smallest aircraft are heavy, and considerable force is needed during retraction to overcome the weight and wind-resistance forces. These difficulties increase with speed. Some of the early aircraft, such as the Avro Anson, had a mechanical screw-jack device for winding the wheels up by hand, a very tedious process. Others, for example the initial marks of Spitfires, used rudimentary hydraulic circuits energized by hand-pumps to achieve the desired result. Neither method was acceptable for the bigger aircraft then in prospect, some of them four-engined, but the development of progressively higher-pressure circuits, energized by pumps driven from the engines, overcame these difficulties, and hydraulic retraction is now universally employed.

Designers have shown much ingenuity in tucking wheels away into increasingly more crowded airframes. In the days of piston-engined aircraft the wheels of multi-engine types were traditionally pulled up into the engine nacelles, a convenient arrangement since the nacelles comprised little more than empty fairings. In many cases the nacelles were not quite deep enough to completely enclose the wheels, so that some of the tyre was left protruding. The loss of performance was quite small as the wheels were of smooth contour and produced little drag. On some planes, notably the Douglas DC-3, the wheels protruded some way below the profile of the lower fuselage and wings so that in an emergency the plane could be landed on them, while still retracted, without causing much damage. On single-engined types the wheels most frequently folded away into the wings. Nowadays the wings of fighters are so thin that they cannot accommodate the landing gear, and very complicated mechanical arrangements are necessary to fold them in such a way that they take up the least possible space in the fuselage.

Failure of the landing gear to retract after take off is usually no more than an inconvenience, but inability to lower the gear for landing can be catastrophic, so safety arrangements have to be made to deal with this emergency. Normally the gear is designed so that when the uplocks, which prevent the undercarriage from inadvertently extending in flight, are freed, the gear falls to the landing position under the influence of gravity.

FLYING BOATS

The practice of flying aircraft off water is almost as old as aviation itself and results from the number of good natural runways available from the world's rivers, lakes and harbours. It releases the aircraft from its greatest limitation, the need for specially prepared strips of ground for take-off and landing. If, however, the seaplane is fitted with retractable wheels to exploit landing strips as well, it becomes the truly liberated amphibian. Even today, when airfields proliferate, there are more seaplanes and amphibians in service than ever before.

The true water plane is the flying boat, with the fuselage itself designed to operate on water with most of the characteristics of a boat. Most small landplanes can be fitted with mini-hulls or floats instead of wheels and, as such, earn the separate designation of floatplane.

The first recorded successful flight from water was made in March 1910 by Henri Fabre of France, just over six years after the Wright brothers achieved the first sustained powered flight of a heavier-than-air aircraft. The next step, in 1911, introduced one of the great names of seaplane development when Glenn Curtiss of the USA flew a novel craft with a single float—to which wheels were soon added to produce the first amphibian. His first real flying boat came out the following year, and suddenly seaplanes gained acceptance. In 1914 the world's first scheduled airline began in Florida, operating between St Petersburg and Tampa.

1913 to 1931 were the years of the famous Schneider Trophy races for seaplanes, whose role in stimulating high performance technology is reflected in the progress of winning average speeds from 47.75 mph (76.8 km/h) for the first meeting to 340 mph (547 km/h) for the last. The final winner, Britain's Supermarine S.6B, later set a world record of 407 mph (655 km/h), and evolved directly into the Spitfire of World War II fame.

Britain's efforts, in fact, led seaplane development of all kinds through the 1920s and early 1930s, culminating in the huge Short Sarafand of 1935 which, with its 150 ft (65.7 m) wingspan, was the largest biplane built. But, by then, such devotion to biplanes had already cost Britain the lead, as faster monoplane flying boats were developed in Europe and America. Germany's 12-engined Dornier Do.X, although

Above top: a Short Calcutta flying boat of Imperial Airways on the Thames. It went into service in 1928, was of all-metal construction and carried fifteen passengers at a top speed of 110 mph (177 kph).
Opposite page: a Consolidated PBY Catalina.
Below: a pre-war Dornier DO-X seaplane.

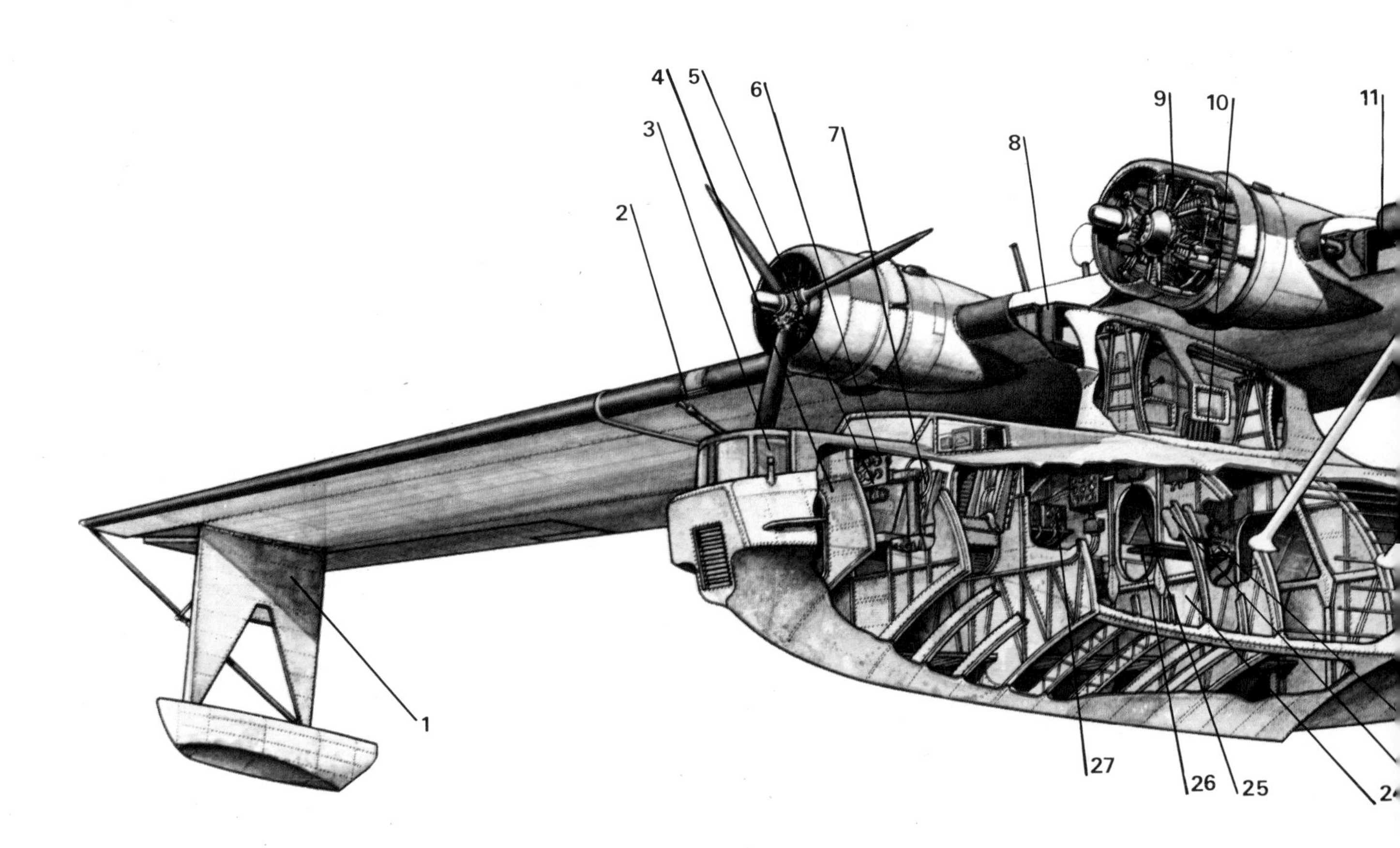
1
2
3
4
5
6
7
8
9
10
11
25
26
27

never entering service, introduced the age of the giants, dominated by the great Sikorsky boats and Martin Clippers of America. Finally came the Boeing 314 Clipper which, in 1939, established scheduled transatlantic passenger services. Largest of all was Howard Hughes' 460,000 lb (208,650 kg) Hercules, with a 320 ft (97.54 m) wingspan, which made its first and only flight in 1947, and could have carried 700 passengers. It is the largest aircraft ever to fly, with an overall length of 219 ft (66.75 m). Among the most famous aircraft of World War II are America's Consolidated Catalina and Britain's Short Sunderland flying boats, used unceasingly for maritime patrol in both the Atlantic and the Pacific.

Opposite page: a Short Sunderland marine rescue and anti-submarine flying boat used in WW II.
Right: the PBY4 Catalina's port blister gun.
Below: RAF Coastal Command Catalina Mk IVA (PBY5 with equipment supplied under Lend-Lease). She had two Pratt & Whitney 14-cylinder radial engines, and carried 7-9 crew. Wingspan was 104 feet (31.7 m).

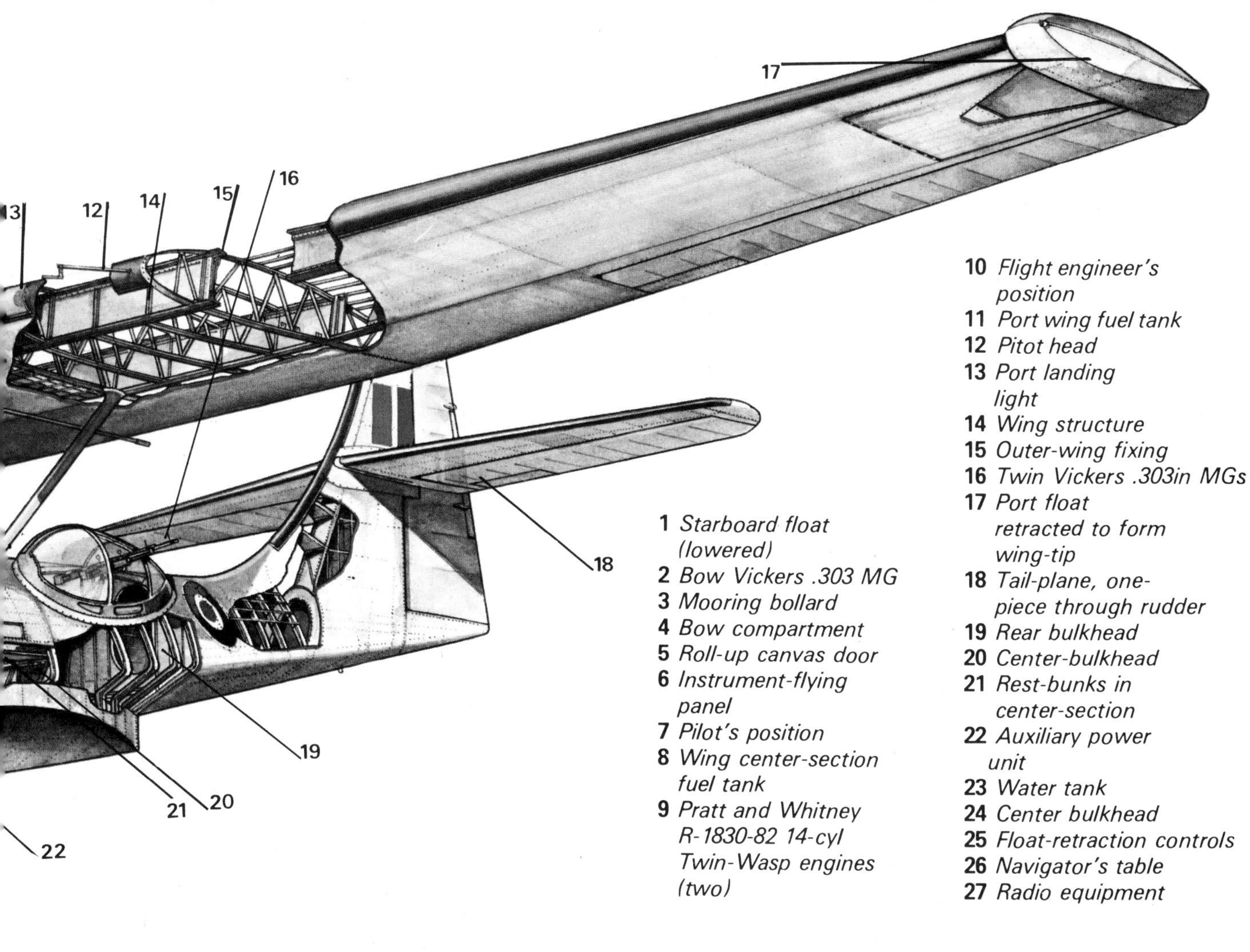

THE AUTOGYRO

An autogyro is a heavier-than-air flying machine which derives its lift from a rotor system mounted above the machine, with blades rotating more or less horizontally.

Autogyros differ from helicopters in that their rotor blades are driven by the air flowing upwards past them (the principle being known as autorotation), whereas the helicopter has mechanically driven blades set at a greater pitch angle, so as to 'screw upwards' through the air.

To maintain height, or climb, an autogyro needs a propulsive system such as an engine and a propeller to drive it forwards. Then, by tilting the lift rotor system slightly backwards, the rotor blades will lift the aircraft, even though the air flows up and through the rotor.

A simple autogyro needs some forward speed to maintain height, so unlike the helicopter, it cannot hover or take off vertically.

The motion of the rotor and the resulting upward thrust, or lift, depends entirely upon autorotation, resulting from the air flowing up and through the slightly tilted rotor blades as the machine moves forward.

Nature has applied the principle of autorotation for millions of years, seen in the whirling flight of the sycamore seed as it falls to the ground. Autorotation slows its descent and the wind has greater opportunity to disperse the seeds over a wider area.

The windmill was probably the first human invention which used autorotation, by harnessing the wind to produce rotary motion. The idea of a flying windmill, where rotating sails produced a wind to lift the machine, had a certain fascination with inventors, and among Leonardo da Vinci's thousands of drawings is an idea for flight along these lines. The real possibility for achieving such a machine was, however, delayed until the development of the aerofoil and the aircraft which embodied this device.

A windmill is basically an airscrew or propeller working in reverse, such that the air flowing over the sails is deflected by them, and exerts a force on the sails pushing them round. The sails effectively 'give way' to the wind and are pushed round by it.

As early as the Middle Ages, however, it was realized that if the sails were set at a very flat angle to the wind they would be made to rotate against the airflow and thus be 'pulled' round into the wind. The principle here is the same as with a sailing ship which can 'tack' close to the wind, meaning it can move forward against the wind, at a shallow angle to it, if the sails are properly set. In much the same way a glider moves forward as it descends through the air.

The rotor blades of an autogyro are shaped to achieve the same effect, and set at a shallow angle of about 3° to the horizontal plane in which they rotate. The shape is that of an aerofoil which enables the blades to turn into the airflow rather than be pushed round by it.

When turning fast these rotor blades offer considerable resistance to the upward airflow, and it is this resistance that can be used to provide lift. The amount of lift created depends upon a compromise between the airspeed of the rotors, and the resistance the rotating blades offer to the airflow past them. In practice, the desired lifting force is only produced when the blade speed greatly exceeds the forward speed of the machine.

To take off the rotor must produce adequate lift and it is necessary, therefore, to bring the rotor up to the required speed. This can be done in two ways.

The first and simplest way is to propel the machine forwards and, by tilting back the rotor system, use the airflow through the blades to build up the rotor speed. This, however, requires a suitably long runway. The second method involves more complex machinery but makes possible very short take-off distances. Here the rotor is brought up to speed by a linkage to the engine used to provide the forward motion. When the rotor has the correct speed, the linkage is disengaged. The machine is then allowed to move forward, and take-off is achieved by tilting back the rotor system. Some autogyros can 'jump-start', by over-speeding the rotor using the engine. The drive is then disengaged, and the rotor pitch increased. The aircraft jumps, using the stored energy, and continues then in autorotation.

When the engine and propeller speed are reduced the forward speed will decrease and the autogyro goes into a steady descent path. The autorotation principle still applies, as the air flowing up and through the rotor maintains the rotor speed. A lifting force is therefore produced which, although insufficient to maintain the machine altitude, prevents it from falling like a stone. Even when the propeller is stopped, the autogyro will descend safely.

In this respect the autogyro is at some advantage over the helicopter, since, in the case of helicopter engine failure the 'climbing pitch' angle of the rotors (about 11°) would quickly stop them, with disastrous results. To keep his rotors turning the pilot will have to quickly reduce the pitch angle of his blades to that which provides 'autorotation' for a safe forced landing, but some valuable height may be lost in the process.

The first successful autogryo was designed by Juan de la Cierva and was flown on 9 January, 1923 at Getafe Airdrome near Madrid. This was his fourth design, the other three suffering from an alarming tendency to roll over.

The instability was due to the use of rigid rotor blades. With the machine moving forward and the rotor turning, the blade turning into the airstream experiences a greater lifting force than the opposite blade moving downstream. With rigid rotor blades, this imbalance is transmitted to the whole machine producing a rolling motion. To overcome this instability, Cierva designed a rotor system with blades suitably hinged at the root, so that rather than transmit the imbalance to the whole machine, it was taken up by the individual blades which could move accordingly.

Opposite page top: Juan de la Cierva standing by one of his first autogyros in 1925. The winglike projections are ailerons, necessary because the rotor was not fully controllable.
Bottom: this Kellett autogyro was taken to the Antarctic by Admiral Byrd in 1933. The pilot, shown in the picture, was William S. McCormick.

At the root of each blade he inserted two hinges. One allowed the blade to flap up and down and was called the flapping hinge and the other permitted sideways movement and was called the drag hinge.

The autogyro (or helicopter) rotor blade is not, by itself, stiff enough to carry the weight of the machine. It is the enormous centrifugal force of rotation that keeps the rotors moving in an almost flat path, and even though they have 'flapping hinges' at their roots, the weight of the machine is carried here.

WORLD WAR TWO

Top of the page: although the Messerschmitt Me-109 had one of the largest production runs of any WW II aircraft, the Focke-Wulf FW190 was the later and more sophisticated aircraft.
Above: an FW190 is caught by the cannon of a Hawker Typhoon.
Right: the pilot's flying gear.

Fighters

The two chief fighter variants in use at the beginning of the war were the light interceptor fighter, exemplified by the Bf 109 and Spitfire, and the heavier, two-engine escort or 'destroyer' fighter such as the Messerschmitt Bf 110 and slightly later Bristol Beaufighter. The two-engined fighter proved not very suitable for air-to-air combat involving single-engined fighters, and was subsequently allocated a different role.

Early fighter combat immediately made it clear that apart from improvements in performance, usually associated with improved powerplants to produce higher speeds, ceilings and rates of climb, fighters needed protection from enemy fire in the form of armour protection for the pilot and engine and self-sealing fuel tanks to prevent these from leaking and catching fire when hit by enemy action. Several of the single-engined types in service in 1939 were still flying in 1945, and the development of aircraft occurred during the war itself. Armament was naturally increased, with larger calibre machine guns and cannon becoming the norm, but at the same time protection was increased, and performance raised from some 350 mph (565 kph) on 1,000 hp to 450 mph (725 kph) on about 2,000 hp. Ranges were also improved by the introduction of underwing fuel tanks that could be jettisoned when empty. The classic examples of fighters that underwent this type of development were Britain's and Germany's standard fighters, the Spitfire and Bf 109. New fighters were also introduced in the war, and these included the magnificent and versatile Focke Wulf Fw 190, North American P-51 Mustang and Republic P-47 Thunderbolt. The Russians, preoccupied with tactical air operations in support of the army, developed simple but robust fighters which were in every way the match for German fighters at the low altitudes at which the Russians operated.

The need for pure interceptors lessened as the war progressed, so many fighters found themselves adapted to the role of fighter-bombers, with engines adapted for low-altitude operations and the capability of delivering up to 2,000 lb (910 kg) of bombs or a mixture of bombs and rockets. The fighter-bomber was soon a vitally important weapon, especially over Russia and the European fronts. The classic fighter-bombers were the Hawker Typhoon and Tempest. Designed as interceptors, their high-altitude performance was disappointing, but they proved fast, manoeuvrable and capable of carrying heavy underwing

Left: from the foreground: two Spitfires (the nearer is the later model), a Hurricane and more Spitfires. Both the Spitfire and the Hurricane had the Merlin engine and were excellent machines. Both could turn inside an Me-109. The Hurricane had a slightly better rate of climb because of its greater wingspan and consequent slightly lower wing loading (in pounds per square inch). It could also carry more weight for the same reason. An Me-109 was faster than either; it could outdive a Hurricane, but not a Spitfire.

loads at low altitude, and were used almost exclusively as fighter-bombers in the second half of the war. In the field of interceptor types, finally, the introduction of the British Gloster Meteor and German Messerschmitt Me 262 jet fighters in 1944, with speeds in the order of 500 mph (805 kph) showed what might be expected from the next generation of fighters.

The heavy fighter of the opening stages of the war was soon evolved into two major roles: bomber-destroying by night, the classic examples being the Messerschmitt Bf 110, Bristol Beaufighter and fighter versions of the de Havilland Mosquito; and as strike fighters, particularly in the maritime role, classic examples of these being again the Beaufighter and Mosquito, in different marks, and the German Junkers Ju 88. The Americans also entered this field, converting many of their medium bombers, principally North American B-25 Mitchells and Martin B-26 Marauders, into strike aircraft. In night-fighting and maritime strike operations, small radar sets on board aircraft came to play a dominant role as the war moved towards its conclusion.

Bombers

With the exception of the United States, which did not enter hostilities until 1941 in any case, most of the combatants in World War II started the war with only medium bombers. These underwent development similar to that of fighters to improve their combat capabilities, speeds rising by up to 100 mph (160 kph) to the region of 350 mph (565 kph) by the end of war. Few new bombers of note entered service after the beginning of hostilities except the extraordinary British de Havilland Mosquito, which was unarmed, made of wood and so fast that no contemporary fighters could catch it; and the Russian Petlyakov Pe-2, a sturdy and versatile two-engined machine that served Russia remarkably well throughout the war.

The German Junkers Ju 87 Stuka dive-bomber performed well in early campaigns; despite horror stories to the contrary, its precision probably caused fewer civilian casualties than mass bombing would have done. The Battle of Britain showed, however, that the relatively slow Stuka, which was vulnerable during its bombing run, could not be used where the Germans did not enjoy superiority in the air. It continued to be useful as a tank killer in North Africa and on the Eastern front. On the same front, the Ilyushin Il-2 Shturmovik, a single-engined ground-attack machine of very robust construction, proved a problem for the Germans. Armed with heavy cannon, rockets and bombs, it operated very well at relatively low altitudes, rarely above 1,600 ft (490 m).

In the sphere of heavy strategic bombing, the British and Americans reigned supreme, the former by night and the latter by day. The British had started with daylight raids over Germany, but losses were so severe that they decided instead to concentrate their efforts on mass night raids to destroy whole areas. Based on the Halifax and Lancaster four-engined bombers, capable of carrying loads upwards of 12,000 lb (5,455 kg) into Germany, raids by forces of over 1,000 bombers became frequent occurrences in the German night from 1942 onwards. With radar aids these missions became more effective in 1943 and by 1944 were straining German industry and communications to the limit.

The Americans prepared daylight raids by large forces on pinpoint targets. Such was the armament of the B-17G and B-24H that flying in stepped-up box formations, the bombers could provide each other with great defensive fire and thus keep down losses to German fighters. Daylight was essential for the pinpoint raids against the small, vital targets considered the best targets by the Americans. The United States' third major four-engined bomber was the

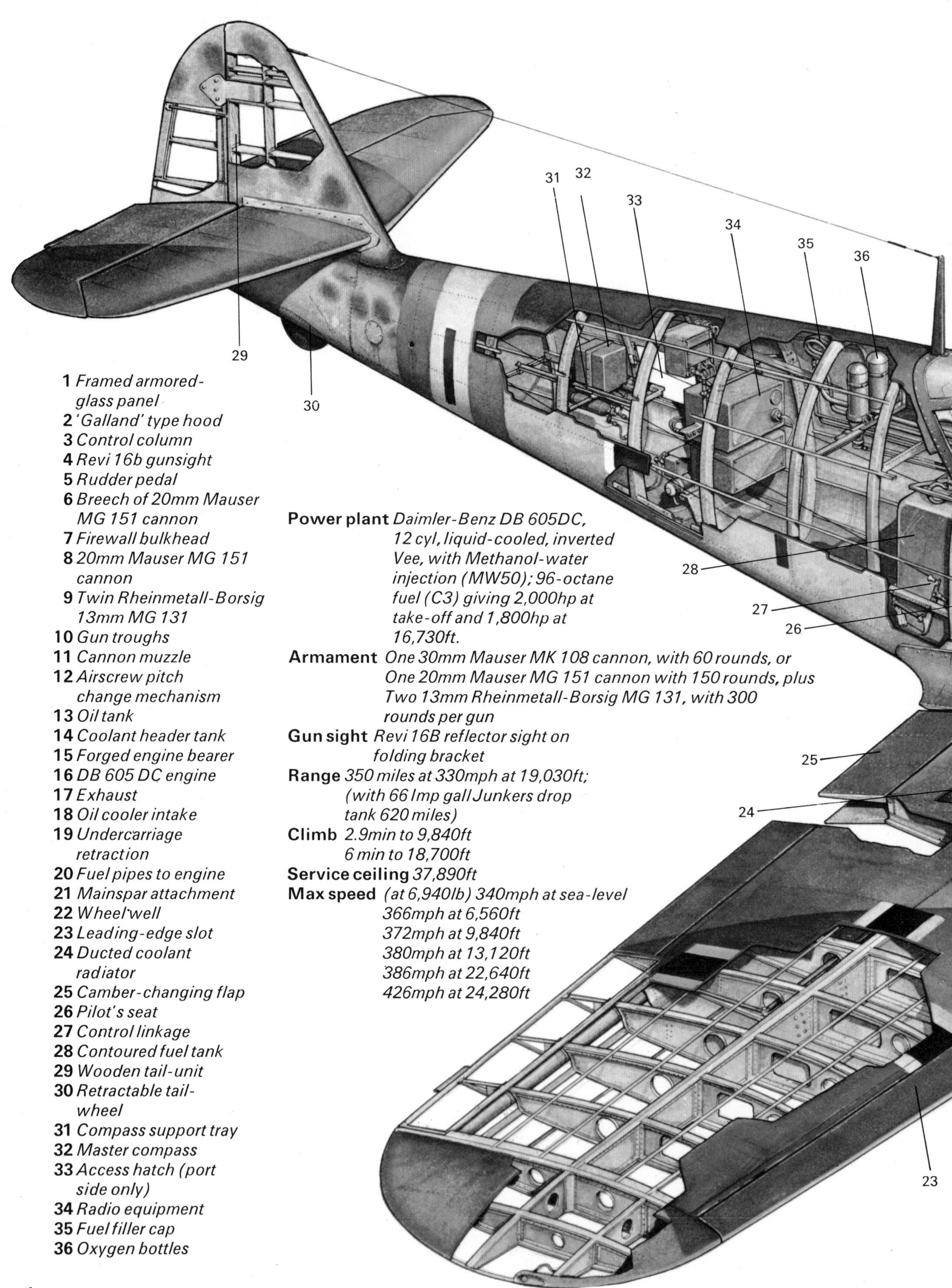

1 *Framed armored-glass panel*
2 *'Galland' type hood*
3 *Control column*
4 *Revi 16b gunsight*
5 *Rudder pedal*
6 *Breech of 20mm Mauser MG 151 cannon*
7 *Firewall bulkhead*
8 *20mm Mauser MG 151 cannon*
9 *Twin Rheinmetall-Borsig 13mm MG 131*
10 *Gun troughs*
11 *Cannon muzzle*
12 *Airscrew pitch change mechanism*
13 *Oil tank*
14 *Coolant header tank*
15 *Forged engine bearer*
16 *DB 605 DC engine*
17 *Exhaust*
18 *Oil cooler intake*
19 *Undercarriage retraction*
20 *Fuel pipes to engine*
21 *Mainspar attachment*
22 *Wheel well*
23 *Leading-edge slot*
24 *Ducted coolant radiator*
25 *Camber-changing flap*
26 *Pilot's seat*
27 *Control linkage*
28 *Contoured fuel tank*
29 *Wooden tail-unit*
30 *Retractable tail-wheel*
31 *Compass support tray*
32 *Master compass*
33 *Access hatch (port side only)*
34 *Radio equipment*
35 *Fuel filler cap*
36 *Oxygen bottles*

Power plant *Daimler-Benz DB 605DC, 12 cyl, liquid-cooled, inverted Vee, with Methanol-water injection (MW50); 96-octane fuel (C3) giving 2,000hp at take-off and 1,800hp at 16,730ft.*
Armament *One 30mm Mauser MK 108 cannon, with 60 rounds, or One 20mm Mauser MG 151 cannon with 150 rounds, plus Two 13mm Rheinmetall-Borsig MG 131, with 300 rounds per gun*
Gun sight *Revi 16B reflector sight on folding bracket*
Range *350 miles at 330mph at 19,030ft; (with 66 Imp gall Junkers drop tank 620 miles)*
Climb *2.9min to 9,840ft*
6 min to 18,700ft
Service ceiling *37,890ft*
Max speed *(at 6,940lb) 340mph at sea-level*
366mph at 6,560ft
372mph at 9,840ft
380mph at 13,120ft
386mph at 22,640ft
426mph at 24,280ft

The Messerschmitt Bf 109G (1945) had a top speed of 340 mph (557 kph) at sea level. Wingspan was about 2 feet (9.3 m) and length was about 29 feet (8.8 m).

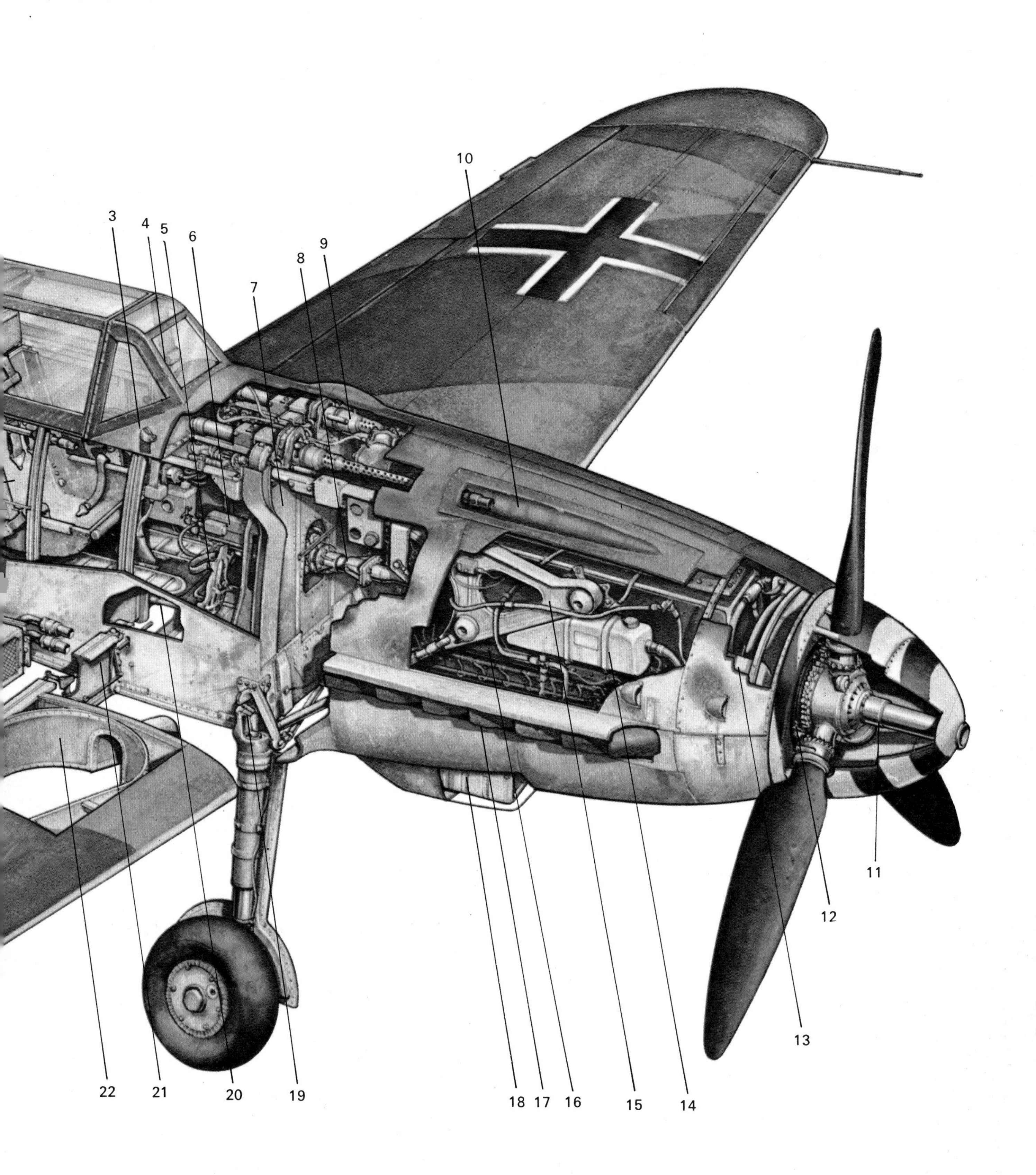

Boeing B-29 Superfortress. This was a large, fast aircraft used for the mass destruction of Japan's cities and industrial capacity. With a top speed of 350 mph (565 kph), it could carry bomb loads of 20,000 lb (9,900 kg) over very great ranges.

At the end of the war, it is worth noting, the Germans had a jet bomber (Arado Ar 234) in service, and were pressing ahead with the development of other advanced types.

With the exception of a few Japanese aircraft, reconnaissance in World War II was undertaken by a variety of converted fighter and medium bomber types. With armament removed, the airframe cleaned up as much as possible, extra fuel tanks and cameras fitted, aircraft such as the Spitfire and Lockheed P-38 Lightning roamed over much of Europe, with help from special photographic reconnaissance versions of the Mosquito joining them later.

Naval aviation

Maritime aircraft came of age in World War II. Some naval battles in the Pacific were fought almost entirely by carrier-based aircraft, without the ships involved coming anywhere near each other. There were two categories of naval aircraft; shore-based aircraft, both landplanes and seaplanes, for use in the anti-submarine and strike roles, and carrier-based aircraft, for use against other naval forces and land targets beyond the range of land-based aircraft.

The two classic British maritime aircraft were the remarkable Fairey Swordfish and the Short Sunderland. The Swordfish was a biplane torpedo-bomber that was by any standards obsolete by 1939. Yet it soldiered on throughout the war, proving a very versatile and able type. The Sunderland flying-boat played an important part in safeguarding the sealanes across the Atlantic towards Britain.

Japan's greatest naval aircraft was the Mitsubishi A6M 'Zero' fighter. This was the first naval fighter to equal landplanes in performance, and its debut into combat against the Americans came as an enormous shock to the Allies. It was 1943 before they finally got the measure of this remarkably agile fighter.

The main protagonists of naval airpower were the Americans: in a war against Japan this was the only offensive method profitable in the Pacific. The standard fighter at the beginning of the war was the tubby little Grumman F4F Wildcat, which had a just about adequate performance. It was soon succeeded, however, by the F6F Hellcat, an excellent aircraft that was complemented late in the war by the superlative Vought F4U Corsair fighter and fighter-bomber. The Corsair has a good claim to the title of best fighter of the war; it was called 'whistling death' by the Japanese. As major offensive weapons the US Navy had the Douglas Dauntless dive-bomber and the Grumman Avenger torpedo-bomber.

One of the lesser-known facts of the Second World War is that the Italians built some very good aircraft. Reggiane, Macchi and Fiat built excellent fighters, but the total numbers of the latest models was less than 2,000, largely because of shortage of engines. In all, Italy had only about 13,800 aircraft, but their pilots fought courageously all over the Mediterranean, the Balkans and North Africa.

Left: the long range of the P-51D Mustang made it ideal for bomber escort.
Above: Lockheed's P-38 Lightning was called 'Fork-tailed devil' by the Germans
Below: the Northrop P-61 Black Widow was a deadly night fighter.

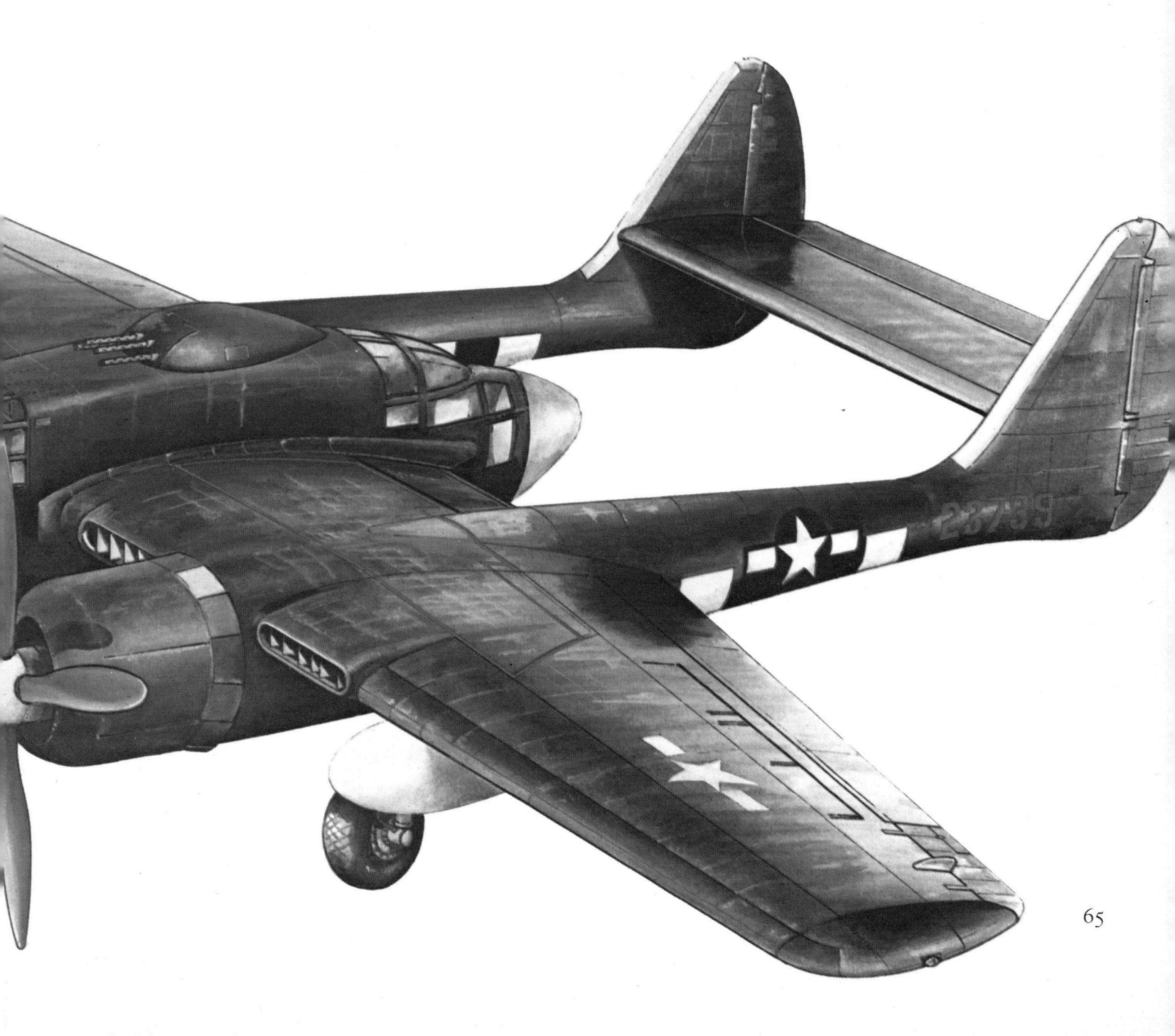

Right: the Douglas SBD-3 Dauntless dive bomber had a crew of two. This drawing shows the rear cockpit closed. Below: a US Marine pilot in the Pacific, 1941.

Above: Mitsubishi A6M2 Zero. Allied pilots were impressed by this fighter. Top right: Grumman F4F-4 Wildcat. First of a series of 'cats', this valiant machine was no match for the Zero. Right: Chance-Vought's F4U-1 Corsair was called Whistling Death by the Japanese. It was one of the fastest fighters of WW II. Below: the USS Hornet.

72-F-3
122

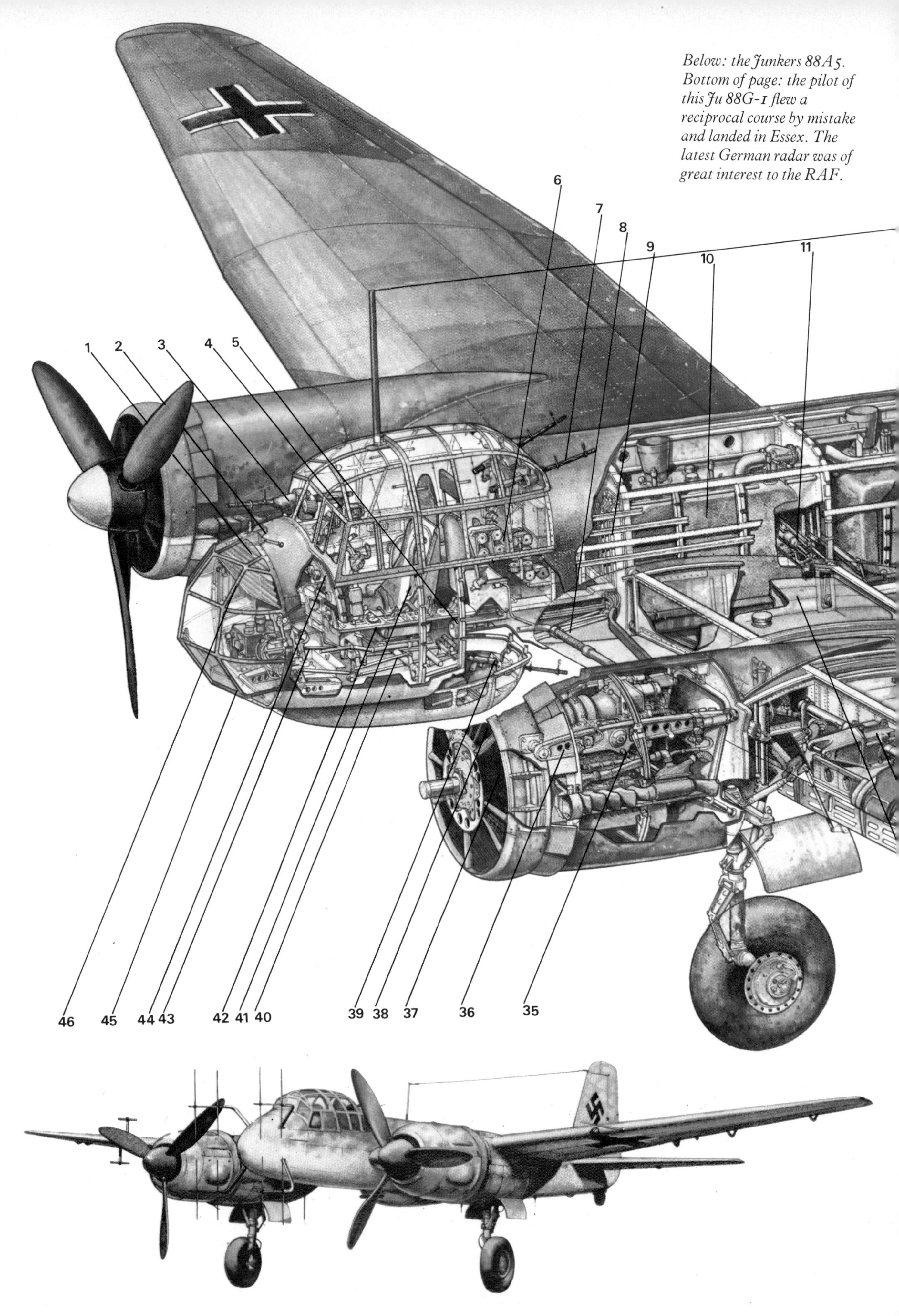

Below: the Junkers 88A5. Bottom of page: the pilot of this Ju 88G-1 flew a reciprocal course by mistake and landed in Essex. The latest German radar was of great interest to the RAF.

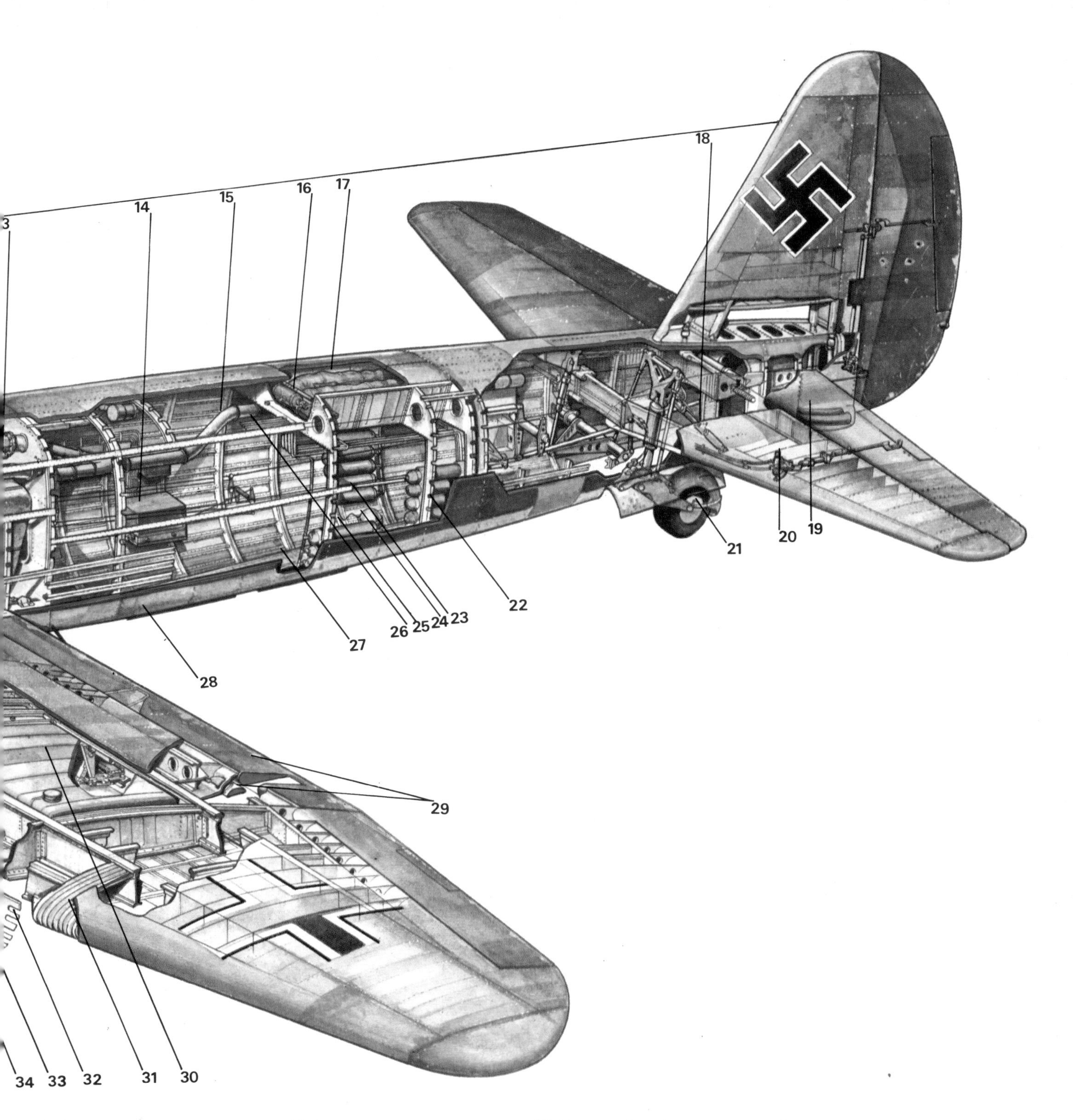

1 *Blackout curtain*
2 *Folding sight*
3 *'A'-stand MG15*
4 *Revi gun-sight*
5 *Power-control link*
6 *MG ammo storage*
7 *'B'-stand MG15s*
8 *Hot-air duct*
9 *Control links*
10 *Fuel tank, 1,220l*
11 *Control surface links*
12 *Fuel tank support*
13 *Fuel tank, 680l*
14 *Computer*
15 *Fuel overflow pipe*
16 *Dinghy-activating cylinder*
17 *Dinghy stowage*
18 *Tail-wheel jack*
19 *Fuel overflow outlet*
20 *Trim-tab operating mechanism*
21 *Retractable tail-wheel*
22 *Oxygen bottles*
23 *Oxygen bottles*
24 *Main compass*
25 *Oxygen bottles*
26 *Oxygen lines*
27 *Access walk-way*
28 *Rail-type aerial*
29 *Slotted flaps*
30 *Fuel tank, 425l*
31 *Corrugated leading-edge*
32 *Retractable slatted dive-brakes*
33 *Dive-brake actuator*
34 *Fuel tank, 415l*
35 *Junkers Jumo 211B-1 engine*
36 *Engine bearer*
37 *Annular radiator*
38 *Oil cooler*
39 *'C'-stand MG15*
40 *Control links*
41 *Pilot's seat*
42 *Pilot's controls*
43 *Rudder pedals*
44 *Instrument panel*
45 *'Beetle's eye' nose section*
46 *Main distributor*

DAN-AIR
COMET 4
DAN AIR

MODERN AVIATION

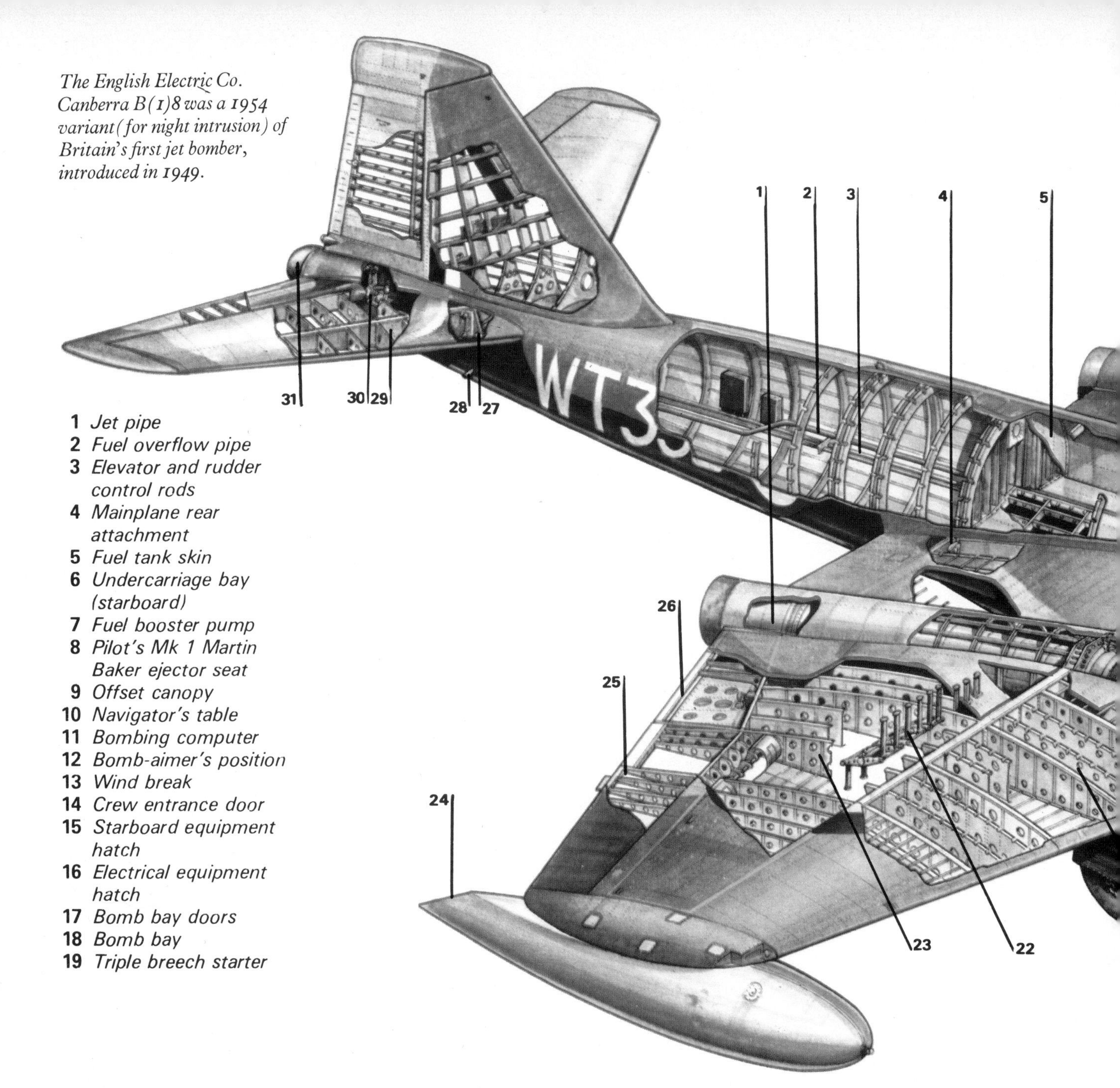

The English Electric Co. Canberra B(1)8 was a 1954 variant (for night intrusion) of Britain's first jet bomber, introduced in 1949.

THE JET ENGINE

The gas turbine and its variant, the jet engine, are the latest developments of old ideas. The word 'turbine' comes from the Latin 'turbo', which means a whirl or eddy. Water wheels, which have been in use for centuries, are turbines.

In 1791 the gas turbine as we know it was described in a patent by John Barber. His drawing showed the essential features of the gas turbine engine: a compressor, from which air is passed to a continuous-flow combustion chamber, in which the fuel is burnt; and a turbine, through which pass the resultant hot gases. The hot gases turn the blades of the turbine and this motion is used to drive the compressor. There is a surplus of power over that needed to drive the compressor, because it is a feature of the behaviour of gases that the work available from the expansion of a hot medium is greater than that required to compress the same medium when it is cold.

Other internal combustion engines work on an intermittent cycle. Any single part of the engine is exposed to combustion gases for only a short time and is then washed by the relatively cool charge of the next cycle. Practically the whole of the oxygen in the air can be utilized, giving temperatures of over 2,500 K (2,227°C, 4,040°F) in the combustion products, while few parts of the engine exceed 500 K (227°C, 440°F).

(K stands for Kelvins, the unit of measure of heat in thermodynamics, in which temperature is measured from absolute zero. Temperatures quoted in Kelvins may be converted to Celsius by subtracting 273.)

By contrast, the blades of a turbine, which experience a continuous flow of combustion through them, can only withstand a temperature of about 1,100 K (827°C, 1,520°F) if they are to be reliable over a useful period of time, even

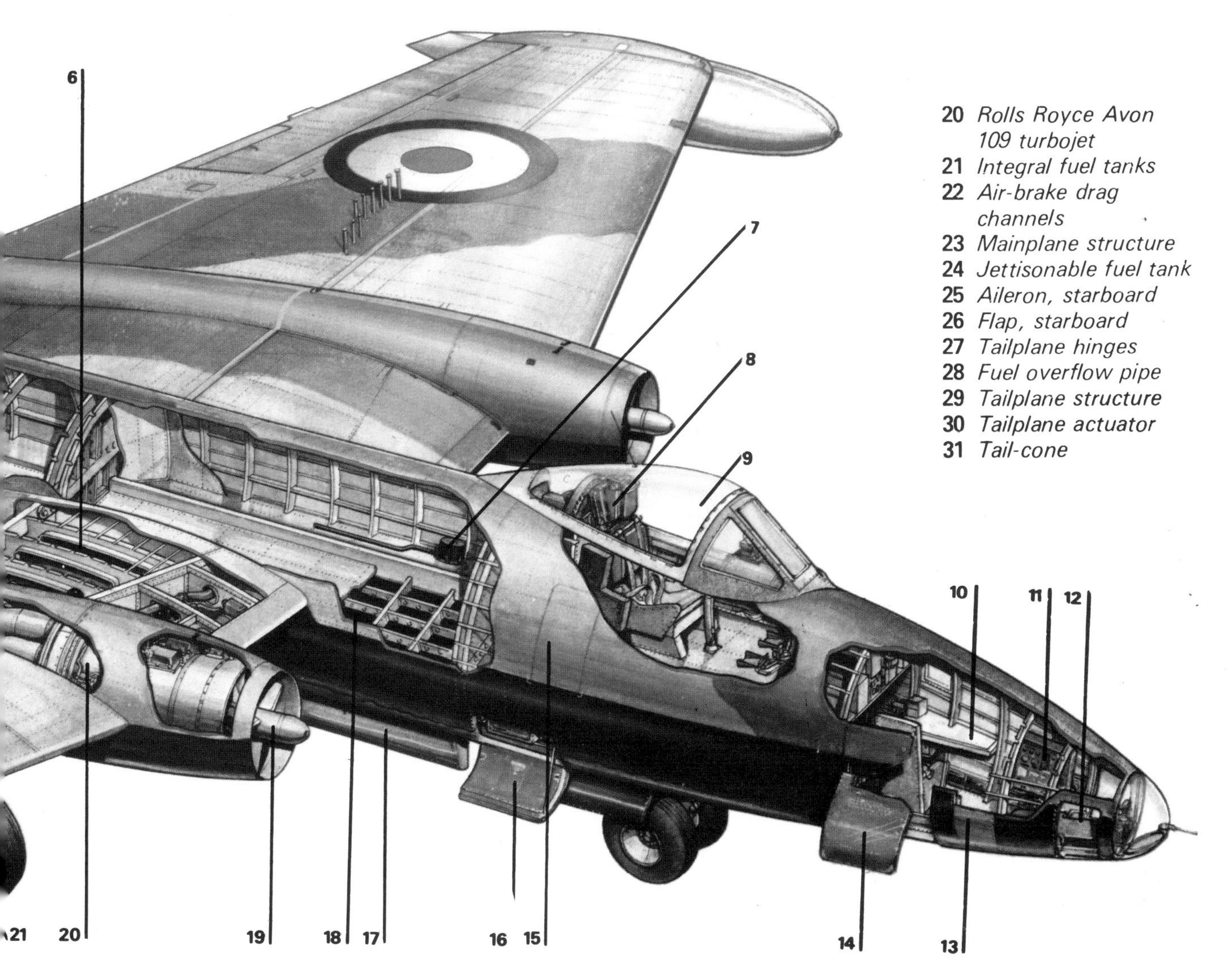

when they are made of complex modern alloys of nickel and cobalt. Only part of the oxygen in the air can be used if the temperatures of critical parts are not to exceed this figure. This fact seriously limits the output and efficiency of the gas turbine and provided a stumbling block for many years. There were no practical developments until the beginning of this century.

The turbocharger was the first successful use of the principles of the gas turbine. It is a variant of the gas turbine which produces no power in itself but increases the power output of the engine to which it is attached. A turbine is operated by the flow of hot exhaust gases from the engine; the turbine operates a compressor which raises the density, and hence the mass flow-rate, of the air charge to the combustion chamber of the engine. The first turbocharger was designed by Alfred Büchi and built by the Swiss firm of Brown-Boveri in 1911. In 1916 turbochargers were first used in aircraft, and were subsequently used in the most successful aircraft of World War II.

The centrifugal compressor was the only machine available when the turbocharger was first developed, and was capable only of low pressure ratios and modest efficiency, insufficient for a power-producing engine.

Just before World War II gas turbine engines were built by Brown-Boveri and installed for electrical generation. These had multi-stage axial-flow compressors, which have rotating blades and stationary blades arranged so that pressure is built up in stages. More efficiency and higher pressure ratios are available from this type of compressor.

The specific power output (the power obtained divided by the air-mass flow rate, a size criterion) and the thermal efficiency (the power obtained divided by the fuel energy rate, a running cost criterion) both increase with turbine inlet temperature, compressor pressure ratio (up to a point) and the efficiencies of compressor and turbine. Efficiency is determined by comparing the power of the actual machine with that of a theoretical machine having no frictional or other heat losses. Efficiencies of both compressors and turbines can be as high as 90% nowadays, but were much lower at the beginning of development.

The first man to envisage the use of gas turbines for aircraft propulsion was Frank Whittle, a Pilot Officer in the Royal Air Force, who was later knighted for his achievement. He patented in 1930 the combination of a simple gas turbine and a nozzle to provide a jet-propulsion device, or turbo-jet. In 1936 he formed a company, Power Jets Limited, to develop it, and in 1939, the company received a contract for a flight engine. The same year a German design, the Heinkel He 178, made a short flight; the Gloster-Whittle E 28/39 was more successful in 1941. In that year a Whittle W1X

Frank Whittle

It is often said that Sir Frank Whittle invented the jet engine and in a sense this is true, but the bare statement does need qualification. The aircraft jet engine is a variant of the gas turbine—a form of power which had been under development since the early years of this century. The first aircraft to fly using a jet engine was the German Heinkel He 178 in August 1939—some two years before Whittle's first engine was ready for flight testing. The Heinkel engine was not developed for production aircraft, however, whereas many of the early British and American jet engines were derived from Whittle's design.

Frank Whittle was born at Coventry on 1 June 1907, and after attending Leamington College he enlisted in the Royal Air Force as an apprentice. He qualified as a pilot and became a flying instructor, but he also developed a deep interest in the technical problems of aircraft propulsion. The idea of adapting the gas turbine engine to power an aircraft seemed a logical development to Whittle, and in 1929 he tried to persuade the Air Ministry that his engine was feasible. They turned it down. Nevertheless he took out a patent in January 1930, then concentrated on his flying career. A few years later, at the age of 27, Whittle went to Cambridge University to study engineering and carry out research. In the meantime a new company called Power Jets Ltd had been set up to develop Whittle's jet engine.

By 1937 Whittle and his colleagues from Power Jets had built the world's first turbojet engine, and on 12 April it was run for the first time in a test bed. Whittle was still an officer in the RAF, but permanently attached to Power Jets, where he remained throughout World War II except for a short time at the RAF Staff College. When Air Ministry officials saw a jet engine working for the first time they were still a little apprehensive but they gave financial support, and in March 1938 an order was placed for a new engine. This engine was to power the Gloster E28/39 experimental aircraft, specially designed to take Whittle's engine.

The Gloster E28/39 made its first flight on 15 May 1941 with Flight Lieutenant P E G Sayer at the controls, although it had made a very short hop previously during taxying trials. The engine on this historic flight was a Whittle W1 fitted with a centrifugal compressor, ten combustion chambers and a turbine to drive the compressor. Both aircraft and engine are preserved in the Science Museum, London. As tests continued they demonstrated that the jet engine became more efficient at high speeds and greater altitudes, whereas the conventional piston engine became less efficient under these conditions. These facts had been Whittle's argument from the beginning, but it had been a long struggle to overcome both the technical difficulties and the lack of interest in some official circles.

In 1948 Whittle retired from the RAF with the rank of Air-Commodore and received a knighthood. After holding several advisory posts Sir Frank Whittle started a new line of research, this time into equipment for the oil industry.

Below left: Whittle (left) explains his jet engine just after WW II.
Below: the Whittle W1 and the Gloster E28/39, which first flew in 1941.

engine was shipped to the USA and the General Electric Company began development; the first American jet aircraft, the Bell XP59A, flew in October 1942.

These engines all had centrifugal compressors; it was not until well after the war that axial-flow compressors were reliable enough for aircraft. The promise of the turbo-jet idea was to provide greater thrust for less weight and with less vibration than the conventional combination of internal combustion aircraft engine and propeller, as well as overcoming the forward-speed limit of the propeller itself. In war-time the advantage of jets would have been their ability to climb quickly to intercept bombers, as well as being able to fly faster than bombers or enemy fighters. The Germans had begun development of axial-flow compressors, but at the end of the war they were only just beginning to develop new alloys which would have made possible longer flying time without overhaul of the engine.

After the war, many successful jet engines were sold with centrifugal compressors, but ultimately they were a dead-end development for aircraft, because not only was efficiency low but the frontal area of such engines was high, leading to engine-nacelle drag. Axial-flow designs made possible better aerodynamic design of aircraft.

In modern jet aircraft which fly at below the speed of sound, modifications to the engine are made. The efficiency

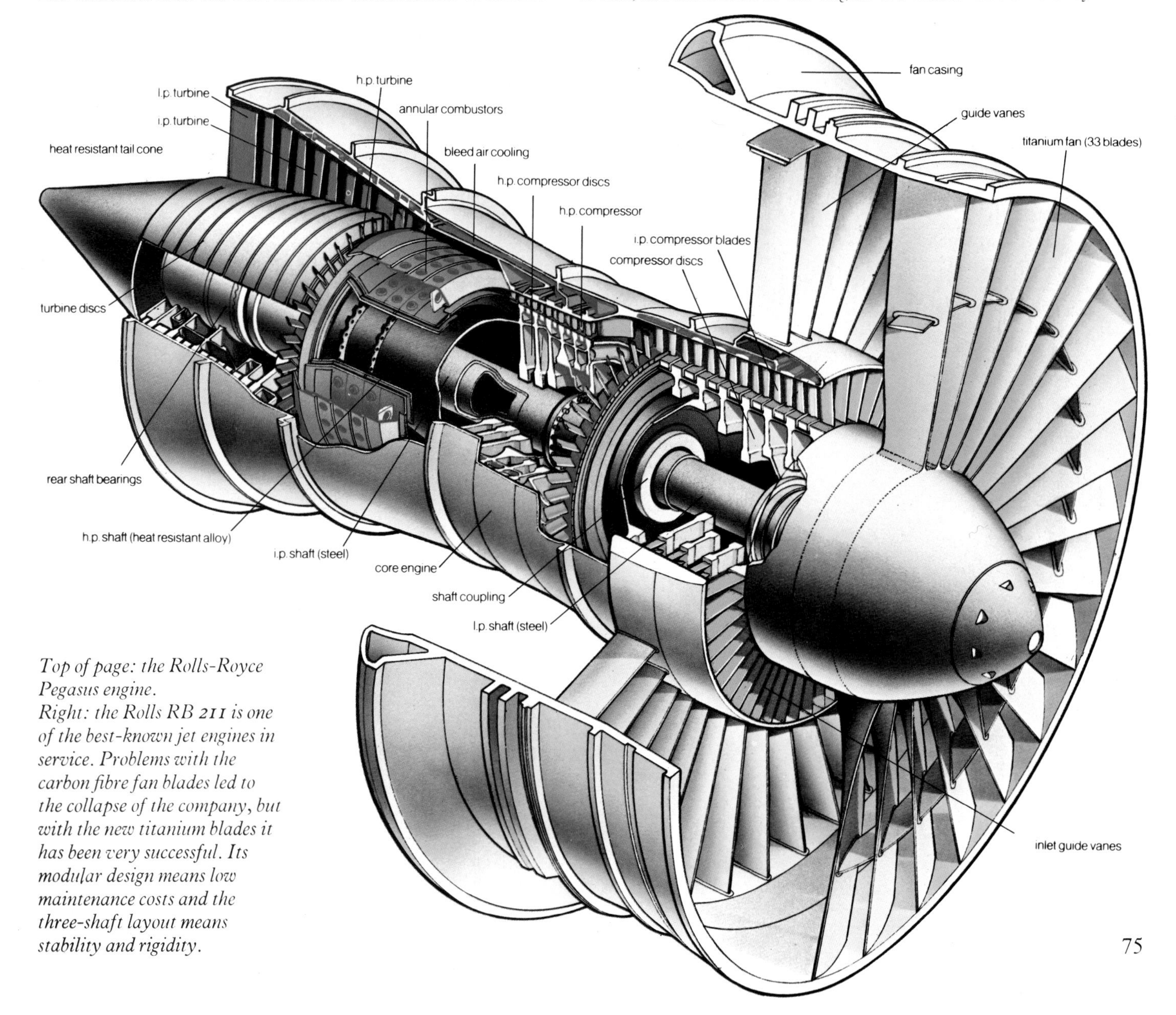

Top of page: the Rolls-Royce Pegasus engine.
Right: the Rolls RB 211 is one of the best-known jet engines in service. Problems with the carbon fibre fan blades led to the collapse of the company, but with the new titanium blades it has been very successful. Its modular design means low maintenance costs and the three-shaft layout means stability and rigidity.

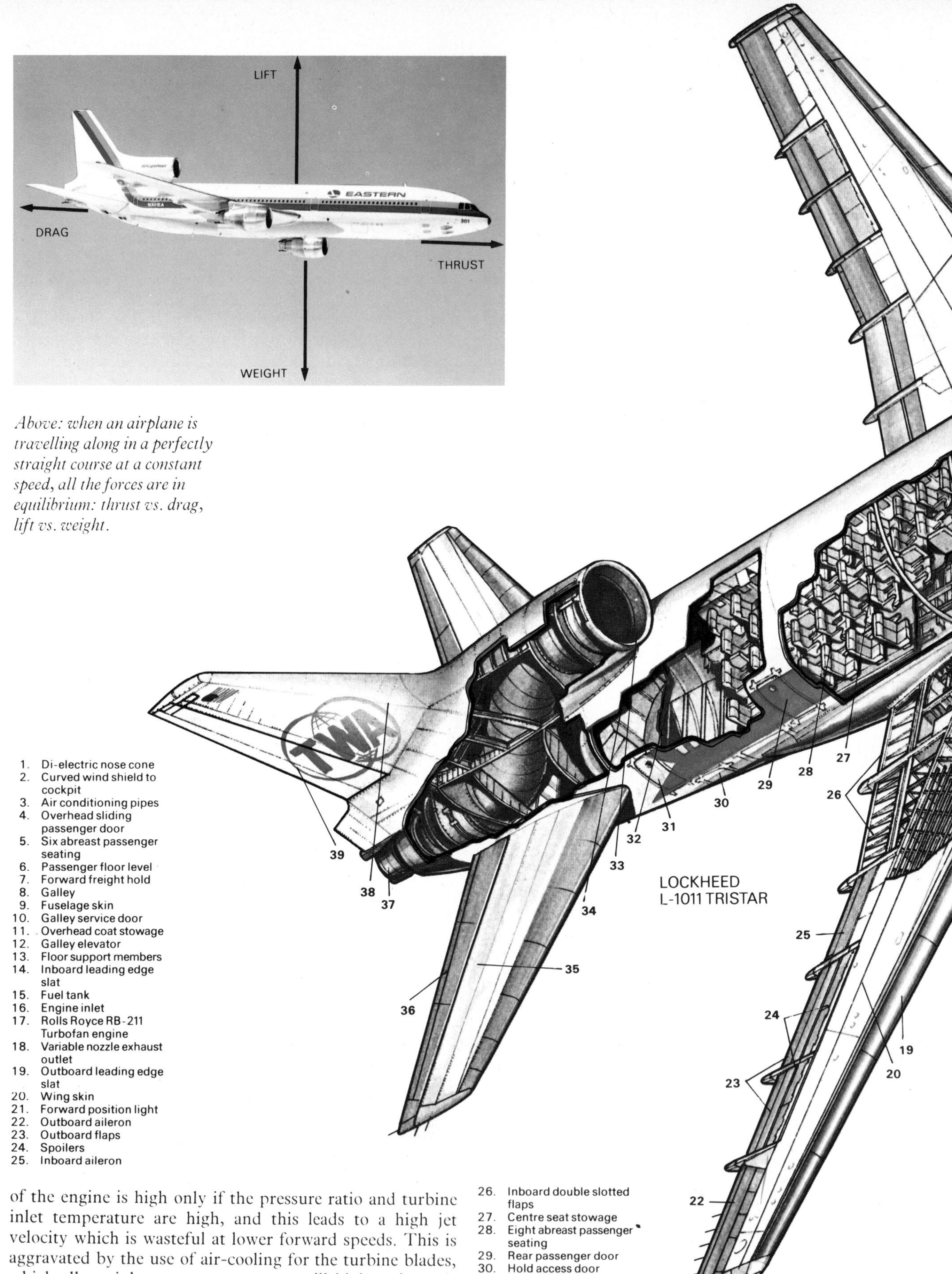

Above: when an airplane is travelling along in a perfectly straight course at a constant speed, all the forces are in equilibrium: thrust vs. drag, lift vs. weight.

1. Di-electric nose cone
2. Curved wind shield to cockpit
3. Air conditioning pipes
4. Overhead sliding passenger door
5. Six abreast passenger seating
6. Passenger floor level
7. Forward freight hold
8. Galley
9. Fuselage skin
10. Galley service door
11. Overhead coat stowage
12. Galley elevator
13. Floor support members
14. Inboard leading edge slat
15. Fuel tank
16. Engine inlet
17. Rolls Royce RB-211 Turbofan engine
18. Variable nozzle exhaust outlet
19. Outboard leading edge slat
20. Wing skin
21. Forward position light
22. Outboard aileron
23. Outboard flaps
24. Spoilers
25. Inboard aileron
26. Inboard double slotted flaps
27. Centre seat stowage
28. Eight abreast passenger seating
29. Rear passenger door
30. Hold access door
31. Emergency exit
32. Rear freight hold
33. Rear engine inlet
34. Toilets
35. Tailplane
36. Elevator
37. Rear engine exhaust
38. Tail fin
39. Rudder

of the engine is high only if the pressure ratio and turbine inlet temperature are high, and this leads to a high jet velocity which is wasteful at lower forward speeds. This is aggravated by the use of air-cooling for the turbine blades, which allows inlet temperature to go still higher. Accordingly, the turbine is extended to extract more energy from the gases, and this energy powers a fan which is placed in front of the compressor. This fan blows air back between the body of the turbine and the outer concentric casing, and a greater flow emerges at lower velocity, giving a greater

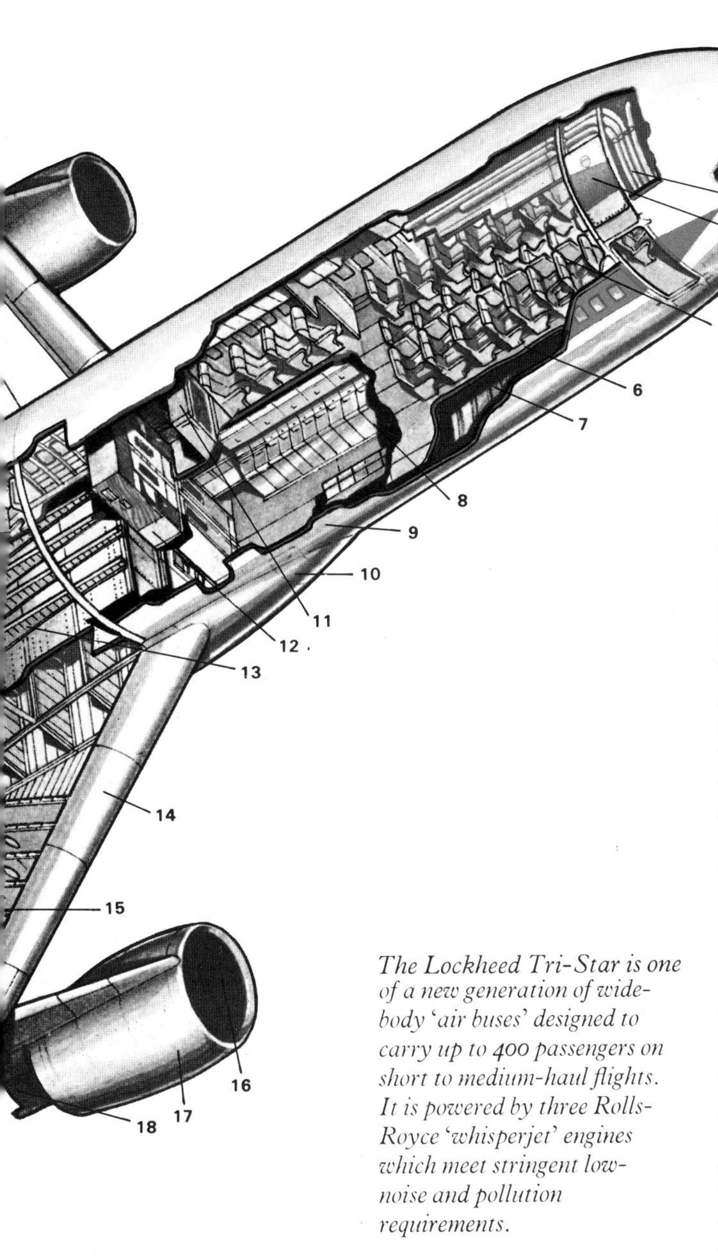

The Lockheed Tri-Star is one of a new generation of wide-body 'air buses' designed to carry up to 400 passengers on short to medium-haul flights. It is powered by three Rolls-Royce 'whisperjet' engines which meet stringent low-noise and pollution requirements.

thrust with the same amount of fuel. An advantage of this type of engine, called a turbofan or fanjet, is that it is quieter because the jet velocity is lower. The ratio of the airflow through the outer duct to that going through the turbine is the bypass ratio. Fanjets with high bypass ratios propel the large airliners of today. This system has been developed with multiple swivelling nozzles for the Harrier 'jump-jet' aircraft.

For supersonic flight the simple jet engine is entirely suitable, as the high jet speeds match more closely the high forward speed of the aircraft. Jet speeds are sometimes increased by burning extra fuel between the turbine and the propelling nozzle, using surplus oxygen left in the turbine gases. This is called afterburning and increases thrust considerably. During take-off, fuel consumption increases faster than thrust, but at cruising speeds afterburning can be quite economical. Afterburning is incorporated in the Rolls-Royce/SNECMA Olympus 593 engines for the Concorde, which cruises at 2.2 times the speed of sound. A characteristic of afterburning is that it greatly increases the noise level of aircraft taking off.

The turboprop engine, like the fanjet, makes use of the extra turbine energy to save fuel, but uses it to turn a conventional propeller rather than a fan inside the engine cowling. During the 1950s turboprops were used on large jetliners, but cruising speeds have increased since then with development of the jet engine, and turboprops are used today only on smaller aircraft. The best turboprop designs are lighter, less noisy and more free from vibration than comparable piston engines; the Rolls-Royce Dart Mk 525, which had a two-stage centrifugal compressor and was used in the Vickers Viscount, was well known for its smooth operation.

An engine similar to a turboprop, but used to drive a transmission shaft rather than a propeller shaft, is called a turboshaft engine. Such engines have been used to drive helicopter rotors, notably by the Bell Aircraft company of the United States, on several models beginning with the XH-13F of 1955. The engine is usually mounted on top of the fuselage directly adjacent to the rotor.

Ramjets and pulse-jets are also called athodyds, an acronym from Aero THermODYnamic Duct. They have no rotating parts.

In the ramjet, incoming air is compressed by a specially shaped inlet nozzle which slows its velocity and raises its temperature. After combustion the hot gases are allowed to expand and leave the rear nozzle at a velocity greater than that of the aircraft, resulting in thrust. The ramjet operates only at forward speed, so a take-off assist is necessary. The ramjet has been used to power guided missiles which do not fly outside the atmosphere. They have been used to power target drones, and have also been fitted to the tops of helicopter rotor blades, with inlet passage on the front edge of the blade. Ramjets are most efficient in the 1,500 to 2,500 mph range.

The pulse-jet, as its name implies, operates intermittently. The air enters through a valve which then closes; combustion then takes place and thrust is produced; when the pressure on the combustion chamber drops, the valve opens and the cycle begins again. Pulse-jets were used during World War II in the German V-1 flying bomb. They were unreliable, extremely noisy and had high fuel consumption, but were simple and inexpensive to build and were a good choice for this application, because they only had to operate for a few minutes to get the bomb to the target. The pulse-jet tends to lose thrust with speed, and is most efficient at subsonic speeds. Since the war, they have been used for target drones, and were also used on the tips of helicopter rotor blades.

THE EJECTION SEAT

Towards the end of World War II emergency parachute escapes from military aircraft were becoming increasingly difficult, and the introduction of jet-powered aircraft with their vastly increased speed virtually eliminated the possibility of a successful 'over the side' bail-out.

In 1944 Mr James Martin (now Sir James Martin) was invited by the then Ministry of Aircraft Production in London to investigate the practicability of providing fighter aircraft with a means of assisted escape for the pilot in an emergency.

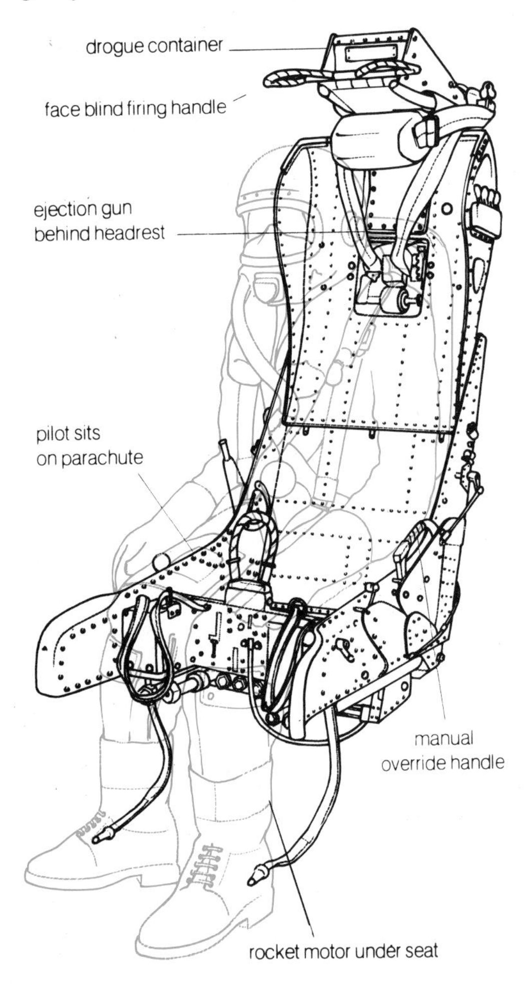

After investigating alternative schemes it soon became apparent that this could be best achieved by forced ejection of the pilot's seat, with the pilot sitting in it, and that the most effective way of doing this would be by an explosive charge. After ejection, the pilot would fall away from the seat and open his parachute by pulling a ripcord in the usual way. This also fitted in with Air Staff requirements at that time, that any ejection system should 'utilize existing safety equipment'.

When an ejection seat is operated in an emergency, the seat, complete with the occupant and carrying a parachute and a pack of survival aids, is ejected from the aircraft by an ejection gun. The ejection gun is secured to the aircraft vertically behind the back of the seat, and is powerful enough to hurl the seat well clear of the aircraft even if it is travelling at high speed, possibly faster than the speed of sound.

Some seats are fitted with a rocket motor underneath the seat in addition to the ejection gun to increase the height attained by the seat. The rocket is fired as the seat leaves the aircraft and the combined force of the gun and the rocket will propel the seat and occupant to a height of about 300 ft (91 m), which is high enough to allow a parachute to open fully, even if the ejection is made from the ground with the aircraft stationary. This feature is a decided asset when installed in modern vertical take-off and short take-off aircraft, and also in conventional aircraft should ejection be necessary with the aircraft in a nose-down attitude at speed near the ground.

To commence ejection, the pilot pulls on a handle located above his head or between his knees, or pulls a screen down over his face which starts the ejection sequence and also protects his face from the air blast. This jettisons the cockpit canopy and fires a cartridge which ignites other cartridges in the gun and, if fitted, the rocket motor, which then provide the thrust to eject the seat.

After the seat has left the aircraft, a drogue (small parachute) attached to the top of the seat is deployed. To ensure quick and positive deployment of the drogue, it is pulled out of its container at the top of the seat with some force by a heavy 'billet' fired from a drogue gun. The object of the drogue is to stabilize the seat and slow it down to a speed at which the occupant's parachute can be opened without fear of it bursting.

When the drogue has slowed the seat sufficiently, a barostatically controlled (pressure sensitive) time release unit releases the drogue from the top of the seat, transferring its pull to the canopy of the occupant's parachute, pulling it out of its pack. Simultaneously the time-release unit releases the occupant's safety harness from the seat, and the occupant is pulled clear by his opening parachute to make a normal parachute descent while his seat falls free.

Should the ejection take place above 10,000 ft (3048 m), the action of the time-release unit is delayed by the barostat control which responds to atmospheric pressure in a similar way to an aneroid altimeter or barometer. (Atmospheric pressure falls as the altitude increases.) By delaying the opening of the main parachute until this height, the seat and its occupant, stabilized by the drogue, descend quickly through the cold, rarefied upper atmosphere. The seat incorporates a built-in oxygen supply for the occupant to breathe, which is turned on automatically during ejection.

This entire sequence is automatically controlled from the time the pilot operates the seat until he lands by parachute, but in the unlikely event of the mechanism failing the pilot can intervene and open his parachute by a manual ripcord.

The use of an ordinary ejection seat is impractical for escapes from aircraft flying at speeds greatly in excess of the speed of sound, as the pilot will be subjected to extremely high and potentially dangerous deceleration forces as he leaves the plane. The force of the air against the pilot

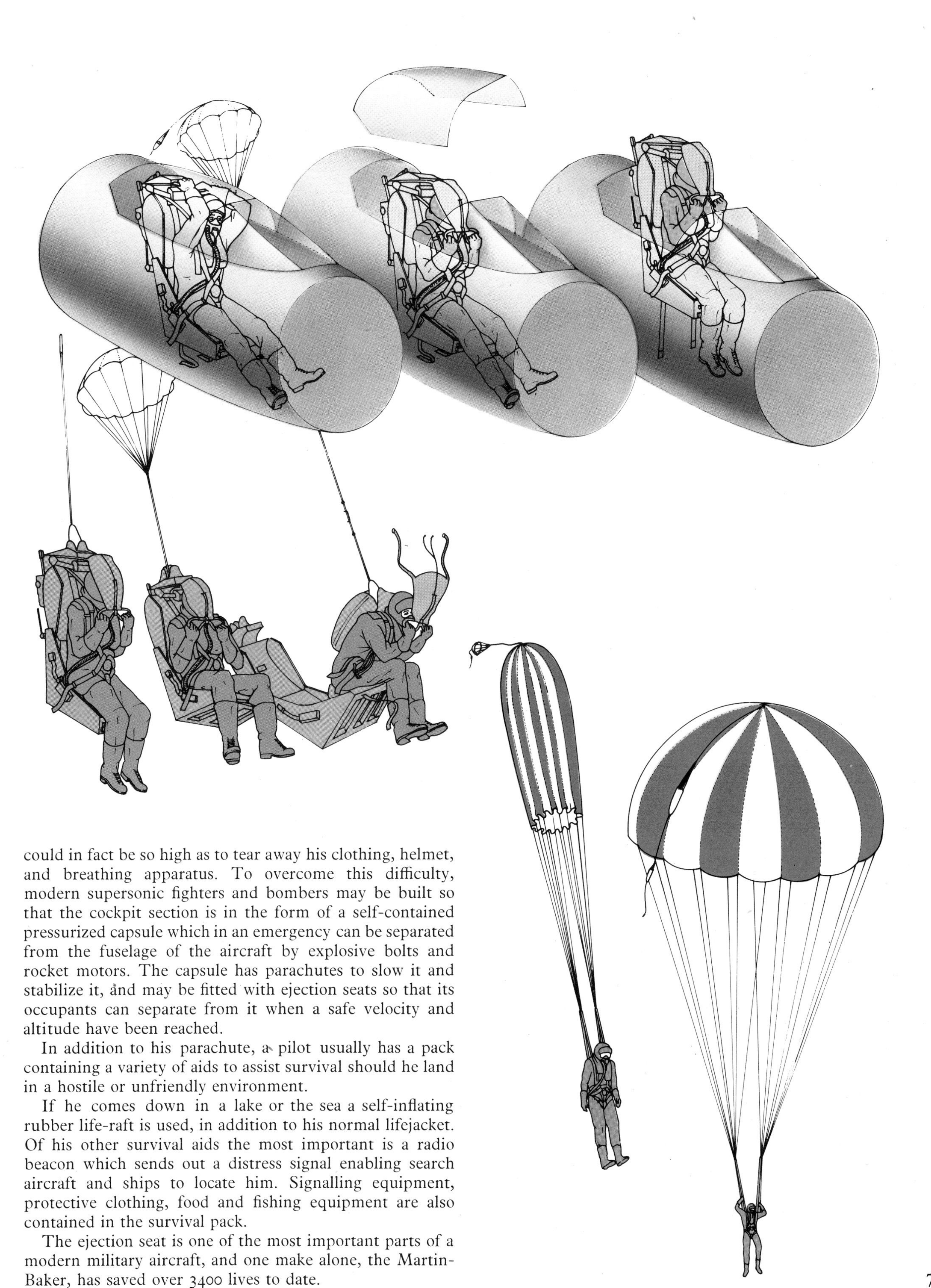

could in fact be so high as to tear away his clothing, helmet, and breathing apparatus. To overcome this difficulty, modern supersonic fighters and bombers may be built so that the cockpit section is in the form of a self-contained pressurized capsule which in an emergency can be separated from the fuselage of the aircraft by explosive bolts and rocket motors. The capsule has parachutes to slow it and stabilize it, and may be fitted with ejection seats so that its occupants can separate from it when a safe velocity and altitude have been reached.

In addition to his parachute, a pilot usually has a pack containing a variety of aids to assist survival should he land in a hostile or unfriendly environment.

If he comes down in a lake or the sea a self-inflating rubber life-raft is used, in addition to his normal lifejacket. Of his other survival aids the most important is a radio beacon which sends out a distress signal enabling search aircraft and ships to locate him. Signalling equipment, protective clothing, food and fishing equipment are also contained in the survival pack.

The ejection seat is one of the most important parts of a modern military aircraft, and one make alone, the Martin-Baker, has saved over 3400 lives to date.

SUPERSONIC FLIGHT

The construction of all aircraft from simple glider to swing-wing supersonic craft has to be carried out with one principal aim in view: to reduce weight as much as possible. Primitive types at the turn of the century adopted a wooden or steel tubular frame covered with canvas or similar material to provide the required aerodynamic surfaces. Such construction methods are still used for some simple light aircraft, though the canvas may also be replaced by glass fibre materials or aluminium sheet.

But for faster high-powered craft, where dynamic forces are involved, such constructional practice would be unsuitable. Most larger aircraft use a reinforced monocoque construction, in which the outer shell takes a lot of the stress but is backed up by a suitable frame of light alloy. The shell is sometimes made of solid light alloy but nowadays tends to be a sandwich of two thin layers glued to a metal 'honeycomb' mesh to give high stiffness with low weight. The aim here is to produce a material akin to corrugated cardboard in cross-section.

For supersonic aircraft, where the stress problem becomes even more acute, wings and other components have to be made by machining outer skin and frame together from solid pieces of alloy. Though giving the strength and heat resistance that are necessary, this method is very expensive and has contributed considerably to the high cost of, for instance, the Concorde project. It seems likely that it will be reserved strictly for military types in future.

Common to all forms of transport is the emphasis on speed. The longer the distance to be covered, the greater the speed necessary to accomplish the journey in a reasonable time for commercial economy, personal comfort and military safety. Since the birth of powered aviation in 1903, speeds have increased from 40 mph (64 km/h) to well over 4500 mph (7242 km/h) and the technology is now available to support any objects envisaged. Costs rise steeply with increases in speed, however, and there exists, particularly for commercial aviation, an economic limit associated with the velocity of sound waves in the air.

Sound is a wave disturbance in the atmosphere, rather like the ripples which spread out when a stone is dropped into still water. The velocity of sound waves in air is proportional to the square root of the absolute temperature. At sea level, in temperature zones, where the average temperature is about 59°F (15°C), sound waves travel at 761 mph (1225 km/h). The velocity falls with increasing height (because the temperature is dropping) until at just over 36,000 ft (10.97 km) it is only 691.3 mph (1112.5 km/h). Further increases in altitude, at least up to about 60,000 ft (18.29 km), have no effect since the temperature of the atmosphere remains constant.

During the last century an Austrian scientist, Professor Ernst Mach, studied the propagation of sound waves, and in recognition of his work the speeds of aircraft flying close to the velocity of sound are described by their Mach numbers. At sea level an aircraft travelling at 761.5 mph (1225.5 km/h) is said to have a speed of Mach 1, and if it is making 1320 mph (2124 km/h) at 40,000 ft (12.19 km), its speed is Mach 2. Flight up to Mach 1 is described as subsonic; that above Mach 1 is supersonic.

During World War II, piston-engined fighters were sometimes flown at speeds considerably above normal during test or in combat, and their pilots would report severe buffeting or even loss of control. The greater performance of the early jet fighters brought with it increasing experience of these compressibility effects, as they were called, though their maximum speed still fell short of Mach 1. The struggle to fly ever faster, and the difficulties involved, gave rise to the popular though erroneous idea of a 'sound barrier'.

Below: the North American F86F-30 Sabre was faster than the MIG-15 below 35,000 feet and would recover from a spin 'hands off'.
Next page top: the Bell X-1 rocket powered plane was the first supersonic craft, October 1947.
Centre: the X-15 rocket plane, here launched from a B-52, reached 4534 mph (7297 kph) in October of 1967.
Bottom: schlieren photo of a Concorde model in a wind tunnel.

AIR FORCE

At low speeds air behaves as if it were incompressible; the passage of a slow aircraft through it does not result in an increase in the pressure of air ahead of it because the molecules of air have plenty of time to move out of the way. But as the speed of the aircraft increases the air molecules have progressively less warning of its approach, and therefore less time to move. If the aircraft is travelling at the speed of sound, its speed is the same as that of the motion of the molecules which warn of its approach. Under these conditions the arrival of the aircraft compresses the air and the disturbance is propagated as a shock wave and the resistance of the air to the motion of the aircraft increases very rapidly. If the aircraft is to travel even faster, more power has to be applied to overcome this drag, or resistance to motion. Associated with the formation of shock-waves is a breakdown in the airflow behind them, which may cause loss of control.

The first aircraft to fly faster than sound was America's little rocket-powered Bell X-1 which, carried by a converted B-29 Superfortress bomber into the stratosphere in order to conserve fuel, attained Mach 1.06 on 14 October 1947. A few years later, employing the German idea of wing sweepback to reduce drag, jet fighters were able to exceed Mach 1 in a dive, though their engines were still insufficiently powerful to take them to the speed of sound in level flight. America's F-86 Sabre and Britain's Hunter were examples of these transonic aircraft.

The first truly supersonic aircraft was the North American F-100 Super Sabre of 1953, which could reach Mach 1.25 in level flight. It had an even more streamlined

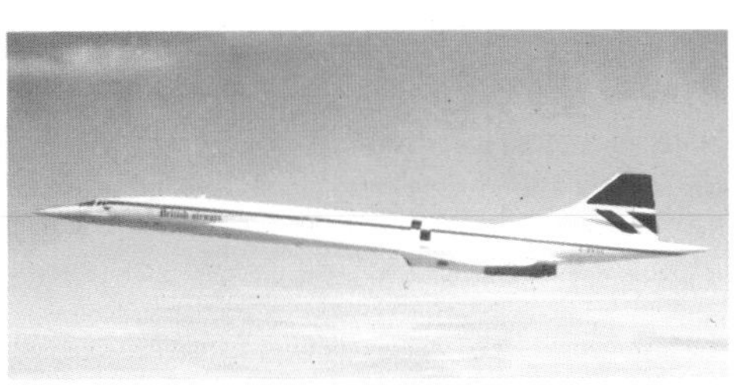

Above far left: two views of the Lockheed Blackbird supersonic reconnaissance plane, which flies the Atlantic in two hours. The black colour helps resist the tremendous heat generated at such high speeds.
Above left: the Russian Tupolev Tu-144 and the Concorde.
Left: the Concorde, a beautiful machine and a great technological achievement, but controversial and incredibly noisy. Despite the claims of its makers, over south London it sounds as though it will make the sky fall down when taking off.

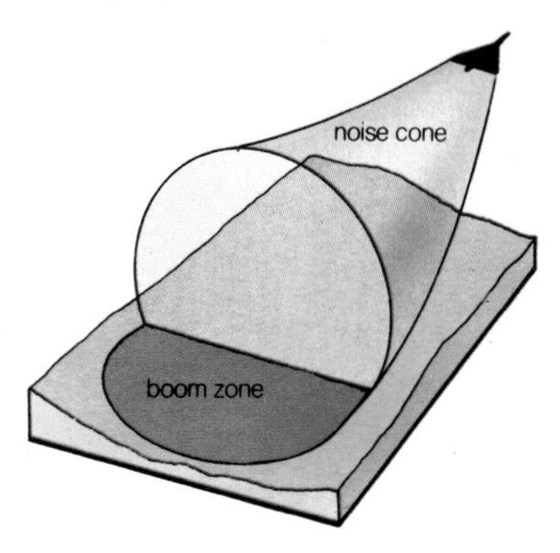

shape than its predecessors with, in particular, an extremely thin wing. Such was the pace of development that only five years later the Lockheed F-104 Starfighter showed sustained speeds of Mach 2 to be not only technically

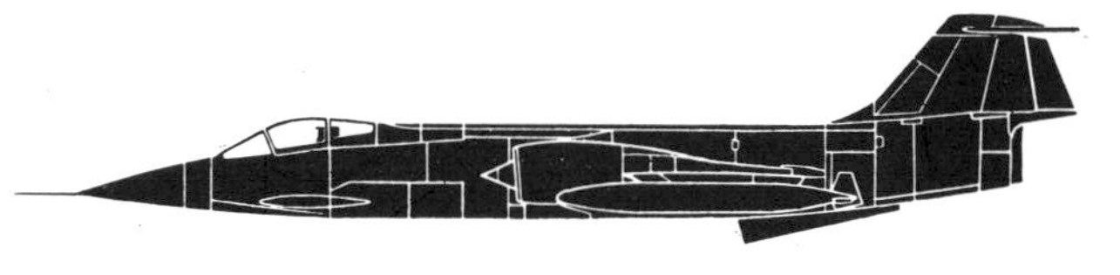

possible but militarily realistic. It had an exaggeratedly small wing, only a few inches thick, and with such sharp edges that they had to be covered with felt when the aircraft was on the ground to prevent people from injuring themselves.

Nowadays there is no particular difficulty in designing a fighter to fly at up to Mach 2.5, though speeds above this call for the use of special metals to resist the high temperatures caused by the friction of air molecules passing over the structure. At the beginning of 1975 the fastest aircraft in the world were the Lockheed SR-71 reconnaissance vehicles and Russia's MiG-25 intercepter, code-named in the West 'Foxbat'; both cruise at heights of over 80,000 ft (24.38 km) at Mach 3, approximately 2000 mph (3218 km/h) at that altitude. Fastest of all, however, was the North American X-15 research aircraft which, on 3 October 1967, flew at 4534 mph (7297 km/h), equivalent to Mach 6.72. The friction heating was so severe that parts of the airframe became redhot, and so tough, very expensive Inconel (nickel-based) alloys were necessary to withstand the heat loads. Speeds above Mach 5 are described as hypersonic, to indicate that the nature of the airflow over the plane has changed again.

Wings designed to fly efficiently at supersonic speeds are invariably inefficient at low speeds, generating high drag and low lift. Landing speeds are much higher than for subsonic layouts, calling for longer runways. In an effort to couple low drag at high speed with high lift at low speed, a number of the newer combat aircraft have variable-geometry wings, the sweepback of which can be varied continuously to provide the best efficiency at any particular speed. But delta-shaped wings are still the cheapest ones to build, and they are also lighter. They were chosen for the Anglo-French Concorde supersonic transport (and the Russian Tu-144), where the weight penalty and the technical risks involved in variable-geometry designs were considered unacceptable at the time of the original design.

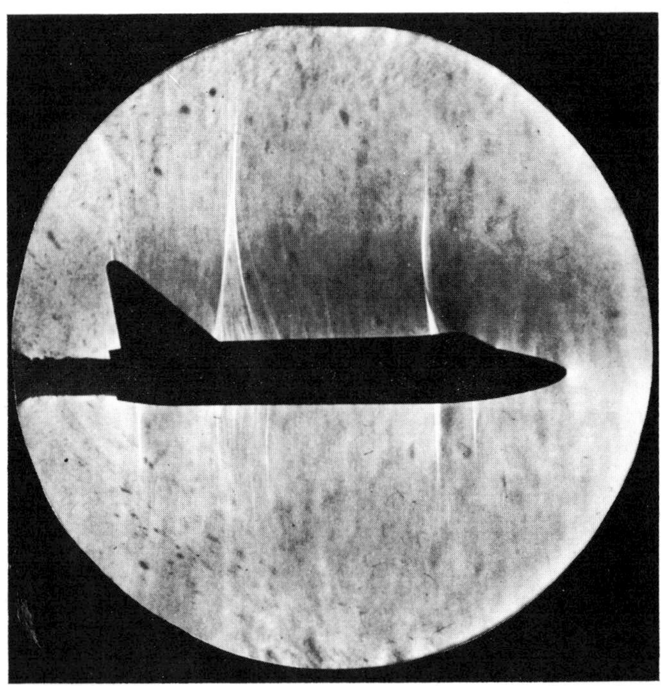

Above: a wind tunnel photograph, simulating flight at just below the speed of sound. The airflow over the canopy and the swept wings reaches supersonic speed locally.
Left: the Anglo-French BAC-Sepecat Jaguar tactical support aircraft (see also picture on page 53). It can fly at 990 mph (1593 kph) at 36,000 feet.
Below: the USSR's MIG-25 intercepter, code-named 'Fox-bat'. It flies at Mach 3 at 80,000 feet.
Opposite page: a proposed space shuttle vehicle. Launched like a rocket, it jettisons its fuel tanks, which burn up in the atmosphere; after delivering its payload it would re-enter the atmosphere at a shallow angle and fly back like an aircraft.

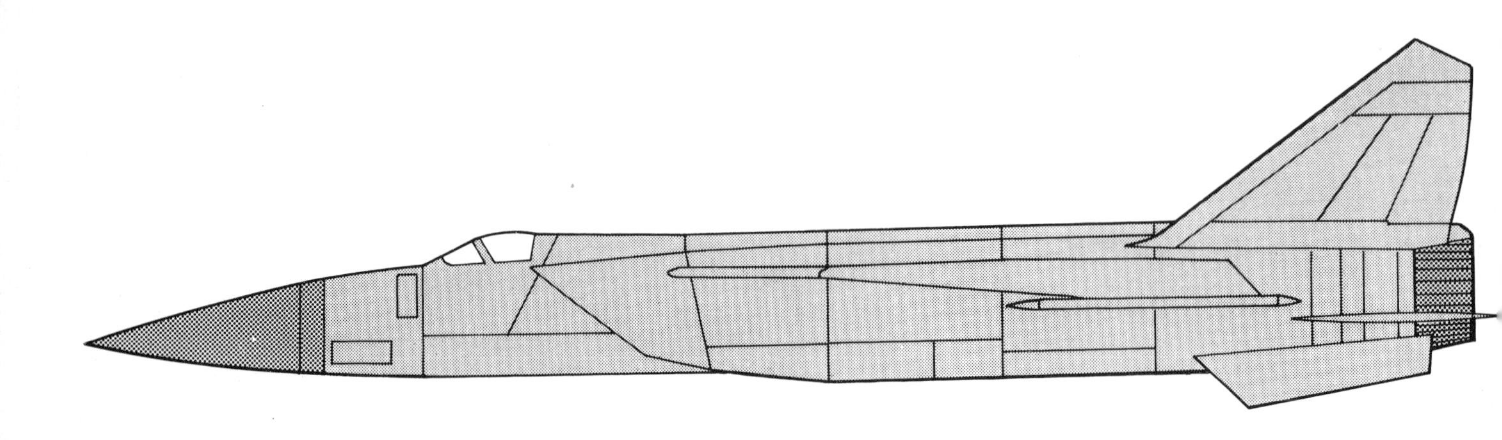

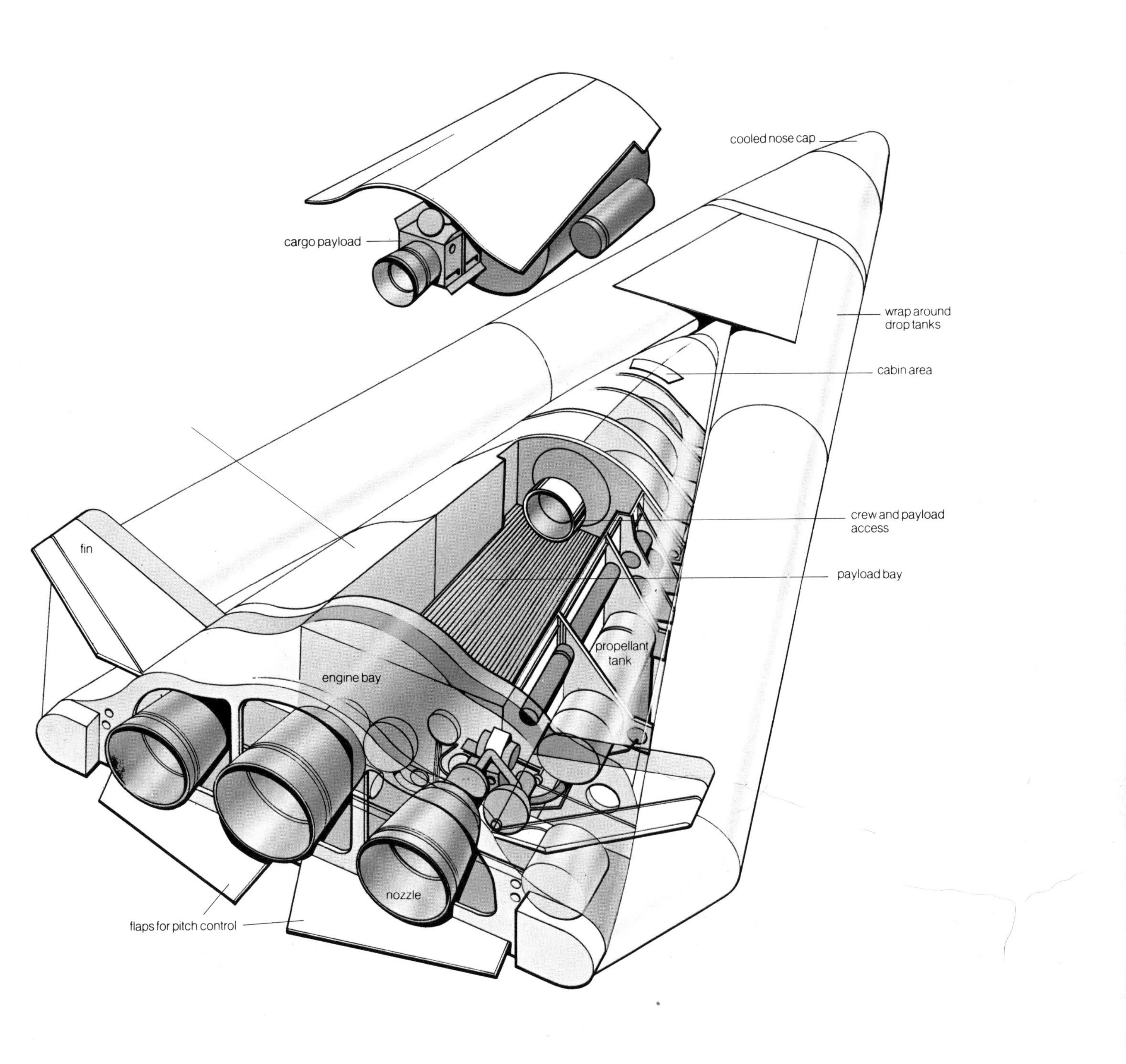
cooled nose cap
cargo payload
wrap around
drop tanks
cabin area
crew and payload
access
fin
payload bay
propellant
tank
engine bay
nozzle
flaps for pitch control

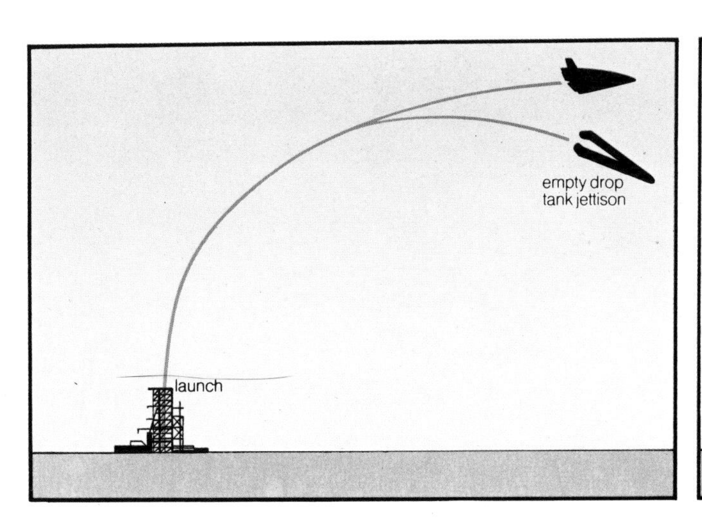
empty drop
tank jettison
launch

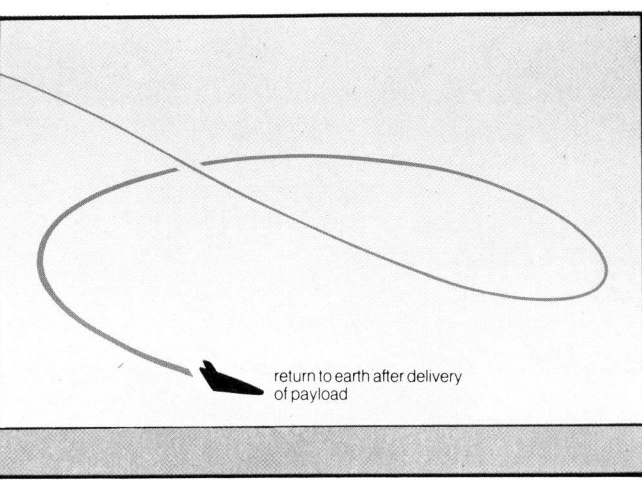
return to earth after delivery
of payload

IN-FLIGHT REFUELLING

Air to air refuelling permits increased range duration for aircraft. Its military application adds significantly to the flexibility of the deployment and use of air power in the tactical and strategic roles, both operationally and economically.

In concept, in-flight refuelling is not new. Early forms of the technique were used in the United States between 1923 and 1934 for the purpose of setting up various endurance records. The first British experiments were made by Squadron Leader Richard Atcherley – later to become Air Marshal Sir Richard Atcherley. He hauled a grapnel on the end of a line from a receiver aircraft. The tanker, flying above and slightly behind, trailed a weighted line. By weaving from side to side, the tanker brought its weighted line into contact with that of the receiver. When it was hooked by the grapnel, the receiver's operator pulled it in. The weighted line attached to the tanker's refuelling hose was then hauled down to the receiver, connected to the aircraft's fuel system, and the fuel transferred. The hose was afterwards disconnected, hauled back into the tanker and contact between the two aircraft broken off.

In 1932 Sir Alan Cobham began to take an active interest in refuelling in flight, and in 1934 he and Squadron Leader Helmore attempted a non-stop flight to India in an Air Speed Courier aircraft refuelled from Handley Page W10 tankers. The attempt had to be abandoned, however, due to failure of the Courier's throttle linkage shortly after completion of the second refuelling. In the same year Flight Refuelling Limited was incorporated as a company for experimental and development work in this field, headed by Sir Alan Cobham. The culmination of his development work came in 1939 when the first scheduled flight-refuelled service was set up to carry mail between London and New York. The aircraft operating the service were Short 'C' class flying boats, having a take off weight of 53,000 lb (24,040 kg) which was increased to 64,000 lb (29,030 kg) when airborne. The tanker aircraft were Handley Page Harrows capable of carrying 1,000 gallons (4546 litres) of fuel. The first flight took place on 5 August 1935 and, in all, sixteen crossings of the Atlantic were achieved before the outbreak of war caused the service to be discontinued.

The advent of the single seat jet fighter presented the problem of establishing contact with a receiver in which an operator could not be employed. To meet this requirement the probe and drogue system of flight refuelling was introduced in 1949. Today it is employed as standard practice by all the major military powers with the exception of Strategic Air Command of the United States, who use the Boeing flying boom method. This calls for an operator in the tanker aircraft to 'fly' the telescopic boom into the

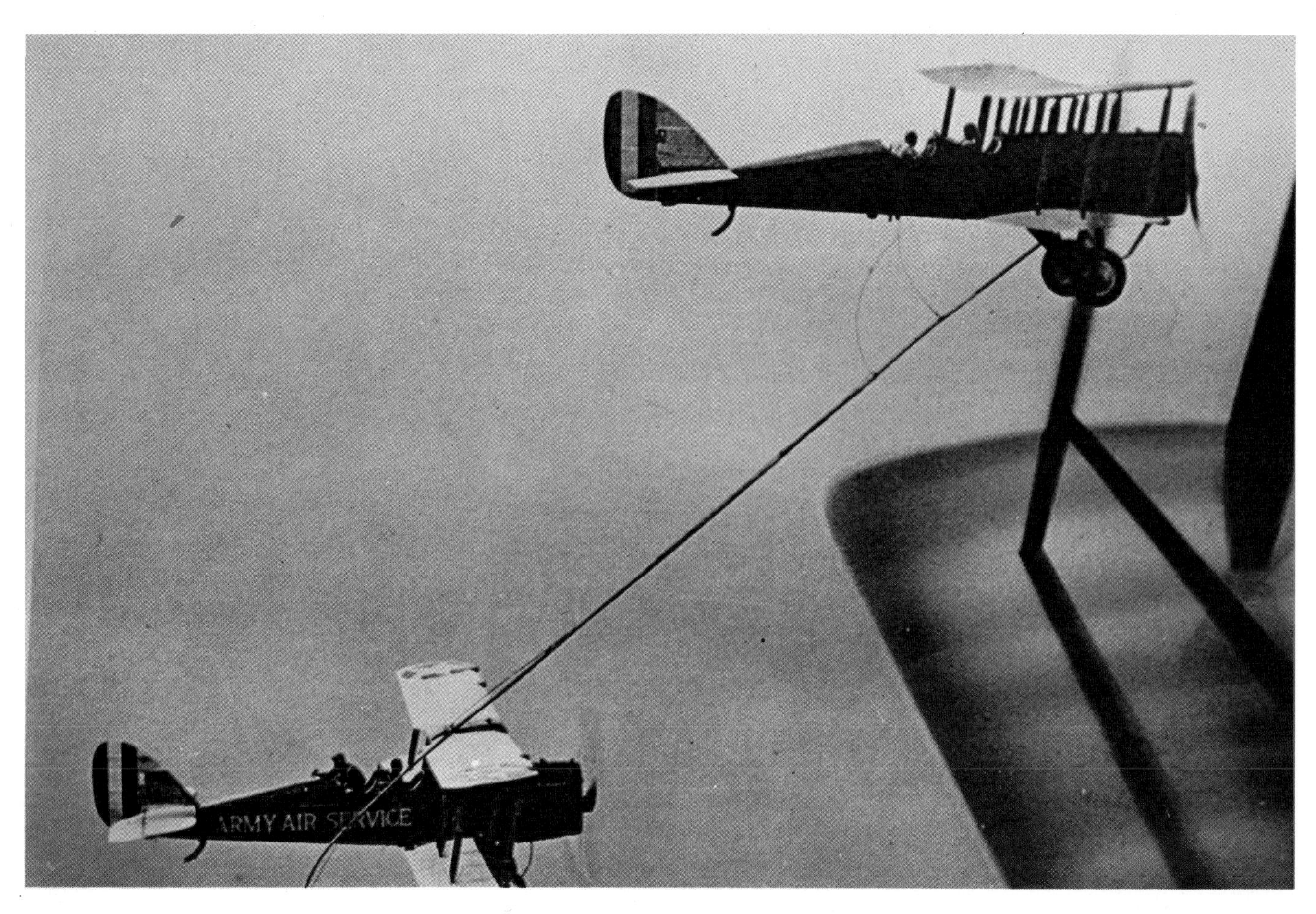

receiver's receptacle fitting. In the former method by Flight Refuelling Limited the pilot of the receiver aircraft is in command of the operation. In the latter, the pilot of the receiver is under the command of the tanker's boom operator. The first experiments with the flying boom system began in May 1949, using a Boeing KB-29P tanker and an EB-29 as the receiver.

In the probe and drogue system, the tanker trails a hose terminating in a reception coupling and drogue, while the receiver has a nozzle fitted to a probe mounted on the nose or wing leading edge. To make contact the receiver merely flies his probe nozzle into the conical drogue while overtaking at 2 to 5 knots. The nozzle automatically opens its valve and that in the reception coupling, thus enabling the passage of fuel between the two aircraft. On completion of fuel transfer, the receiver pilot has only to close his throttle slightly and drop back until the hose reaches its full trail position when the probe nozzle withdraws from the reception coupling. Thus the receiver pilot has only to switch on his fuel system and fly in formation to receive fuel while the tanker pilot flies straight and level. The tanker equipment is automatic apart from simple system selection by the tanker operator. This is best illustrated by the Mark 20 refuelling pod which can be fitted to a fighter or convert it into a tanker and can be used on single seater types, in which case the pilot operates the tanker equipment.

A fail-safe philosophy is applied in the design of the hose unit such that in the event of any single failure the unit will discontinue fuel transfer and apply the hose unit arrester mechanism or wind in the hose. The main considerations are the safety of the two aircraft during the transfer of fuel. In the event of any hydraulic failure a secondary compressed air system is provided to allow the hose to be fully trailed and jettisoned – whereas an electrical failure will cause the hose to automatically rewind and stow itself.

Among the many aircraft currently in use as tankers are the Handley Page Victor 1 and Victor 2 (UK), Boeing KC 135 (USA) and the Tupolev Tu-16 (USSR). In the case of single and two seat fighters, almost any type can be converted to the tanker role by fitting a Mark 20 FR pod.

Above top: two Lightning intercepters of RAF strike command taking fuel from a Handley Page Victor.
Above: the Boeing 'Flying Boom' system.
Opposite page: transferring fuel between two DH4B bombers of the United States Army Air Force. The plane was designed by Geoffrey de Havilland, first flew in 1917 and was license-built in the USA.

AERIAL PHOTOGRAPHY

Photographs have been taken from the air almost since the beginnings of photography itself. The first aerial photograph known was taken from the basket of a balloon over France in 1856. By the 1880s, photographs were being made from balloons, kites and even rockets in the course of experiments in Europe, and in 1909 from aircraft, both in France and America.

The first practical, rather than experimental, use of the technique was in the American Civil War – it is significant that this was a military use, for aerial photography has been dominated by the demands of military reconnaissance ever since. In 1862, at Richmond, Virginia, the Federal army sent up a photographer in a tethered balloon to take pictures of the opposing positions.

The French were early pioneers in both aviation and photography, and when the war began in 1914, they already had some aerial photographs taken in peacetime of the very places the Germans were invading.

The French photographs provided the inspiration for better aerial photography. J. T. C. Moore Brabazon (later Lord Brabazon), a keen photographer in charge of the British army's air reconnaissance team, experimented with old-fashioned bellows cameras but found them useless. They could not be kept still in the slipstream of an aircraft flying at 80 mph. So he designed a camera suitable for fitting in the floor of an aeroplane – the first purpose built aerial camera.

By the end of the war, these had developed into huge devices with a focal length as great as 6 ft (1.83 m) to give fine detail. Angled mirrors were installed inside the fuselage to 'fold up' the path of the light rays between lens and plate.

Moore-Brabazon introduced the use of a stereoscope to view pairs of pictures taken from slightly different points, giving an exaggeratedly three-dimensional effect that allowed the heights of objects taken from above to be measured. He also attempted to bring some routine into the taking and interpreting of pictures, so that sequences of events could be followed in successive shots of a place and logical deductions made. At this time, though, the system was still primitive.

At the end of the First World War, the newly developed techniques of aerial photography were applied to peaceful uses – though a certain amount of spying still continued. The main applications were mapmaking and surveying, but there were also other uses.

In Canada, forests being grown for timber were photographed from the air as early as 1921. This was an ideal method of checking on the state of the trees.

Another use of aerial photography was discovered in the United States in the 1920s and 1930s, where the Agricultural Production and Marketing Board regularly photographed farms from the air to check what crops were being grown. In this way, they were able not only to compile statistics, but also to detect false claims made by farmers for the subsidies that were paid for growing certain crops. This unusual peacetime spying made them extremely unpopular.

By 1938, it had become obvious to everyone that Germany was preparing for war. In Britain, the Royal Air Force commissioned the brilliant Australian aerial photographer Sidney Cotton to get as many pictures of military installations as he could without attracting attention.

Cotton had been taking aerial photographs since the early 1920s. His method of tackling the job was most ingenious. First of all, he used RAF funds to buy a Lockheed Electra, a fast civil aircraft which was the latest model and therefore of interest to aircraft enthusiasts.

He modified this by installing three cameras under the floor; they were hidden by a close-fitting sliding panel when not in use. He also arranged for a stream of warm air to be blown into the camera compartment from inside the aircraft. This prevented the cameras from fogging up or freezing at high altitudes and low temperatures, a problem that had dogged aerial photographers for years.

The next step was to go on a tour of Germany, where his new aircraft attracted a lot of attention. He often gave joyrides to high-ranking Nazi officers, at the same time photographing the very installations they were in charge of. None of them ever became suspicious.

When war broke out again, Sidney Cotton was given the job of organizing and running the first British photographic reconnaissance unit. Before the end of 1939, he had an Spitfire – the fastest aircraft of the time – fitted with a camera in each wing. It was used to reconnoitre the German frontier from a height of 33,000 ft (10,000 m).

To interpret the detailed and well organized pictures from these missions, he used a Wild photogrammetric machine, a highly sophisticated device for taking accurate measurements from aerial photographs. This had been developed in Switzerland before the war and was intended for mapmaking.

The photographic Spitfires and the larger Mosquitos that

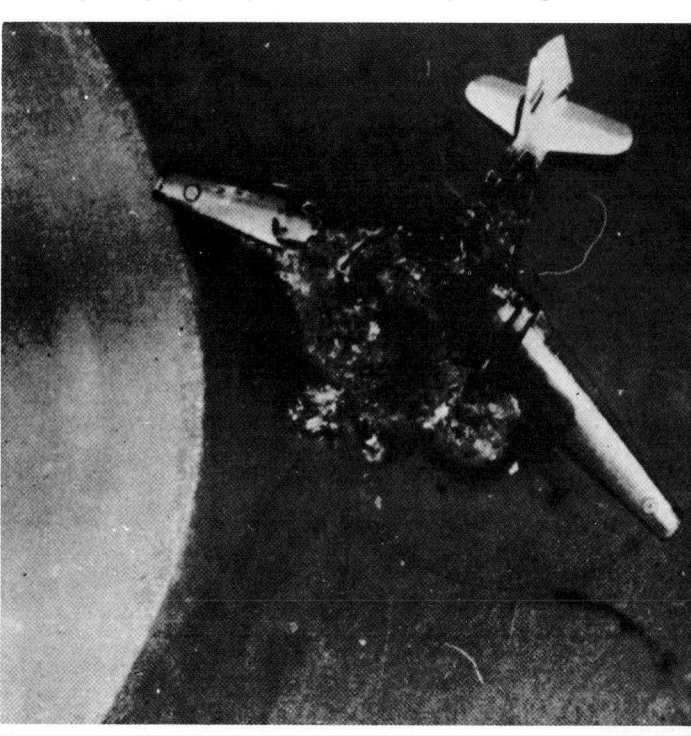

joined them later in the war were completely unarmed. Removing the heavy guns and armour plating gave them extra speed, height and endurance, which made them almost impossible to shoot down. This advantage lasted almost until the end of the war, when the German jet propelled Me262 and rocket Me163 fighters equalled their performance. Their relative invulnerability allowed them to make regular returns to the same place and thus to keep up regular coverage.

The regularity with which photographs were taken proved vital. Frequent pictures enabled a reference file on a place to be built up, so that troop movements, new buildings and unusual events could all be observed. This enormously increased the value of reconnaissance.

The early successes of Cotton's unit included the detection of V-1 and V-2 launching sites, the forecast of the planned German invasion of Britain and its later abandonment.

When the Americans joined the war in 1941, they adopted a system of photographic reconnaissance closely similar to the British one and achieved comparable success. In contrast, the Germans never got their system properly organized, which was a drag on their efficiency.

Since the war, great advances have been made in photographic techniques. One of the most important of these has been infra-red photography.

Infra-red light behaves just like visible light and can be picked up on a suitable type of photographic film. There are two differences, however. One is that infra-red light penetrates haze much better than visible light, which makes photographs taken from high altitude much clearer.

The other difference is that the amount of infra-red light emitted by an object changes with its temperature. This makes it possible to distinguish between warm and cold water, for example, so that the discharges from factories into rivers can be monitored to make sure they are not overheating the water. The amount of heat absorbed from the sun by living and dead vegetation is different, so the state of a field or forest can be seen at a glance.

Infra-red pictures cannot be printed in infra-red, so 'false colour' film is generally used. This renders infra-red as red, red as green and green as blue. It is sensitive to blue light. Another device, the airscan thermograph, uses an electronic scanner similar to a television camera to record infra-red light only, ignoring visible colours altogether.

More detailed information can be obtained with the multi-band camera, a device which takes nine simultaneous pictures of the same scene. It is loaded with nine different combinations of film and colour filters.

Pictures can also be taken with side-looking airborne radar which has the advantage that it works in complete darkness or fog. This makes it particularly suitable for military use. Unfortunately, the quality of the picture is not very good, though it is being improved.

All these devices are used for both civil and military purposes. For high-altitude military reconnaissance specialized types of aircraft have been developed, such as the notorious U2, an American spy plane one of which was shot down over Russia in 1960. Its successors can fly faster, higher and farther. Much of their equipment is still secret.

Today aerial photography is also used in archaeology. In Britain, ancient sites have been discovered in farmers' fields; from the air, a pattern of slight elevation or difference in vegetation may be observable which could indicate, for example, the buried wooden foundation of an ancient building or fortification.

Above: a reconnaissance pod made by EMI contains radar and an infra-red scanner as well as an ordinary camera. Here it is fitted to a Phantom. Left: photographic proof of the accuracy of the Israelis during the 1967 war: Egyptian Ilyushins destroyed on the ground.

THE HELICOPTER

Helicopters and autogyros are superficially similar to one another in that both are wholly sustained in flight by the lift generated as a result of the rotation of long thin wings, or rotor blades, in a horizontal plane.

The blades of an autogyro, however, are caused to rotate by the action of air blowing through them, while those of a helicopter are driven by an engine. Autogyros cannot therefore land or take off vertically in calm air. Helicopters, on the other hand, can take off or land vertically, hover, fly forwards, backwards or sideways irrespective of the wind.

The principles of helicopter flight have been known for centuries. Many helicopter models were made by early flight pioneers such as Sir George Cayley (in 1792). The first helicopter capable of carrying a man was built by Paul Cornu in France in 1907, powered by a 24 hp engine, but insurmountable stability and engineering problems held back helicopter development compared with that of conventional aircraft.

It was not until January 1942 that the world's first practical helicopter, the VS-316A, was built by the Russian-born American engineer Igor Sikorsky. This machine, designated the R-4 by the armed services of the USA and

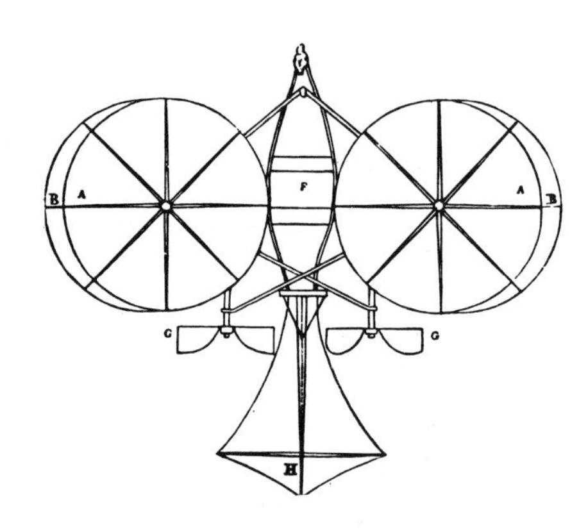

Above: designed by George Cayley in 1834, this early idea had rotors for lift and propellers for thrust. It was intended that the fan-like rotors would flatten out and become wings in forward flight.
Above right: this machine was built in France in 1907 by Paul Cornu, and reached a height of six feet (2 m). It had a 24 hp Antoinette engine.
Right: the helicopter produces lift by forcing air downwards, creating the ripple patterns on the water in this photo.

Britain, had the simplest possible configuration for a helicopter and one that is still the most widely used today.

The main structural element of a helicopter is the fuselage, housing the crew, payload, fuel and powerplant, which until the mid-1950s was a piston engine but is now usually a gas turbine. The output shaft from the engine, turning at several thousand revolutions per minute, is connected to a main gearbox, which steps down the speed to between 300 and 400 revs/min to drive the rotor (the assembly carrying the hub and attached blades).

The reaction of the rotor spinning in one direction would cause the rest of the helicopter to rotate uncontrollably in the opposite direction. In order to prevent this a secondary rotor, of smaller diameter, is mounted on the rear end of the fuselage and driven by a second shaft from the gearbox at such a speed that it exactly neutralizes the turning action of the main rotor.

Each of the blades of the main rotor (modern helicopters have any number from two to seven) is inclined (with its leading edge upwards) so that it meets the air at a small angle to the horizontal. This is the pitch angle, analogous to the pitch of a propeller or a screw thread.

When in hovering flight the combination of rotor speed and the pitch of the blades provides a lift force which exactly balances the weight of the helicopter. In order to climb, the rotor has to generate more lift, and this is achieved not by increasing the speed of the rotor (the rotor speed of a particular helicopter at all times remains virtually constant, irrespective of what the aircraft is doing) but by increasing the pitch of the blades. More lift, however, also means more drag (wind resistance) and so extra power is needed from the engine.

The pitch of the blades is controlled from the cockpit by means of the collective pitch lever, so called because it changes the pitch of all the main rotor blades by the same amount. This lever is mounted on the floor, and is one of the very few differences between the cockpit of a helicopter and that of a conventional fixed-wing aircraft. Operated by hand, it is moved up to gain height and down to descend.

Since most manoeuvres, including climbing and descending, necessitate changes of power, the collective pitch lever has a twist-grip throttle control at the top so that engine power and blade pitch can be controlled and co-ordinated with one hand.

Helicopters have no wings or tailplane and so the main and tail rotors are required to generate between them not only the forces needed to provide lift but also those needed to control it. In order to make the helicopter travel forward, or in any other horizontal direction, the rotor has to be tilted in that direction. Its reaction, or total lifting force, is then inclined away from the vertical and can be considered as being made up of two components: one acting vertically to balance the weight, and the other, much smaller force, acting along the direction in which the pilot wishes to travel.

To make the helicopter travel faster, the rotor blade has to be tilted further so that more of the reaction of the rotor acts in the desired direction. At the same time the vertical component of lift must be maintained, so more engine power has

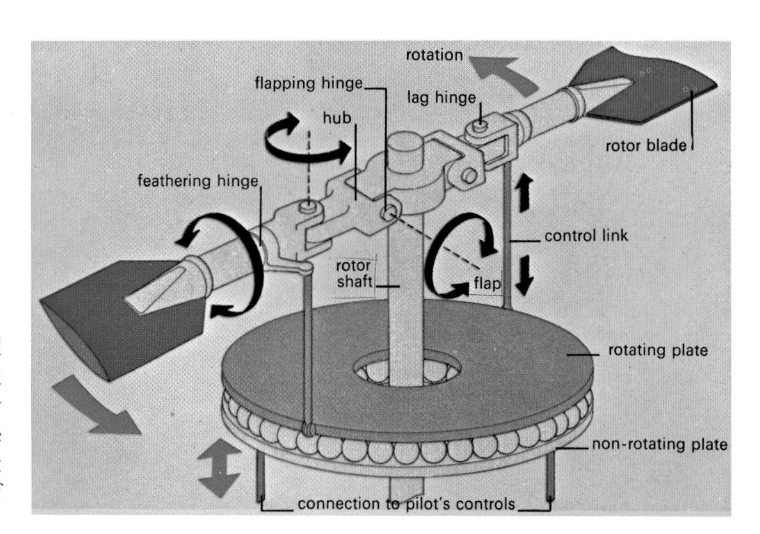

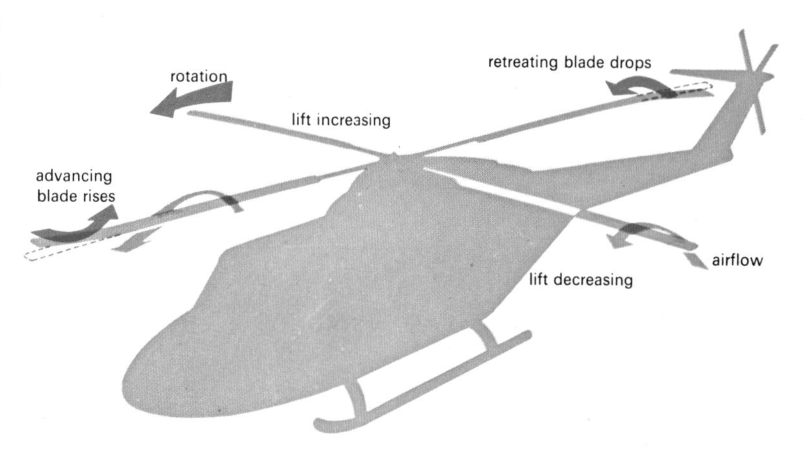

Above top: changes in blade pitch are provided by the swash plate, which moves up or down for collective change or tilts for cyclic change.
Above: the rotor blades flap upwards when they are moving towards the front of the machine, and downwards when they are moving towards the rear, in order to make the lift equal on both sides. This is necessary because of the forward speed of the aircraft.

TOW Cobra (plan)
1 TOW guidance control
2 TOW sight stabilization amplifier
3 TOW power supply
4 Main rotor
5 TOW launcher pods (two missiles each)

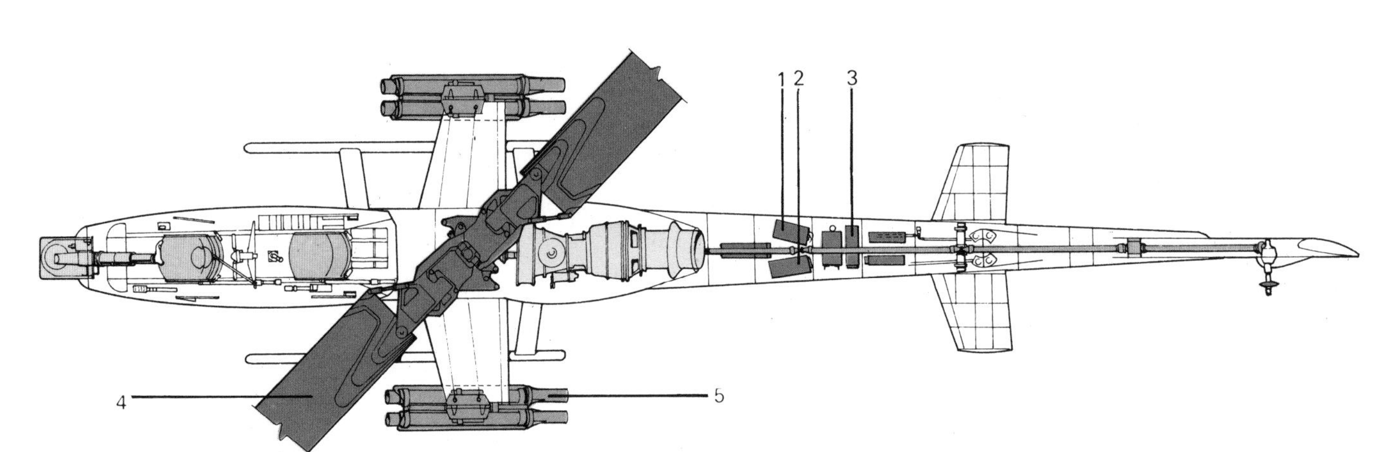

Above: the Bell AH-1G Huey Cobra, as used extensively by US forces in Viet Nam. Used mainly for casualty evacuation, it was also fitted as a gunship. It has a Lycoming turboshaft engine. The main rotor length is 44 feet (13 m) and range 230 miles (370 km).
Far right: a Huey gunship in the Mekong Delta, 1967. There was close liaison with river patrol boats in search and destroy missions.

to be applied.

The rotor is made to tilt by arranging that one half of the disc traced out by the rotating blades generates more lift than the other half, and this is achieved by increasing the blade angle on one side and decreasing it on the other. Thus the pitch of a blade goes through a complete cycle, from maximum to minimum and back again, during one revolution.

The cyclic pitch control, which determines where on the rotor disc the variations of lift shall occur to perform the desired manoeuvre, or change the speed, is commanded by a conventional control column in the cockpit. Changes in heading (the direction in which the helicopter is pointing relative to north) are made by collectively altering the pitch of the tail rotor blades by means of conventional rudder pedals.

As the forward speed of the helicopter increases, the velocity of the forward-moving blade is increased by an amount equal to the speed of the aircraft, while that of the rearward-moving blade is decreased by the same amount. Eventually a situation is reached when the forward-moving blade is approaching the speed of sound over a considerable portion of its travel. Undesirable aerodynamic effects then cause the drag of the blade to increase rapidly and its lift to

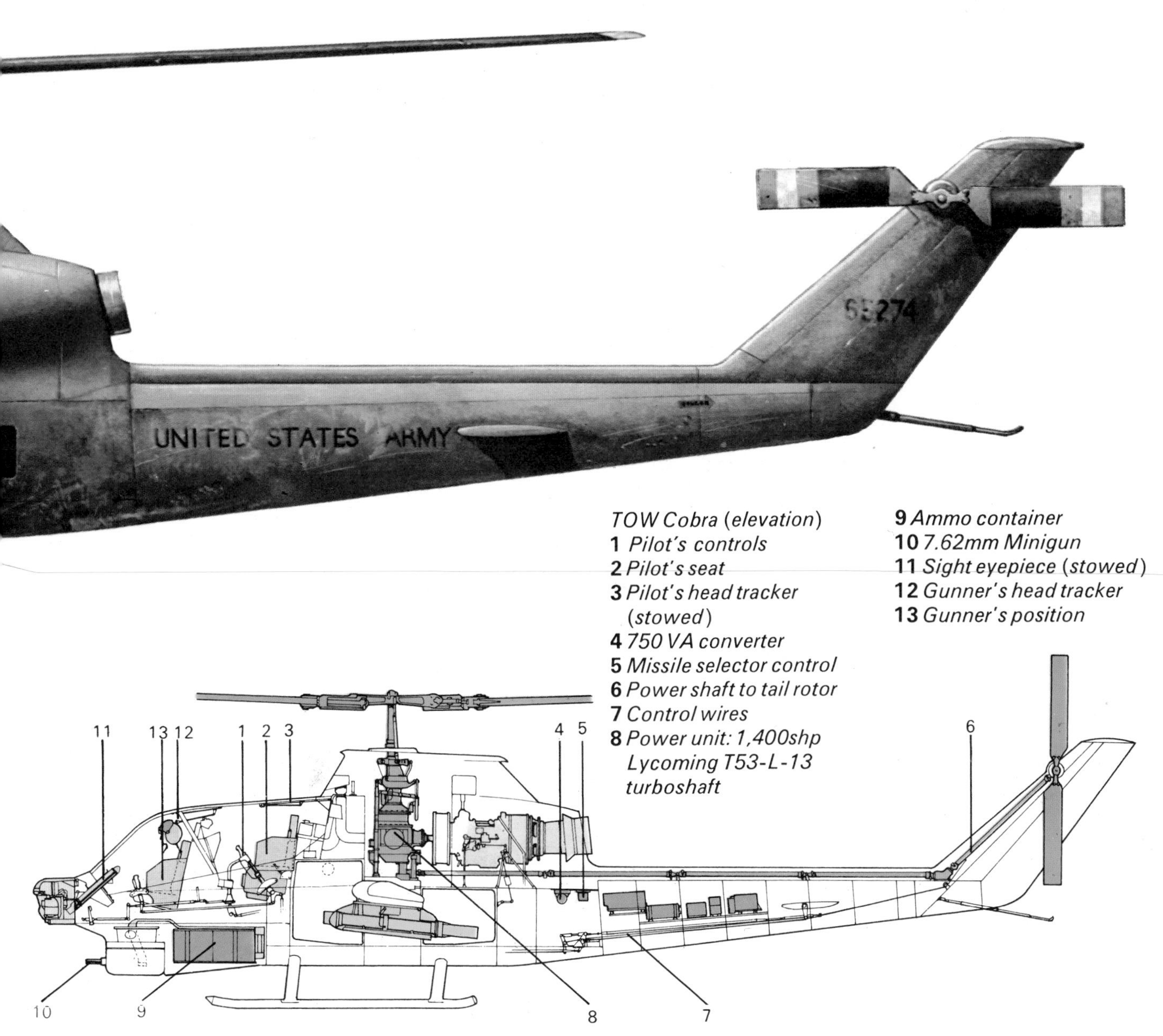

TOW Cobra (elevation)
1 *Pilot's controls*
2 *Pilot's seat*
3 *Pilot's head tracker (stowed)*
4 *750 VA converter*
5 *Missile selector control*
6 *Power shaft to tail rotor*
7 *Control wires*
8 *Power unit: 1,400shp Lycoming T53-L-13 turboshaft*
9 *Ammo container*
10 *7.62mm Minigun*
11 *Sight eyepiece (stowed)*
12 *Gunner's head tracker*
13 *Gunner's position*

Above: Royal Marine Commandos enter a Westland Wessex HU5 aboard HMS Fearless. *Such units are being formed in case of terrorist attacks on North Sea oil rigs. Sea King helicopters, with twice the endurance of the Wessex, may be used.*

decrease. At the same time the relative velocity of the retreating blade, travelling momentarily in the opposite direction to that of the helicopter itself, is too low to provide useful lift and it may become stalled. These effects limit the speed of a conventional helicopter to about 250 mile/h (400 km/h).

If engine power is suddenly removed, the rotor slows very rapidly, lift is lost, and the helicopter begins to drop. To prevent loss of rotor speed the collective pitch lever has to be rapidly lowered, so as to set the blades at a negative pitch angle. This means that the leading edges of the blades are inclined slightly downwards from the horizontal, but as the air is moving upwards through the rotor, the blades still meet the airflow at a small upward angle.

As the helicopter begins to descend, usually in a forward glide, the air blowing up through the rotor disc generates forces on the blades which keep them spinning. This is called autorotation. As the helicopter nears the ground the collective pitch lever is raised slightly so as to reduce the rate of descent, using the kinetic energy stored in the rotor to provide, for a short time, the extra lift necessary to decelerate the machine for touchdown.

The use of two smaller main rotors in place of a single large one can be an advantage, particularly with bigger helicopters. The rotors are arranged to spin in opposite directions so that the reaction torque of one cancels that of the other. There is thus no tendency for the fuselage to rotate, so the tail rotor can be dispensed with. This reduces the weight somewhat and enables all the power developed by the engines to be put to useful work in lifting and moving the aircraft.

The rotors may be mounted transversely across the fuselage as on the Mil-12, the world's largest helicopter, or they can be located at either end of the fuselage as on the Boeing Vertol CH-47 Chinook. They may be set one above the other and driven by concentric shafts, as on the Kamov Ka-26, or they may be carried on separate shafts mounted at a slight angle to one another; in this case (as with the Mil and the Boeing) the rotors intermesh with each other and the drives to them have to be synchronized so the blades do not collide with one another.

The general adoption of gas turbine propulsion for helicopters in place of piston engines in the mid-1950s resulted in a tremendous improvement in performance. Nowadays piston engines are only to be found on the older or very smallest helicopters. Instead of generating a high-velocity stream of hot gases to thrust the aircraft through the air, as in the jet engine, the power of the engine is extracted mechanically by fitting it with extra turbines and connecting these to the shaft which drives the rotor. This type of powerplant is known as a turboshaft engine, and only a small proportion of the gas energy emerges as thrust.

VERTICAL TAKE-OFF

V/Stol, standing for vertical or short take-off and landing, is a term used to describe the ability of a special class of aircraft to ascend or descend vertically, so permitting them to operate from very confined spaces on the ground. Helicopters and balloons are obvious examples, but the description has come to apply more specifically to aircraft having a more or less fixed-wing layout, but possessing special features which permit them to hover or land or take-off without significant forward motion. The term Vtol, for vertical take-off and landing, is synonymous with V/Stol, and was current some years ago. But designers now recognize that significant increases in payload or range may be secured where circumstances permit a short ground run, and the newer term more accurately reflects this benefit. The term Stol in isolation denotes a type of aircraft which, though capable of operating from very short runways, cannot land or take off vertically.

V/Stol aircraft share some of the benefits and penalties of both fixed-wing types and helicopters. They may be regarded as extending the low-speed capability of the former and improving the high-speed performance of the latter.

Though of outstanding versatility, helicopters have the fundamental disadavantage of being slow. While a few can attain 250 mph (400 km h), most can cruise at only half that speed. They are essentially therefore short-range vehicles, and their value as a means of transport has been largely overshadowed by their usefulness for tasks demanding an ability to hover or fly slowly for long periods, or land and take off from restricted spaces or unprepared surfaces. Efforts to improve their maximum or cruising speeds have so far met with little success, and their relatively small payloads make commercial operation unrewarding except for specialized tasks such as oil-rig servicing and the maintenance of remote or inaccessible equipment. Their special abilities are obtained at the expense of generally low structural, aerodynamic and propulsive efficiency.

Since the 1950s, many attempts have been made to improve the speed of helicopters by adding engines and propellers to give forward thrust, and small wings to relieve the load on the rotor so that at high speed it provides no lift, but simply 'freewheels'. By these means some of the more undesirable effects of compelling the rotor to generate lift and thrust simultaneously at speed are postponed. Although a number of compound helicopters, as they are called, have been built and flown experimentally, their performance has not justified the extra complexity and cost.

The next step was the convertiplane, the simplest form of which has a conventional fuselage and tailplane and a rather small wing having two rotors at its tips, similar to those of a helicopter but of smaller diameter. For take-off and landing these rotate horizontally, as with a helicopter, but are turned to spin in a vertical plane for forward flight, when they act as outsize propellers. Convertiplanes have been investigated in more detail than, probably, any other form of V/Stol configuration, because in the opinion of many designers they offer a more acceptable set of compromises.

Below: the experimental 'flying bedstead' of 1954, now in London's Science Museum. The Rolls-Royce test vehicle was stabilized by compressed air nozzles.

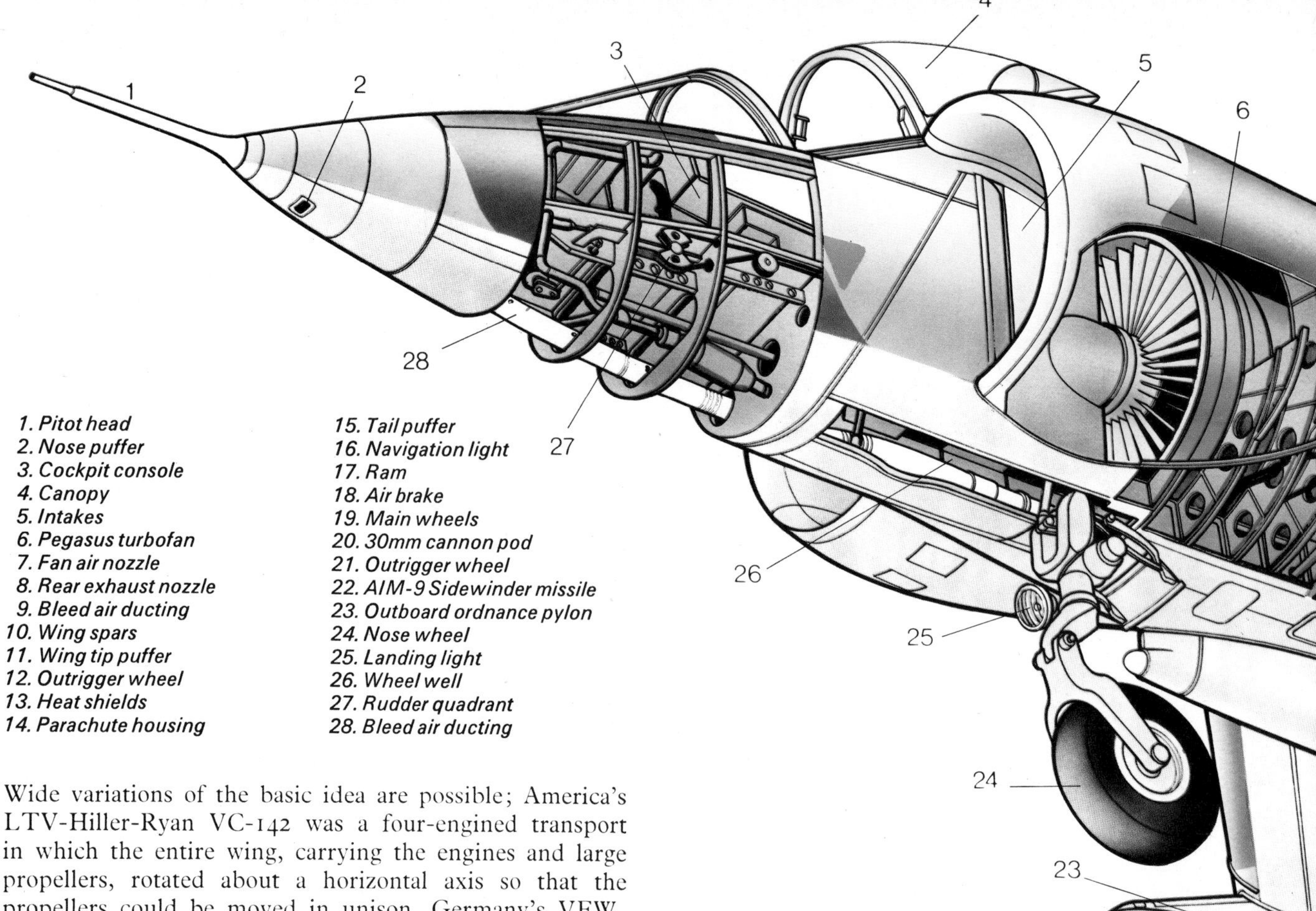

1. *Pitot head*
2. *Nose puffer*
3. *Cockpit console*
4. *Canopy*
5. *Intakes*
6. *Pegasus turbofan*
7. *Fan air nozzle*
8. *Rear exhaust nozzle*
9. *Bleed air ducting*
10. *Wing spars*
11. *Wing tip puffer*
12. *Outrigger wheel*
13. *Heat shields*
14. *Parachute housing*
15. *Tail puffer*
16. *Navigation light*
17. *Ram*
18. *Air brake*
19. *Main wheels*
20. *30mm cannon pod*
21. *Outrigger wheel*
22. *AIM-9 Sidewinder missile*
23. *Outboard ordnance pylon*
24. *Nose wheel*
25. *Landing light*
26. *Wheel well*
27. *Rudder quadrant*
28. *Bleed air ducting*

Wide variations of the basic idea are possible; America's LTV-Hiller-Ryan VC-142 was a four-engined transport in which the entire wing, carrying the engines and large propellers, rotated about a horizontal axis so that the propellers could be moved in unison. Germany's VFW-designed VC-400, though it never flew, had two rotors on the tips of each of its tandem wings – four in all. Again, there are no production aircraft of this layout flying at the present time.

In all the configurations described, lift and thrust has been obtained by the use of rotors or propellers. However an equally large number of experimental types have been built and flown on the power of conventional jet engines. Perhaps the most ambitious of these was Dornier's Do31, a medium-sized transport which used a combination of special vectored-thrust and lift engines supplied by Rolls-Royce, and was thought in the late 1960s to have commercial possibilities. (In a vectored-thrust engine, the thrust can be directed downwards for lift or rearwards for propulsion.)

Interest in V/Stol reached a peak about 1970. The West German Air Force and the German airline Lufthansa together held a competition to select a 100-seat transport suitable for both civil and military application. No fewer than four projects were put up by industry, and one of them was chosen as the winner. However when the design was analyzed in great detail the drawbacks and technical difficulties were seen to be insuperable, and the idea was shelved.

At about the same time in Britain investigations were being made into V/Stol airliners with virtually the same operational requirements, and Hawker Siddeley made a proposal for a 100-seat transport with a range of 500 miles and a speed of Mach 0.85. The propulsion system was based on the discrete lift/thrust technique, which for any V/Stol aircraft is the alternative to vectored thrust. Instead of varying the direction of thrust of one or more engines to give the required proportion of lift to propulsive force, the two forces are generated by separate sets of engines. The Hawker Siddeley HS.141 was designed around two large engines for cruising power and a battery of 16 small engines to be switched on at the beginning and end of the flight to generate the lift required to keep the aircraft in the air when the small, swept wing could no longer generate sufficient lift. The evaluation showed, again, that despite the application of very advanced technology, the design would be technically risky and commercially unattractive.

At the present time there is only one V/Stol aircraft in service: Britain's Hawker Siddeley Harrier fighter, designed for the close support of troops in the field. This apparently conventional (at first sight) fighter is powered by a single Rolls-Royce Pegasus jet engine in which the propulsive exhaust is ejected through four vectored-thrust nozzles. This fighter is not dependent on runways vulnerable to bombs, but can fly from any small clearing a few miles or so from the battle. The time taken to fly a mission, return to the operating site and prepare for the next mission is considerably less than for a more conventional type, which may have to fly up to 20 times the distance to reach the target, and then spend more time making a normal landing and then taxying back to the refuelling and rearming bays. The Harrier has a greater productivity; it can deliver a greater load of bombs on the target in a given time. The engine is sized to lift the aircraft vertically at take-off and is about twice as powerful as the powerplant fitted to a conventional fighter of equivalent size and performance; accordingly, for a given fuel weight the Harrier can fly only

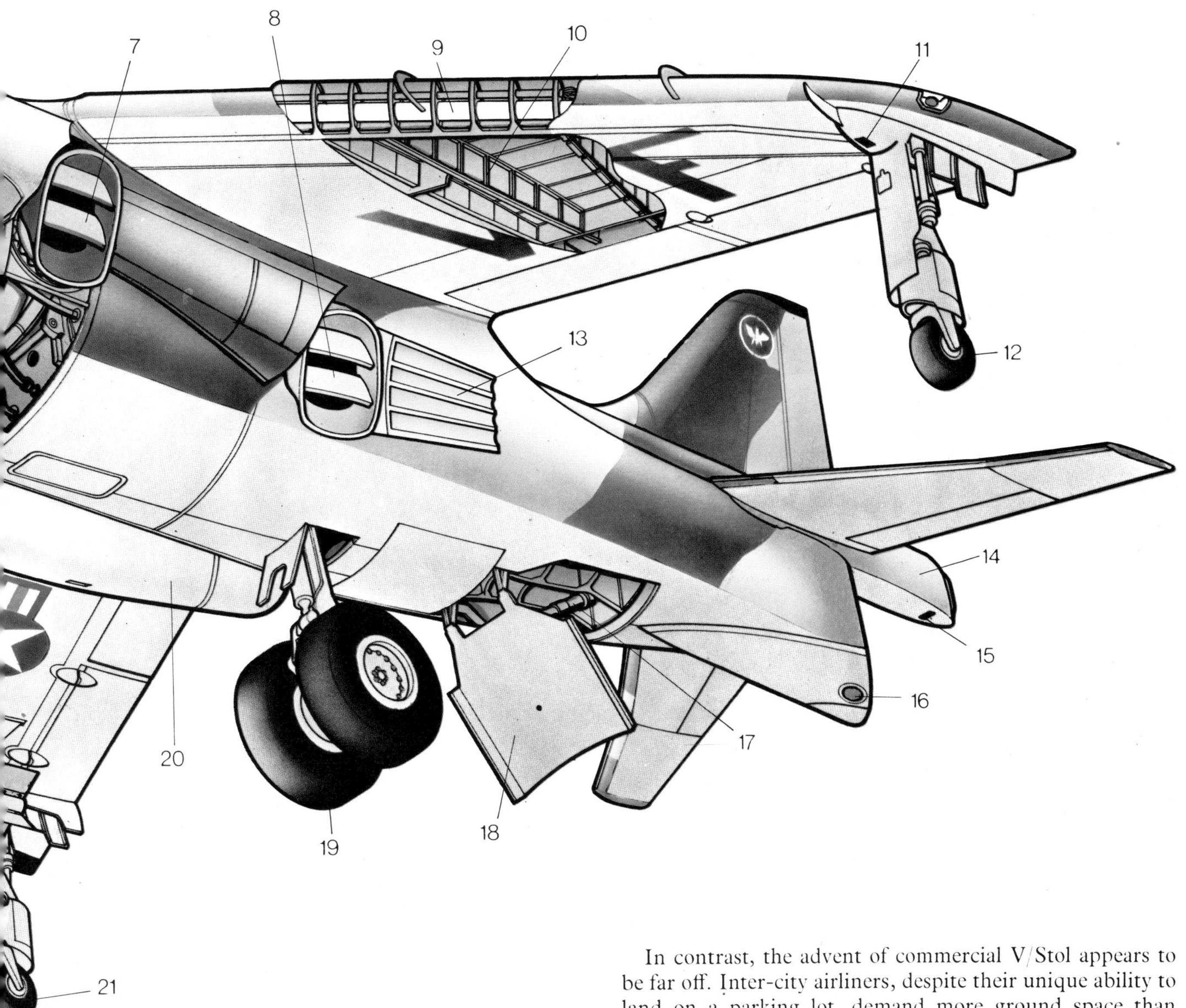

Above: the Hawker Siddeley Harrier AV-8 A (USMC). The US Marines like the aircraft, but orders for it have been cut because of budget considerations.

half as far. However in view of its flexibility this is no penalty. If a ground roll of 1,000 ft or so is available – and conventional fighters need 10,000 to 12,000 ft – a much heavier bomb load can be carried, and since situations in which this amount of space cannot be found are rare, Stol performance is a more realistic guide to the military effectiveness of the Harrier than its Vtol capability.

The Harrier 'jump jet' has been sold to the US Marines, who soon discovered a new flexibility in its design. They have developed a technique called VIFF (vectoring in forward flight). This makes the aircraft more manoeuverable than conventional fighters. If an enemy plane is in pursuit, for example, the pilot of the Harrier can swivel the exhaust nozzles, causing the aircraft to slow down very suddenly, so that the enemy pilot must overtake whether he wants to or not.

In contrast, the advent of commercial V/Stol appears to be far off. Inter-city airliners, despite their unique ability to land on a parking lot, demand more ground space than might at first be thought. For example the take-off and touch-down points have to be isolated to some extent from the terminal area, with its passengers, servicing facilities and vehicles, because of the destructive effect of the jet efflux. The minimum size of such a V/Stol port might be about 50 acres, and a site of such an area is not easily acquired in the central regions of a city such as London or Zurich, particularly when the collision hazards of tall buildings are taken into account. Again, new types of conventional aircraft can use existing facilities, so the cost of introducing them is not increased by such overheads. With V/Stol types, however, the introductory costs would be associated with the cost of building terminal facilities, servicing areas, refuelling points and the many other peripheral activities needed to ensure the smooth flow of perhaps 5 million passengers a year. The biggest technical problems are the reduction of noise and the development of special navigation techniques to enable planes to come down steeply in all weather conditions and at night. Even for military transports, where safety levels may be relaxed a little and the profit motive is absent, the next generation of transports will be designed for Stol, and not V/Stol, operation.

GLIDERS

In the early days of aviation the lack of suitable lightweight engines hampered the general advance and exploration of flying. As a result, gliders have a much longer history than powered aircraft.

The first gliders were made by Sir George Cayley who, after a series of models, constructed at Brompton, near Scarborough, Yorkshire, gliders to carry a boy in 1849 and Cayley's coachman in 1853. Other gliders were made around the turn of the century by Otto Lilienthal in Germany, Percy Pilcher in England, and Wilbur and Orville Wright in America, culminating in the first flight of a powered aircraft on 16 December 1903. From that date, apart from people learning to fly, gliding was mainly ignored until competitions were organized at the Wasserkuppe in 1920 and 1921.

From these meetings the sport of gliding grew throughout Europe. It reached England in 1929, although a brief meeting had been held in Sussex in 1922. The first International Competition was held in Germany in 1937, but during World War II large transport gliders were built to carry up to 60 troops or small vehicles. After the war, sporting gliding spread throughout the world, and international competitions have been held on a regular basis in the various continents since the 1948 competition in Switzerland.

There are two basic methods of launching a glider into the air. The first is winch launching, in which a long steel cable is wound on to a powered drum and the glider pulled into the air in a similar manner to the launching of a kite. The other launching method is using an aircraft to tow the glider up to any desired height. An earlier method, using an elastic rope to catapult the glider into the air from the top edge of a cliff or high hill, is now rarely used. Gliders may also be launched by towing them behind a car or truck.

Once in the air, a glider cannot maintain a steady horizontal flight path indefinitely, and the line of the flight path will slope downwards relative to the horizon. The angle between the horizon and the flight path is known as the gliding angle, and the minimum value for each glider, known as the best gliding angle, is used to give a direct comparison as to the efficiency of each type of glider. Before the last war a high-performance glider had a best gliding angle of around 1:25. By 1955 gliders had improved, and the average gliding angle of 1:35 was being achieved. This was due to improved surface finishing and the use of laminar aerofoils, although the gliders were still made from the traditional wooden materials of spruce or pine with birch or gaboon plywood covering. Nowadays best gliding angles of 1:50 are being obtained but the constructional materials used are usually glass fibre with synthetic resins. These plastic materials give the very smooth surfaces necessary to suit the specialized aerofoils used on modern competition gliders in order to achieve best gliding angles at higher speeds than were previously possible.

Minimum 'sink' at high speeds is nowadays very important in a glider, as competitions usually consist of triangular courses around which the competitor has to fly as quickly as possible. After launching, usually by aero-towing, the pilot has to find a thermal or any other air that is rising upwards faster than the glider is sinking through it. Having thus climbed to a suitable height, the competitor sets off on the desired course as fast as possible, gradually losing height until another thermal is found, and so on until the course is completed. In addition to thermals, other types of rising air currents can be found when air is blowing up the face of a steep hill, or when waves are set up as air masses pass over mountainous countryside.

A glider is controlled in exactly the same manner as an aircraft, including the use of flaps when these are fitted. Most gliders are also fitted with airbrakes to limit the maximum speed and to assist landing the glider in small fields. Some gliders also have tail parachutes to act as air-brakes. Competition gliders carry a very comprehensive range of flying instruments, including an airspeed indicator, an altimeter and a variometer to show the vertical rise and sinking speeds. Oxygen equipment and radios are also carried, and jettisonable water ballast inside the wings to increase the speed, when weather conditions are good, and to achieve the best gliding angle.

At an average gliding club today a visitor would find several different types of glider in use, and these would be

either single or two seat machines. The two seat gliders are, usually, used for instructional flying, either showing students how to operate the controls of the glider or how to make circuits of the airfield to be able to land correctly. Gliders used for this type of flying may be quite old wooden machines, although new motorized gliders have recently been introduced into some clubs for this purpose. The engine is quite small but, by using powered gliders, a club can offer instructional flying at any time regardless of the weather. Other two seat gliders, of higher performance and built of light-alloy metal, are used to give lessons in advanced techniques of gliding.

Single seat gliders may be found in many different sizes and shapes. The modern glass fibre competition machines have wing spans of either 15 m (49.2 ft) to suit the Standard Class rules, or up to 23 m (75.5 ft) for the Open Class competitions. Many other older competition gliders, of wooden construction, are now used for practice and

Far left: a modern sports glider about to land, using a drogue parachute.
Left: in this picture, the pilot has just run down a slope into the wind. The airspeed is a combination of the pilot's running and the wind; if it exceeds 14 to 16 mph (23 to 26 kph), the craft is lifted into the air.

pleasure flying. Occasionally a pre-war vintage glider may be seen, but these rarely take to the air nowadays, except at special events and displays.

Paragliders

With the appearance of paragliders, which are also called hang gliders, the age-old dream of strapping on a pair of wings and emulating the birds has almost come true. Countless pioneers down the ages have fixed feathers or fanciful wings to their bodies in attempts to fly, but their lack of technical expertise has been reflected in the toll of deaths and injuries. Lilienthal in Germany and Pilcher in England in the late 19th century showed that this method of aviation was at least feasible, though both men eventually lost their lives during experiments.

The technical basis for what is probably the fastest-growing sport in the world was put on a sound footing by Francis M Rogallo, a scientist at America's National Aeronautics and Space Administration, who investigated the possible uses of kites as recovery devices for manned spacecraft. The idea was not taken up, but the data provided the foundation for the new sport which has been developing in California since 1970.

The basic hang glider, and the most commonly used at the present time, is a direct descendent of the design tested by NASA, and is known as a rogallo, after its designer. It is the simplest possible flying machine, comprising a keel about 18 ft long (5½ m) with a cross-member of about the same length mounted horizontally halfway along it. Two sharply raked leading-edge members are attached by their forward ends to the keel and are each braced by the cross-member to form an A-shaped structure. The frame is covered by a lightweight material such as nylon. The pilot hangs vertically below the intersection of the keel and the cross-member in a harness which supports the seat and shoulders so that he cannot fall out. Hanging just in front of him is a control bar, called the trapeze, which is attached to the keel and braced to the corners of the craft by means of cables.

The pilot controls the glider by pulling or pushing the bar or moving it to one side or the other. He contributes by far the greatest proportion of the total airborne weight – the glider weighs about 40 lb (19 kg) – and so, acting as a pendulum, he is able to move the trapeze to make the craft take up the desired attitude. By pushing on the trapeze the pilot causes the nose to rise, so reducing the speed, for example.

To fly, the pilot straps himself into the harness, raises the craft to his shoulders, and runs down a slope. If the angle of the slope is greater than the gliding angle, the craft lifts itself into the air when the airspeed has risen to 14 to 16 mph (23 to 26 km/h). On a calm day the pilot steers his machine to a landing at the bottom of the hill, pulling up and losing speed so that he lands on his feet. But if a wind is blowing up the hill, its strength may be sufficient to sustain the glider, and the pilot is able to turn parallel to the hill as soon as he has taken off, and fly along in an area of rising air. This is known as slope soaring, and can be continued as long as the wind blows.

Rogallos are simple and cheap to build and fly, and they can be folded up into a small bundle for carrying under the arm. However, owing to their shape they are inefficient. The conventional glider can now achieve glides of 50ft for every foot lost in height, while the figure for most hang gliders is about 4:1. In an effort to improve the performance, enthusiasts have been experimenting with hang gliders having wings more like those of conventional aircraft and glide angles of about 10:1. So rapidly is the sport developing that these newer craft may supplant the rogallos, despite their increased cost and greater difficulty of transport and assembly.

SEAPLANES

Small seaplanes still play an important role, particularly in Canada and Alaska and other countries with many lakes and harbours and limited surface access such as Norway, Finland and the USSR. Seaplanes are the only practical means of transport around the Canadian north where they serve in hundreds as taxis, freighters, ambulances and fire-fighting water-bombers.

Water is as demanding an element as the air. Seaplane pilots must also become sailors. Likewise seaplane designers must understand hydrodynamics as well as aerodynamics. Both must appreciate the complex forces of water and wind on water. The variations and conflicts in design, both past and present, are as numerous as those of the boat industry.

The aerodynamic factors differ little except for a preference for keeping wings, tailplane and engines high and as far as possible from spray. The seaplane's greater bulk forward usually calls for a larger vertical tail area to control it. But the 'landing gear' requires unique considerations such as good flotation and stability, ruggedness and lightness plus hydrodynamic lift with minimal spray.

Like an ordinary boat, a flying boat must have its centre of buoyancy beneath its centre of gravity (cg), enough displacement for its gross weight, enough freeboard to prevent swamping and a high bow for low-speed taxying. It differs only in the greater stability offered by wing-tip floats or other outrigger-type stabilizers, which compensate for a high cg and a minimal keel. Retractable water rudders are usually fitted to assist low-speed taxying.

For take-off, the hull must rise quickly out of the water and start planing like a speedboat if flying speed is to be attained, and so the hull bottom is designed to push the water downwards. A shallow 'V'-shaped bottom is now almost standard, often slightly concave to flatten out the spray and improve lift. Fluted bottoms with an intermediate chine or ridge running between keel and side improve these characteristics and are now popular on floats and small flying boats.

Unlike a speedboat, where the cg is near the stern or transom, an aircraft also needs hull support well behind the cg, to cope with displacement when at rest and to give lift during early acceleration. So slightly behind the cg, the flying boat hull has a sharp up-break called the 'step', corresponding to the transom of a boat. The step reduces skin friction on the hull afterbody while planing and allows the aircraft to tilt up at lift-off to achieve a suitable flying angle for the wings. When planing, the aircraft is described as being 'on the step' and can also taxi at speed like this with low throttle setting while manoeuvring tightly yet safely.

The floats fitted to landplanes to convert them into float-planes are little more than small, sealed hulls. Modern floats also have some aerodynamic shape to give lift and reduce the weight penalty. Twin floats are now standard, although a single float was popular before the war and a tail float was carried on some early seaplanes. The high stance of float-planes, however, gives them a high cg and sensitivity to crosswinds.

Helicopters, not needing hydrodynamic gear, are often fitted with light, inflated-rubber pontoons or have these strapped to landing skids ready for inflation by compressed gas. Some larger modern helicopters even have full boat hulls or amphibious operation. A new concept now under test exploits vertical sponsons to provide a smoother ride in heavy seas for air-sea rescue craft. Fixed-wing aircraft could swivel such floats to the horizontal for take-off and landing, Possible use of lightweight water skis and hydrofoils has also been receiving attention in recent years.

Above: the Canadian de Havilland DHC-2 Beaver is an example of the hundreds of small craft which serve isolated communities in Canada and Alaska.

AIRCRAFT INSTRUMENTS

The instrumentation system of an aircraft is a means of providing the pilot and crew with the information necessary to control the aircraft. This information basically concerns navigation, engine performance and airframe controls.

The physical quantities being measured, such as temperature, speed and pressure, are known as parameters. Most modern systems are electrically based, and therefore the parameters are sensed by transducers which produce signals (data) analogous to the parameter values.

Many of the electrical indicator movements are of the moving coil (D'Arsonval) type and another frequently used system is the ratiometer type of instrument. This instrument has two coils wound on a common former, and its deflection is proportional to the ratio between the currents flowing in the coils, each coil being connected to a separate signal. As the instrument is responding to current ratios, it is relatively independent of supply voltage fluctuations.

The ratiometer type of instrument is used in conjunction with variable transducers (typically used for oil and air temperature measurements), or the many pressure and displacement transducers which have a potentiometer output. Many circuit variations are possible, for example engine pressure ratio (EPR) measurement where a pair of transducers measure the inlet and outlet air pressures of a jet engine. Although the data is in fact the difference between the two pressures, the instrument is calibrated in terms of ratio.

The moving coil principle may be reversed by using a moving magnet, mounted between fixed coils, in place of the moving coil. An extension of this principle is the desyn indicator, which responds to the ratio between the currents in a three wire DC circuit. This type of instrument has the ability to indicate through a full 360°, making it particularly useful for navigational bearing indications. A more modern version is the synchro indicator which works from a three wire AC system where the data is in the form of varying phase relationships between the AC waveforms in the circuit. Both of these types are relatively insensitive to supply voltage variations.

Servo mechanisms are used in many advanced instrument designs, particularly those used with air data computers, This method can give greater accuracy, which is particularly useful when the readout is directly in numeric form. This type of instrument usually works from the aircraft 400 Hz electrical supply, and the data is in the form of phase variation rather than voltage or current. The data is sensed by synchros or selsyns, devices which produce signals proportional to the angular position of a shaft, and which signal the servos within the instruments to move the indicator mechanisms to the correct readings. Some instruments, such as encoding altimeters and airspeed indicators, use servos in conjunction with shaft encoder digitizers which generate data in digital form.

Fuel management

Small aircraft generally require only a simple instrument set for their fuel systems, comprising a float type fuel contents gauge and perhaps a fuel pressure indicator. In a large aircraft, however, the fuel load is much greater and it is stored in a number of irregularly shaped tanks throughout the structure. It is important to control the fuel level in each tank to maintain the aircraft's correct centre of gravity. The fuel may surge about during manoeuvres, and to maintain a high degree of accuracy it is usual to measure the contents by means of a number of probes in each tank.

The important parameter is fuel mass and therefore the change in specific gravity with temperature has to be taken into account. Fuel flow is generally sensed by a small impeller within the fuel feed system which transmits electrical pulses at a frequency proportional to the fuel velocity. These pulses are electronically processed and presented in terms of pounds per hour (on a meter) and pounds used (on a numeric counter).

Above: the cockpit of an airliner. Many of the instruments are duplicated, with separate displays for the pilot and co-pilot.

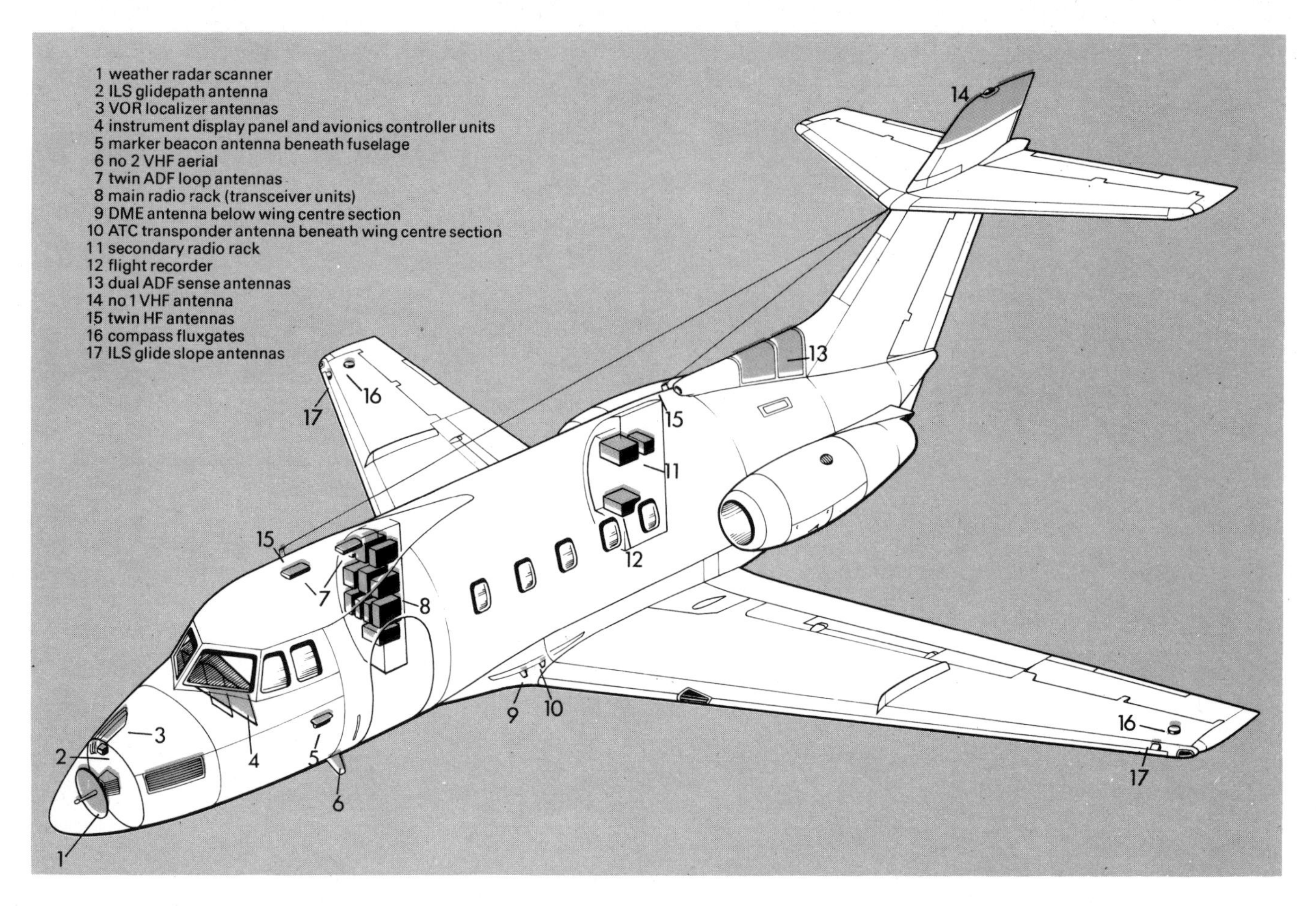

Engine instruments

The basic engine instrumentation of a light piston-engined aircraft comprises gauges showing the cylinder head temperature, oil pressure and temperature, and engine speeds in revs/min. The jet engine, however, needs additional instrumentation covering jet pipe temperature (JPT) and engine pressure ratio (EPR). The JPT has to be critically balanced between the engine running efficiently hot or completely burning out. The outlet gas temperature, usually between 500 and 850°C (932 and 1562°F), is measured by thermocouples, their signals being used both for indication and for automation engine control.

Engine power is a vital parameter during take-off, and with propeller aircraft this is frequently indicated by a hydraulic pressure gauge operated by a transducer in the drive mechanism, or by engine inlet manifold pressure gauges. Jet engine power measurements are derived from EPR, JPT and engine speed measurements.

Hazard warnings

Hazard warnings usually take the form of lamp or audible warnings rather than instruments. Stall warning, for example, is frequently presented by an obvious warning light plus a mechanism which shakes the pilot's control column. Undercarriage faults and fire warnings are usually indicated by lights and an audible warning.

Artificial horizon

The artificial horizon provides indication of aircraft attitude in both pitch and roll and is particularly valuable for 'blind' flying conditions. The heart of the instrument is a vertical free gyroscope acting as a fixed reference about which the aircraft rotates.

In the basic instruments the gyro is inbuilt, and presentation is usually in the form of a moving bar attached to the gimbal assembly, which is read with reference to a fixed 'gull's wing' type of symbol that relates to the banking position of the aircraft's wings. Additional information, such as roll angle in degrees, is often presented.

In aircraft with more advanced equipment, where the gyroscope is remote from the instrument, further information may be combined, often with the horizon as a background shown in the form of a moving sphere coloured appropriately to represent earth and sky.

Turn and slip indicators

These are two-part instruments which enable the pilot to first set a required rate of turn (for example a 'rate 1' turn is 180° in one minute), and then to relate this to the correct bank angle. When turning there are two components of acceleration, one due to the Earth's gravity (vertical) and the other due to the turning motion (lateral). The correct bank angle of an aircraft is when the resultant of these accelerations is acting perpendicular to the aircraft floor. If the aircraft is wrongly banked, it is said to be 'slipping' or 'skidding', and apart from this being an inefficient flight path, an uncomfortable sideways force is exerted on the occupants.

Although the more complex instruments derive their signals remotely, the basic instrument relies on an inbuilt gyroscope coupled to a pointer to indicate the rate of turn, and an inclinometer consisting of a ball in a fluid-filled curved tube to indicate the axis of acceleration. The inclinometer is similar in principle to a spirit level except that a mass is used rather than an air bubble, so that it is sensitive to acceleration forces.

Flight director systems

This is a generalized title for a family of instruments where the purpose is to combine many of the navigational and flight control readings into a common display. Superimposed upon this display is a number of director bars and pointers which automatically move into alignment when the aircraft is brought on to a predetermined flight path.

This type of equipment is also known as an Integrated Instrument System, Flight Control System, or Pictorial Navigation System. These systems consist of two basic instruments, the Horizon Flight Director, which represents a rear view of the aircraft, and the Course Flight Director which represents the aircraft viewed from above.

The data driving the instruments is obtained electrically from other systems including the aircraft compass, radio navigational aid and altimeters, and remote gyroscopes similar to the artificial horizon or rate of turn indicator. Height error sensing devices may also be incorporated, or other aircraft systems which may be of simple nature or may include a complex air data computer and inertial navigation system.

The Horizon Flight Director is generally based upon an artificial horizon display represented by a moving sphere, and to this may be added a rate of turn indicator, radio altimeter and inclinometer and command bars indicating speed and altitude.

The Course Flight Director is principally a compass indicator, with the addition of course director bars and pointers which correlate magnetic compass headings with the relationship to radio beacons. The system may also include distance measuring equipment (DME) and flight path indication.

Speed indication

The speed of the aircraft may be expressed in terms of distance travelled per hour or, in the case of high speed jet aircraft, by the Mach number (the ratio between the aircraft speed and the speed of sound). These instruments compute the aircraft speed from the difference between static air pressure and the pressure of airstream, using a pitot head transducer to determine the airstream pressure.

A pitot tube is primarily used for the measurement of speed or velocity of a fluid, either gas or liquid. The instrument is named after Henri Pitot, who recorded work in 1732 on the measurement of water flow. In principle, if an open-ended tube faces the flow of the fluid, a pressure will build up which will increase with the velocity of flow; thus, if a pressure gauge is attached to the outlet of the tube, the gauge will indicate fluid velocity. The pitot tube is used to measure the speed of aircraft.

The tube facing the fluid is known as the head and is required to sense a total pressure, which is the addition of the surrounding (static) pressure and the pressure due to flow (dynamic pressure). The face of the tube creates an obstacle to the flow; this is known as a stagnation point and creates a stagnation pressure, and it requires very careful design to make the stagnation point give the required total pressure.

To derive an indication of velocity a pressure difference must be measured between the total pressure and the surrounding static pressure, which is sensed by static vents. In a simple system the vents are holes pierced in the side of the outer tube assembly, but in large installations such as aircraft, the airflow is complicated and therefore static vents are placed at a number of positions and the average pressure is taken.

Total pressure is directly dependent upon the density of the fluid, which is directly dependent upon absolute temperature (temperature measured in Kelvins, where 0°C is 273 Kelvins – 273°K). The error on measured velocity due to temperature change is approximately 0.2% per °C in air and therefore compensation must be included for high

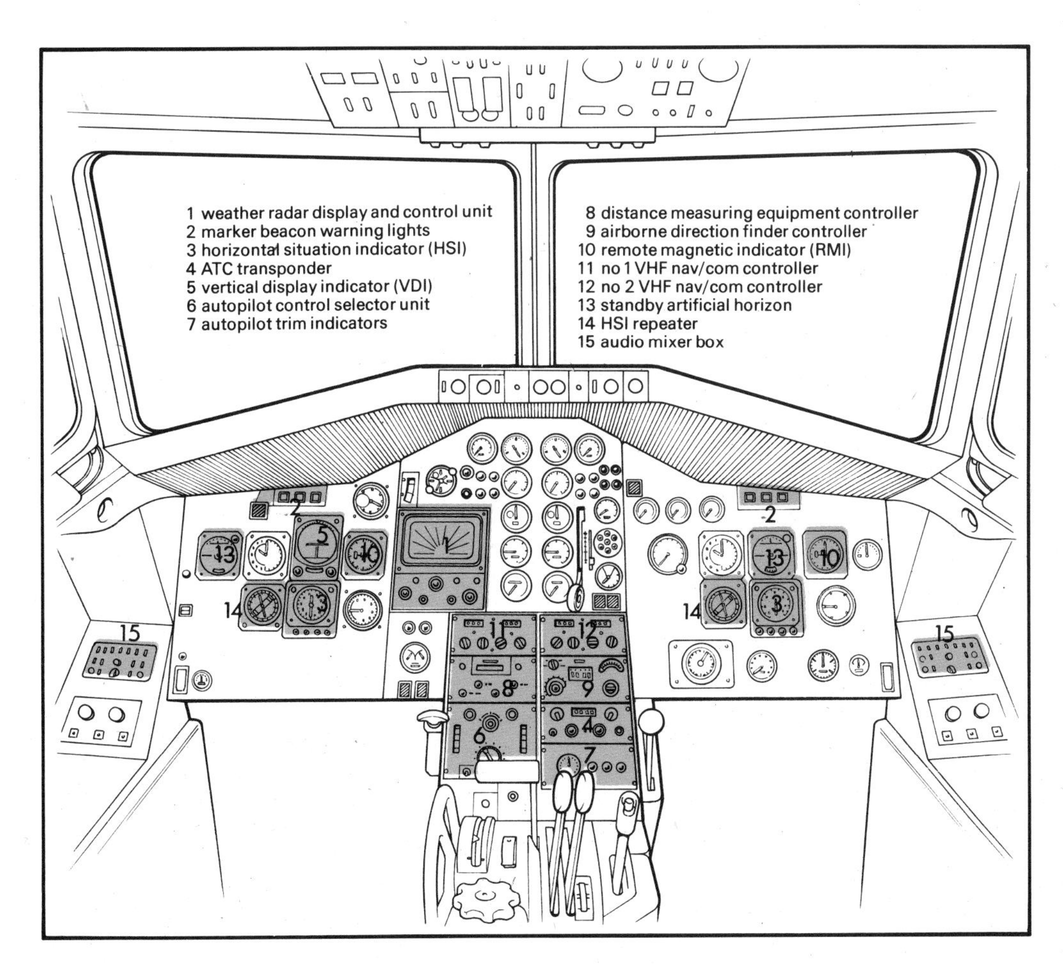

Left: diagrams showing the layout of avionics components in a Hawker Siddeley 125 series 400 executive jet, which seats 8 to 10 people. Some of the antennas are duplicated, so that more than one station can be received simultaneously. The compass fluxgates are electronic magnetic field sensors, and are in effect the main magnetic compass on the plane.

accuracy. Aircraft air speed indicator (ASI) systems do not usually have temperature compensation because first the error is not serious in this application and second the aerodynamic properties which control flight are all affected in the same manner.

A typical design is the L shaped tube, which is satisfactory where the fluid flow is straight and not swirling, that is, there is no turbulence. This design will begin to give significant error if the flow deviates more than about $\pm 10°$, but by shaping the inlet hole, flow angles of up to $\pm 60°$ are acceptable. A general purpose pitot static tube would be about 8 mm (0.3 inch) diameter and have a smooth surface. The nose must be carefully tapered or shaped to give both minimum disturbance to flow and achieve a good total pressure. Smaller and larger versions are made for special purposes, often with in-built temperature sensing elements; also, very special shapes are necessary for supersonic conditions. A number of pitots may be grouped to measure angles of incidence or turbulent flow and if icing is probable, electrical heating may be added.

The basic tube is usually metallic, either non-ferrous or stainless steel and the mounting and surrounding assembly is often plastic or of a fibrous material. In conditions where damage may occur a protective shield may be added but this must not interfere with the flow; additionally, the nose may be hardened to prevent abrasive action disturbing the shape.

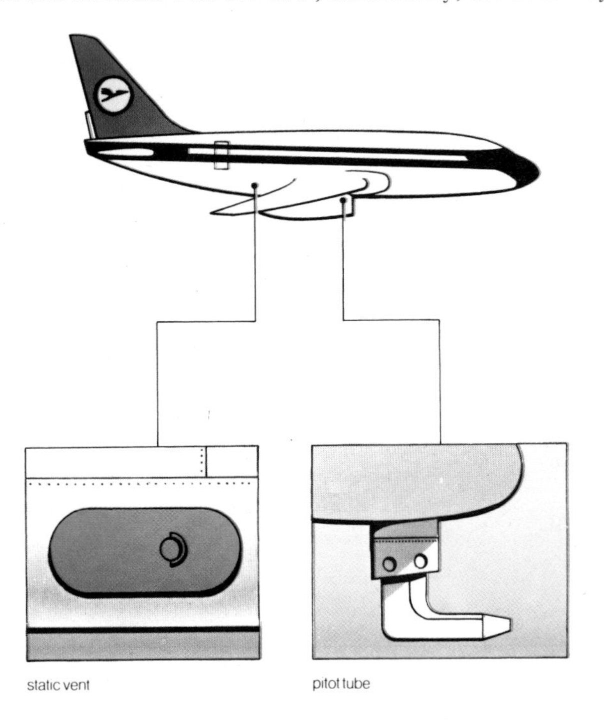

Above: the pitot tube measures the velocity of a fluid, in this case the airspeed of the plane.

In subsonic conditions, the pressure difference sensed by the pitot-static system is proportional to velocity squared, that is, every time the velocity is doubled the pressure difference increases by a factor of four. As velocity increases towards the speed of sound in the fluid, shock waves begin to build up until supersonic conditions are reached, where the pressure can in some circumstances decrease with increased velocity. At these speeds, there is a need for special tube shapes.

At low air velocities, the pressures are extremely small, for example, at 2 mph (about 3 ft/sec, 1 m/s) the pressure is only about 0.0001 psi; at 200 mph (100 m/s) this increases to about 1 psi. Thus for faster moving vehicles such as aircraft, the pitot becomes a practicable method of air speed indication. Complications arise, however, because, due to air density changes with altitude and temperature, the indicated air speed (IAS) is not the true air speed (TAS). At 3,000 ft, the TAS is approximately twice the IAS.

To obtain accurate calibrations, the pitot system must be placed in a fluid flow which is directed accurately along the axis of the tube, without disturbance or turbulence. This is known as laminar flow. A common method is to use a whirling arm rig, which consists of a rotating arm, perhaps 10 to 20 ft (3 to 6 m) long, whose outer end travels in a circular trough. The pitot is mounted on the outer end of the arm and although the travel is circular, the radius is large enough for the fluid flow to be considered laminar. This method is useful for the lower velocity calibrations and has the advantage that the fluid velocity is known directly from calculation of the arm speed and does not require reference to any other fluid flow instruments.

Air traffic control

For most of his route, the pilot of any aircraft uses on-board navigational instruments and sometimes electronic assistance from the ground to find his own way and make his own decisions. But when he is flying into or out of a congested area, the pilot is subject to the binding decisions of the air traffic controller.

Air traffic control, or ATC, must determine the minimum safe spacing between aircraft, both horizontally and vertically, in his zone. His flight progress board is kept up to date partly by means of the flight plan required by each flight. He also receives information from adjacent zones about aircraft about to enter his zone, and provides such information about aircraft leaving his zone. His plan position radar (PPI) gives the exact position and distance of each aircraft in his zone. He communicates by radio-telephone with aircraft as far away as 200 miles (300 km). An electronic direction finder gives the compass bearing of any incoming radio signal.

Using all this equipment, the controller must be constantly aware of changing situations and moving traffic. At a big airport the controller is responsible for the safety of hundreds or perhaps thousands of passengers at any given moment. At times of great congestion it is the controller who directs aircraft to a holding or stacking area, where the planes fly round and round but separated from one another by a safe vertical distance of about 1000 feet (300 m). As the lowest plane in the stack is allowed to land, the others descend to a lower level; new arrivals take the uppermost position.

Computers are beginning to play a large role in air traffic control. By providing information efficiently, computers can relieve the workload on the controller and allow him to concentrate on decision making.

The Eurocontrol Maastricht Automatic Data Processing System (MADAP) is a modern air traffic control system which is multinational in scope. It controls the upper air space of the region covering Belgium, Luxemburg, the Netherlands and the northern part of Germany. It receives data from four radar centres, has more than 80 controller positions and deals with 200 flight plans.

Avionics

The word avionics comes from AVIation electrONICS, the technology of electronics used in aircraft communications, navigation and flight management. In military aircraft it also covers electronically controlled weapons, reconnaissance and detection systems. In its broadest sense, avionics includes the ground equipment used with aircraft, such as radar, test and training equipment.

Avionics equipment has undergone a revolution in design since the invention of the transistor and, later, the integrated circuit. Space, weight and power consumption are a fraction of that required for earlier equipment using valves [vacuum tubes]. As a result, today's equipment is far more complex and reliable, and more can be carried in the aircraft.

Communications

Short distance air to ground communication is usually on VHF (very high frequency) channels in the aviation frequency band 118 to 135.975 MHz. The power transmitted by airborne equipment is usually up to 25 watts. The signals travel only in the line of sight, so the range depends on the aircraft's altitude. With aircraft flying at 30,000 ft (9,000 m), ranges of 250 miles (400 km) are normal. Military aircraft also use UHF (ultra high frequency) channels in the range 225 to 399.95 MHz giving a similar air to ground range and up to 600 miles (965 km) air to air range.

World wide communication is allocated to aircraft in certain channels in the band 2 to 30 MHz. Powers of up to 400W are used with a choice of telemetry methods, such as voice and telegraph. Low frequency (60 to 160 kHz) radio teleprinter equipment is sometimes fitted on large commercial aircraft.

So that the flight crew does not have to listen constantly to the radio system for incoming calls, a selective calling system is used. In the SELCAL mode, the calling station

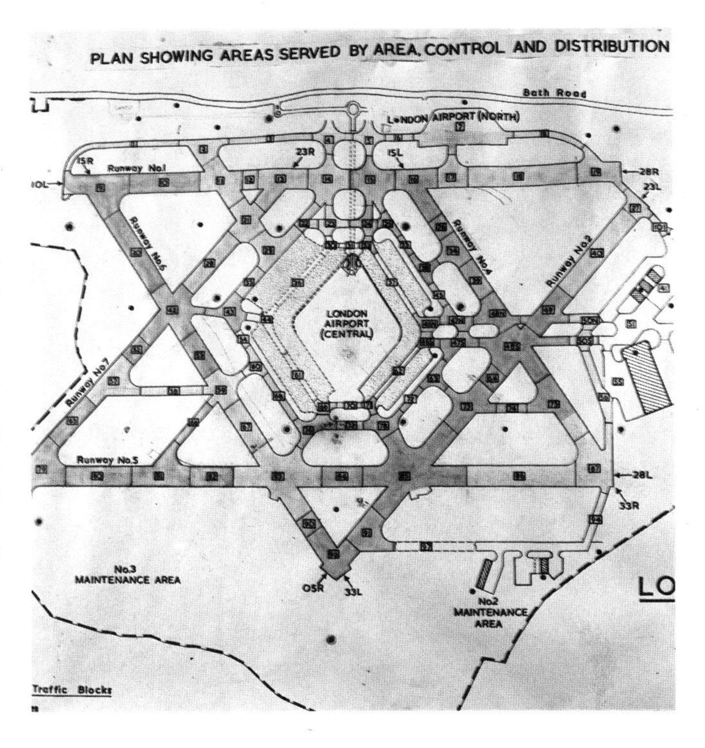

Above: a map of London's Heathrow airport. An airfield surface movement radar reproduces the same map but also making moving aircraft visible.
Below: the precision approach radar. This enables a controller to watch the exact path being taken by an aircraft from ten miles (16 km) out (left-hand screen) and in greater detail from three miles (5 km) (right-hand screen).

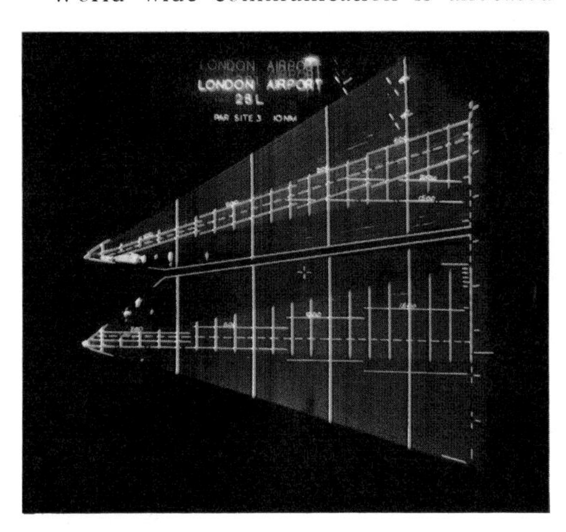

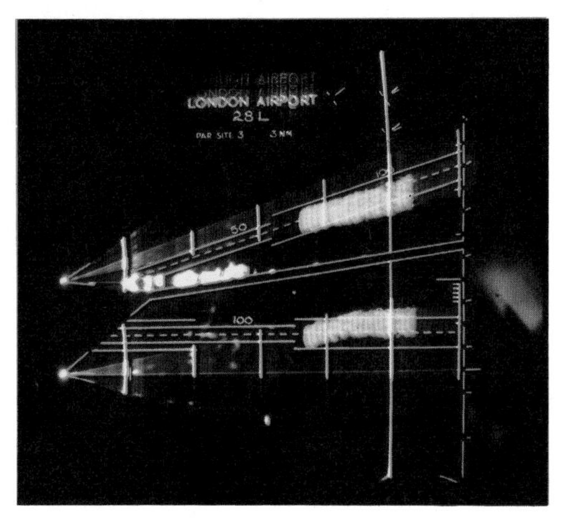

Right: the cockpit of a Piper private aircraft, showing the Decca Navigator flight log. Far right: a 'head up' display, which projects information into the pilot's line of sight.

sends out a two-tone signal, coded for the particular aircraft being called. The airborne receiver is left tuned to the calling frequency, and can be heard all the time. When the aircraft code is received and decoded, the flight crew are alerted by a visual or audible signal, and only then need give their attention to the radio.

A crew intercommunication system is generally linked to a passenger address system on passenger aircraft so that the flight crew can communicate with passengers.

Automatic pilot

The automatic pilot was demonstrated as early as 1914 when Lawrence Sperry, son of Dr Elmer Sperry, the gyroscope pioneer, won a substantial prize offered for the first 'hands-off' flight. The autopilot senses any deviation from an aircraft's flight pattern and automatically adjusts the ailerons, elevator, rudder and trim tabs (these are small extra surfaces mounted on the other control surfaces) to compensate for the deviation. The basis of the system is a gyrocompass which controls the aircraft's direction and a vertical gyro which controls pitch and roll. Early autopilots had air-driven gyroscopes with the aircraft controls activated pneumatically or hydraulically. Today, nearly all autopilots have electrically driven gyros. Even the simplest autopilot will keep the aircraft on a selected heading in level flight far more accurately than a human pilot and this is still the autopilot's main function, but through the years many refinements have been added. Turns may be selected by the pilot through his autopilot: if a new altitude is chosen, the aircraft will climb or descend automatically until it has been reached; and the autopilot may be coupled to radio navigation systems (see below) so that the aircraft will automatically 'home' on to a radio beacon or lock on to an instrument landing system.

A modern addition to the autopilot is the autothrottle, which provides automatic speed control throughout the cruise, descent and final approach to landing. Not only does the autothrottle reduce the pilot's workload during the critical moments before landing, but it also improves flight path holding accuracy, especially with swept wing jet aircraft where the lack of stability at low speeds can be very demanding on the pilot.

Navigation devices

The navigation equipment on an aircraft may be entirely self-contained, operating entirely without external aid, or it may work in conjunction with ground-based aids such as radio beacons and area radio navigation systems. Most navigation equipment can be coupled to the automatic pilot to fly the plane, the flight crew watching the overall system and taking manual control only during take-off and landing, or in an emergency.

When an aircraft is flying between airports, it may use a system such as Loran, Decca Navigator or Omega. Each of these employs its own network of fixed ground stations which radiate a pattern of radio signals. From this, positions can be determined by measuring time or phase differences between the radio stations.

Loran (Long Range Air Navigation) is widely used by aircraft on long-distance routes. The most refined version can give positions accurate to within a few hundred yards or metres even in mid-Atlantic. The Decca Navigator can give a higher accuracy but has a shorter range. Planes on short haul flights and helicopters tend to use Decca Navigator rather than Loran. Both systems use frequencies of around 100 kHz.

Omega uses a much lower frequency, 10 to 14 kHz, and is being brought into use mainly because its signals will penetrate underwater, so it can be used by submarines. A few aircraft are equipped to make use of the system.

Doppler navigators have been developed for use in addition to Loran-type systems. The Doppler effect is the change in pitch of waves—such as sound, light or radio waves—as their source approaches or recedes. It is most often noticed when a car goes past at speed, its pitch being higher as it approaches and lower as it goes away.

In the case of a Doppler navigator, a microwave radio signal of known frequency is sent downwards to the earth's surface. It is reflected back at a slightly different frequency, since the ground is moving relative to the aircraft, and this difference is measured to give the speed. Typical systems have four fan-shaped radio beams which are transmitted in sequence forward, aft and on each side of the aircraft to provide measurement of ground speed, drift angle and total miles travelled. The transmitted frequency is centred around 8.8GHz (8,800,000,000 cycles per second) and the power transmitted is typically one watt.

Doppler systems are entirely self-contained and can be

programmed to provide information on the distance and time, to go to preselected points on the route to show latitude and longitude, to operate the pilot's steering indicator, or to drive moving map displays.

Inertial guidance

Inertial guidance is a navigational technique employing inertial sensing devices whereby a vehicle is guided, without external aids or influence, from one place to another. The term 'Inertial Navigation' is also frequently used to describe this process.

Inertial sensing devices measure the vehicle's acceleration, direction and attitude by making use of Newton's laws of motion. Additionally, simple computations derive speed and position from the acceleration measurements and thus complete the information required for navigation and guidance. Accelerometers, as the name implies, are used to measure the vehicle's accelerations and very sensitive gyroscopes indicate changes in vehicle and direction.

The foundation for inertial guidance was laid in 1852 by Leon Foucault who showed that a gyroscope, because it tends to remain fixed in attitude with respect to the stars, can measure the rotation of the earth. This discovery lay dormant for fifty years awaiting development of the gyroscope to a precision suitable for navigation. In 1908 a German inventor named Anschutz-Kaempfe produced the first sea-going gyrocompass, but difficulties were experienced with the device during ship manoeuvres. Gyrocompasses indicate true north but act like pendulums when upset. Max Schuler, a German professor, recognized that the gyrocompass would not be affected by the ship's motion if its swing, or period, were deliberately adjusted to conform with the earth's radius and gravitational attraction. He proposed the combined use of a gyroscope and velocity-measuring device for this purpose.

Other gyrocompasses were produced in the United States and England, but the first true inertial guidance system was invented for the German V2 in World War II. This was crude but effective. It consisted of attitude-controlling gyroscopes and a single accelerometer which was constructed to cut-off the rocket engine at a present speed. By 1948 the United States had taken the lead by developing gyro-accelerometer principles into full inertial navigators. Ten years later, one of these complex systems accurately navigated the USS Nautilus under the Arctic ice-cap.

It is sufficient to travel in any form of transportation to experience the phenomenon of inertia. As the vehicle accelerates from rest, brakes or corners, the passenger experiences a force accelerating or decelerating him in sympathy. If the force is absent, or too small, the passenger may be thrown about within the vehicle.

As physical objects, by virtue of their mass, require a force to accelerate or decelerate them, the property of inertia, or sluggishness, is attributed to mass because it resists changes of motion. Using this principle, a simple accelerometer may be constructed of a metal weight held centrally in a case by two springs, one in front and one

Right: a miniature inertial guidance system weighing 25 lb (11.3 kg) and 11 inches (28 cm) long, for rockets, ships, submarines and aircraft.

behind. As the case (and vehicle) accelerates, the inertia of the weight compresses the trailing spring. This compression is proportional to the acceleration and is easily detected electrically. Provided that the accelerometer is pointing in a known direction, this electrical signal can be used for computing speed and distance travelled in that direction.

Acceleration accompanies a change in the vehicle's speed. In other words, if the speeds at two instants are different an acceleration has occurred. This may be calculated from the speeds by subtraction. Conversely, and this is the order adopted in inertial guidance, speed may be calculated from acceleration by a process of addition—the opposite of subtraction. The method of continuous addition called integration is used.

Similarly, speed is accompanied by changes in the vehicle's position. So, just as acceleration is integrated to give speed, the speed is itself integrated to give position.

A single accelerometer mounted lengthwise in a vehicle can only sense motion in one direction at a time—north-south or east-west, for example. Furthermore, it must be kept level, or otherwise compensated, to remove the effect of gravity. Useful information is available from such an arrangement but complete inertial guidance systems need two more accelerometers in order to detect motion in all directions. One of these points to the side and the second points downwards, at right angles to the others like the corner of a cube. The three mutually perpendicular accelerometer directions are called axes.

A support for the accelerometers, called a stable platform (or inertial platform), ensures that the three axes point constantly in set directions, isolated from the changes in attitude of the carrying vehicle. For this purpose, the platform is mounted in gimbals. These are bearings which allow almost perfect rotational freedom about the platform.

Three gyros are fixed to the platform in order to maintain its alignment with the Earth's north and east directions, or with the Sun and stars in the case of a spacecraft. If the platform tilts out of alignment for any reason, the gyros sense the movement and activate motors which return the platform to its original position.

The stabilized accelerometers, then, provide the speeds and distances along known fixed axes, while electrical instruments mounted on the platform gimbals measure the vehicle's pitching, rolling and turning. These quantities are used to guide the vehicle to its correct flight path and destination without aid or interference from any external source.

Sadly, no measuring instrument is perfect; all to some extent suffer from errors. The accuracy of an inertial guidance system is almost totally dictated by the sensitivity of the three gyros. Numerous small imperfections, which cannot be removed from the gyros during manufacture, cause the gyros to wander, or drift, thereby tilting the platform out of the desired orientation.

The resulting inertial guidance errors are very complicated but they can be reduced by ingenious alignment techniques, and good systems navigate accurately to within a few miles for many hours. Additionally, some applications of inertial guidance employ position and speed references from external navigation aids to correct the guidance errors.

Direction finding

Most aircraft still carry Automatic Direction Finding (ADF) equipment for finding their position in areas where there is poor coverage by other systems. They use a simple loop aerial which picks up transmissions from radio beacons. The loop picks up the strongest signals from stations which are at right angles to it, so it can be used to find their direction.

An improvement on this very simple system is the VOR or VHF Omnidirectional Range. VOR transmitters radiate a VHF radio beam which rotates in the same way as the light beam from a lighthouse. It does this 30 times a second, while transmitting a signal which varies at 30 Hz, so that each rotation of the beam corresponds to a single cycle of the transmission. Another transmission, which does not rotate, is sent out also at 30 Hz arranged so that the two are in phase when the rotating beam points to magnetic north, on which all navigation systems are based. Equipment on the aircraft is tuned to the VHF transmission, and receives the two signals which will be out of phase to an extent which depends on their direction. By coupling this direction information to the autopilot, the plane will fly automatically to the beacon. VOR beacons are located at suitable inervals along established air corridors.

Distance Measuring Equipment (DME) and Tactical Air Navigation (TACAN) are also available on much flown-over routes, and use airborne interrogator-receiver equipment. Simple DME systems transmit a signal to a ground radio beacon, automatically triggering a reply signal. The time interval between the original transmitted pulse and the reply is directly related to distance and is read off by the receiver in nautical miles. TACAN is a military form of DME and normally gives the beacon's direction as well as its range.

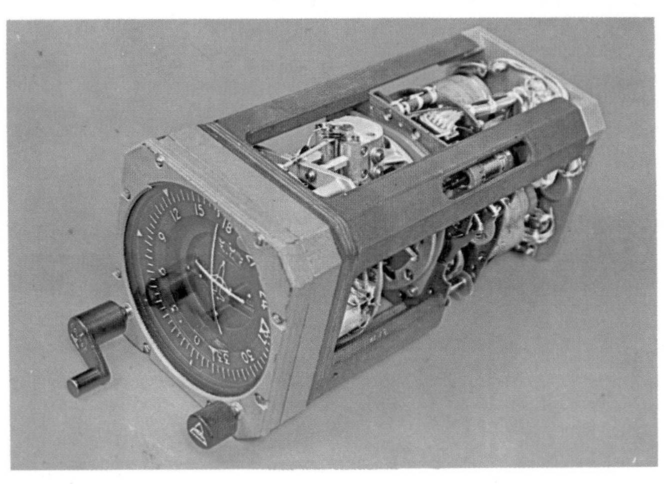

Left top: a flight director system. The horizon director is on the left, the course director is on the right, and the inclinometer is at the top between the dials.
Left: a Bendix course director indicator. The moving coil instrument movements are in the front half, the servos in the rear.

TACAN is also used air-to-air to give range and direction between suitably equipped co-operating aircraft. Ranges of DME and TACAN are typically 200 miles (320 km).

Landing

Near an airport are the ILS (Instrument Landing System) beams used in air traffic control. Equipment on the plane uses the ground-based localizer, marker and glide path transmitters to guide the pilot to the airport and help in the landing procedure. Outer, middle and inner marker beacons give the distance from the runway threshold, and glide-path signals provide guidance on the correct angle of descent. The airport localizer beacon is picked up some 20 to 30 miles (30 to 50 km) away and the aircraft approaches to start the landing run at an altitude of some 2,000 ft (600 m). When the glidepath signal is picked up the pilot follows this down, his progress being indicated by successive marker beacons. Visual and audible indications are given on the sequence of events and of any corrective action to be taken.

Weather radar

Most large commercial aircraft are fitted with weather radar which provides the flight crew with a picture of cloud formations and other atmospheric disturbances ahead. The equipment consists of a forward looking radar mounted in the nose of the aircraft and a display unit in the flight deck. The radar scanner can be tilted downwards to provide ground mapping as an extra navigation aid when crossing coast lines, estuaries or other prominent geographical features. For weather radar, ranges of up to 300 miles (480 km) are possible. Good interpretation of the radar picture depends to some extent on the skill and experience of the crew.

Military electronics

Electronics has revolutionized air warfare as much as the jet engine. Its first applications were in the field of flight safety and accuracy, in which radar and miniature computers helped to take the load of such tasks from the aircrew, giving them more time for basic decision making. With performance figures for aircraft climbing so fast, it was thought in the mid-1950s that what was needed was a weapon that could think for itself. The homing missile with its miniaturized computer 'brain', could be locked onto its target and fired, leaving the pilot of the aircraft to break off the action. So great were the hopes pinned on the missile that the end of the manned aircraft was foressen. As is always the case in such matters, however, electronic counters to the new weapons were swiftly developed, and the electronic warfare race was on. Crew were still needed in aircraft, it was realized, for only men had the necessary mental equipment for high-speed intuitive decision making.

With the realization that both crew and extremely sophisticated electronics are necessary, and the design of aircraft to meet the new requirements, we have entered a new era of air warfare. No longer do we talk of combat aircraft, but rather of aircraft as weapons delivery systems, with the avionics (airborne electronics) as important as the airframe itself. The combination has indeed revolutionized the science of air war, as amply demonstrated in the American involvement in the Vietnam conflict and the last two wars between the Arab states and Israel. In these wars the gun has made something of a comeback, albeit in an advanced form with radar and electronic aiming aids, but the main emphasis has been on the missile, for both offensive and defensive purposes. And as much as in anything, in present day aircraft, defence against the missile lies in electronic counter-measures to confuse the attacking hostile 'brain' as in performance and manoeuvrability. It is worth noting, moreover, that offensive loads can now also be delivered with a degree of accuracy undreamed of in World War II. Free fall bombs are placed with pinpoint precision with the aid of radar and computers, and advanced weapons, both bombs and missiles, can be guided onto special targets by a variety of advanced means, including homing onto the reflections of a laser beam shone onto the target by the attacking aircraft, and control from the aircraft with the aid of a television camera mounted in the nose of the weapon.

Electronics have also been responsible for another development, that of all-weather aircraft. In World War II and before, poor weather frequently grounded aircraft, with the result that ground operations were seriously affected. But now radar can replace the pilot's eyes, and computers can react with the speed necessary to keep the aircraft flying in even the most inclement conditions, leaving the pilot and crew to make the fighting decisions. Allied to this field is that of very low level operations. Whereas in World War II a pilot flying at treetop height would have had to concentrate on avoiding obstacles, present day machines can be flown at very high speed 'on the deck', with the computers flying the aircraft on the basis of the information fed to them by radar looking forwards, downwards and sideways. This is of particular importance in strike operations, where high speed at low level is of considerable importance in evading enemy detection and countermeasures, and securing tactical surprise over the target.

As may be imagined from the above factors, aircraft have increased enormously in cost, complexity and weight since the end of World War II. The avionics often cost as much or more than the basic aircraft. Even Russia and the United States are finding it hard to finance the numbers and types of aircraft needed by their air forces. This cost factor has therefore gradually led to the erosion of the old differentials between aircraft as fighters, bombers or other types of military aircraft. Today aircraft have to be capable of doubling or tripling their roles to make them more cost effective. With the exception of the large strategic bombers employed by the superpowers, aircraft have to operate as strike aircraft with conventional or nuclear weapons, reconnaissance machines, fighters and even trainers. With even the superpowers having to do this, it is understandable that other countries are finding the burden too heavy on their own. Thus have been born in the 1960s and 1970s international projects such as the British-German-Italian Multi-Role Combat Aircraft (MRCA), the British-French

Above: a US Navy McDonnell Douglas Skyhawk A4E about to take off from the USS Forrestal. *Such an aircraft is packed with military electronics. Opposite page: the Aerospatiale Caravelle* Sven Viking *prepares for take-off.*

Jaguar, and the British-French Puma and Gazelle helicopters. It seems almost certain that if aircraft continue to increase in size and complexity, and therefore in cost, multi-national co-operation will become the norm. The basic airframe, the engines and a proportion of the avionics will be standard, with individual national buyers finishing the aircraft to their own particular requirements.

The three main types of military aircraft in use today are the manned bomber, the multi-role support aircraft and the 'radical' types such as the Harrier 'jump-jet' and gunship helicopters. It is likely that the manned bomber will continue as a first-line weapon for some time to come. Although not as potent in destructive potential as surface- or submarine-launched intercontinental ballistic missiles, aircraft still have the capability of great destruction with thermonuclear weapons, and also considerably more flexibility than guided weapons.

AIRPORTS

At one time, airports were located in convenient fields as close as possible to the city they were to serve, without much regard to environmental problems. It was difficult in those days to envisage the growth potential of civil aviation and the complexity of air services and airports to handle them. Today, the spread of cities and the greater importance of air travel mean that airports have to be planned to meet a careful balance of aviation and environmental needs.

A major airport requires a good highway and rail links with the city centre. Passengers should be able to park their cars within a short walk of the berth in which their airliner is docked. They do not want to have to park a long, confusing walk away, struggling with baggage through rain, traffic and disembarking passengers to the terminal building.

In between the car and the airliner, the airport, airlines and control authorities like immigration and customs must provide the embarking passenger with, in order: ticket and check-in counters, passport checkpoints for international flights, concourses with lounge and general consumer services such as duty-free shops and a pier connecting the terminal with the door of the aircraft. The disembarking passenger wants to get out of the airliner as quickly as possible and either leave the airport or get to another berth to catch a connecting airliner. If he is catching a connecting flight he wants to get to the appropriate berth—though it might be literally miles away—without a long walk and without bothering about his baggage. All this has to be accomplished without mixing inward and outward-bound passengers.

To these passengers' requirements the airport designer must now add those of the airlines. An airport like London's Heathrow employs about 50,000 people whose jobs include dealing with passengers and their baggage, servicing and refuelling aircraft, air traffic control and so on. Nearly as many workers may go into and out of an airport each day as passengers. They want car parks and offices, and separate access for service vehicles to the airliners.

JAL
JAL
JAL

JAPAN AIR LINES

The aircraft themselves make great demands on space. Runways 12,000 ft (3.7 km) long and 150 ft (45 m) wide are required for modern commercial jets. Ideally there should be at least two runways, each aligned with the prevailing wind and with turn-offs and taxiways for the least taxying time to and from the terminal.

A modern airliner berth requires a terminal frontage of at least 300 ft (90 m). During rush hours at big airports there may be as many as 50 airliners in dock. This represents a frontage of some three miles. If each airliner has 350 seats it may generate a hundred cars; half a dozen airliners a day may dock in that berth and so parking for 600 cars has to be found near each berth.

The aircraft also need parking and maintenance space. Planes these days are designed for 'on-condition' or 'on-wing' maintenance, in which replacements for faulty units are simply fitted while the plane is parked.

Airliners have to be 'turned round' as quickly as possible between flights to reduce costly time spent on the ground, when they are not actively earning money. The time between flights may be as little as twenty minutes, during which passengers have to be disembarked, the aircraft refuelled, maintained, cleaned and re-provisioned and the next lot of passengers embarked. These activities have to be carefully scheduled to avoid clashes, or the fire risk of passengers embarking during refuelling.

Fog dispersal

Fog dispersal techniques were studied seriously during World War II to enable military aircraft to land under what would normally be hazardous conditions. Nowadays several systems are in operation, and are found at certain military and civil airports in various countries, but with the development of automatic landing facilities, which do not depend on weather conditions for their successful operation, it is doubtful if they will ever become more commonplace.

The air always contains a certain amount of water in the

Far left: an aerial view of New York's John F Kennedy airport. The curving shell of Eero Saarinen's famous TWA terminal is at right centre.
Above left: the Frankfurt air terminal, in the city centre, allows passengers to check in before going to the airport itself.
Above right: security check at Copenhagen: the metal detector.
Left centre: airports have miles of lights.
Right centre: night scene at Cologne airport.
Left bottom: when an accident happens, the important thing is to get there as fast as possible.

form of water vapour—water in its gaseous state rather than liquid (water) or solid (ice). At a given temperature there is a maximum amount of vapour that the air can 'hold' without it becoming 'saturated' and condensing into water droplets. The measure of water vapour in the air is called humidity (measured in grammes of water vapour per cubic metre of air) and the lowest temperature at which a given humidity can be maintained without condensation is called the dewpoint.

The higher the temperature the more water vapour that can be held before condensation occurs. Colder air is normally 'drier' than warmer air, that is, it contains less water vapour.

When droplets do form, they usually do so around minute 'dust' particles and gaseous nuclei that are always present in the atmosphere. Smog, which is an extremely 'dirty' form of fog, occurs in industrial environments.

Two different approaches in fog dispersal are precipitation and vaporization. Precipitation involves making the water droplets grow in size until they fall to the ground (precipitate). Vaporization involves raising the air temperature until the droplets vaporize.

Precipitation depends on whether the fog is 'warm' or 'cold'—that is, above or below freezing point.

Cold fog generally contains some ice particles and if the fog is cooled further then the ice particles tend to grow. In some conditions, the growth is fast and snowflakes form, which fall to the ground. One way to create this necessary cooling is to introduce an agent such as propane gas, which, when released from pressurized containers in which it is kept in liquid form, absorbs a great deal of heat from the atmosphere in changing to a gaseous state. Propane gas dispensers have been installed at some airports where cold fogs are sufficiently prevalent – for example, Paris (Orly). In Britain such conditions are rarely encountered.

With warm fogs, a technique known as electro-gas

IR FRANCE
Vercors

AIR FRANCE
AIR FRANCE

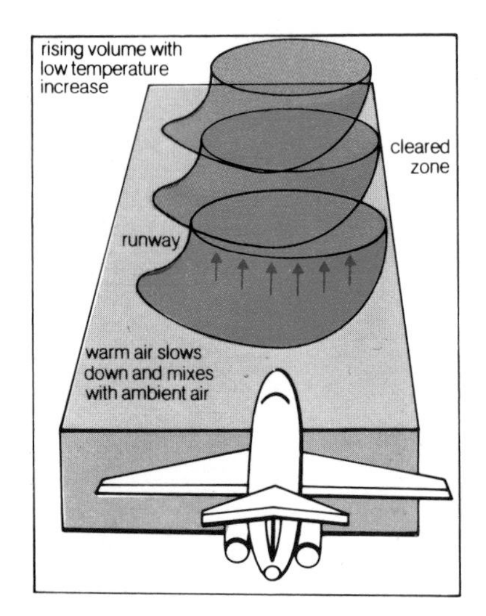

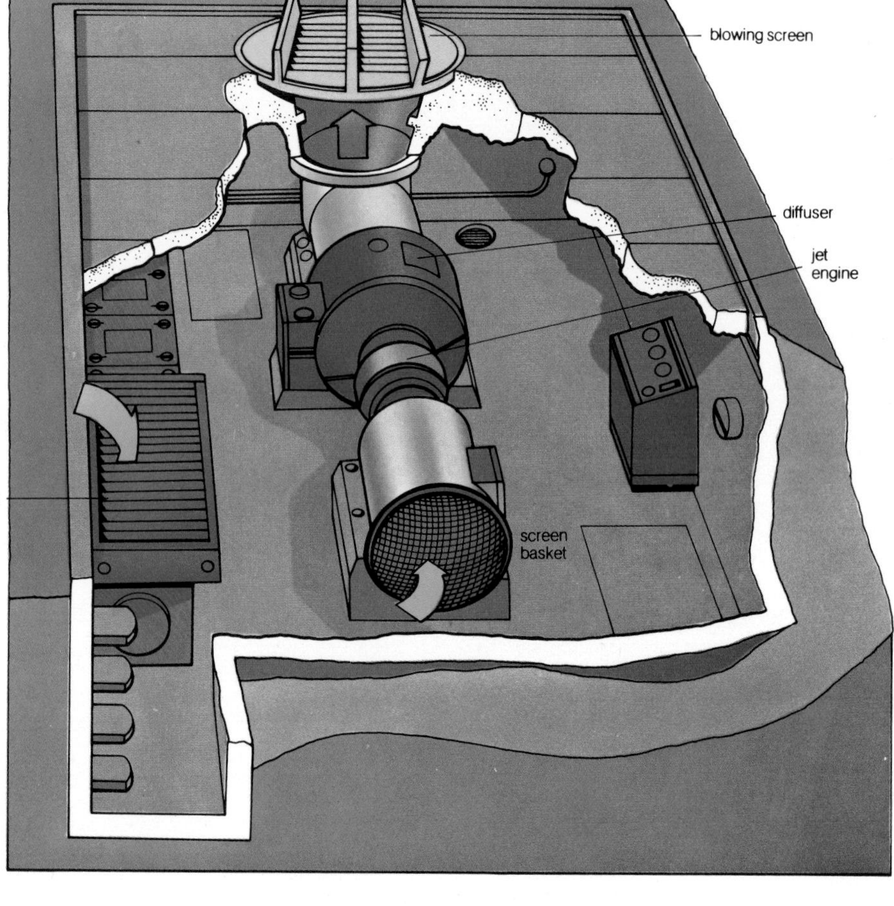

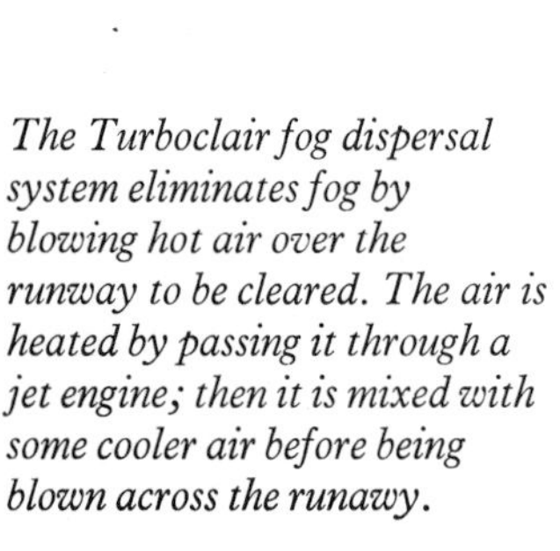

The Turboclair fog dispersal system eliminates fog by blowing hot air over the runway to be cleared. The air is heated by passing it through a jet engine; then it is mixed with some cooler air before being blown across the runawy.

dynamics has been used. This has had a limited success in tropical fog conditions, but the physical principles involved are not fully understood. Electrostatically charged water droplets are projected into the fog. It is assumed that these charged droplets attract other droplets of opposite charge and so 'coagulate' and grow until they fall to the ground.

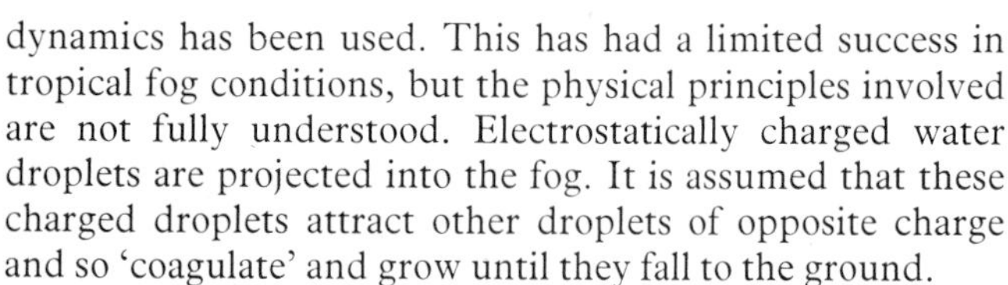

Fog vaporization involves heating the air from 2 to 3°C above its dewpoint so that the water droplets evaporate. Several systems have been devised including petrol [gasoline] and gas burners along the runway, infra-red heaters and heat exchangers (which make use of the latent heat of water vapour), but none has proved to be satisfactory.

For visibility on modern runways a volume of fog 300 ft (90 m) wide, 7,000 ft (2,100 m) long and 200 ft (60 m) high must be cleared. It has been estimated that, under the worst conditions, this would require 2,000 MW (2,000 million watts)—roughly the entire output of one of the largest power stations in Britain. Under less demanding conditions, it is possible to obtain clearance using smaller amounts of power.

At both Orly and Charles de Gaulle airports in France, for example, jet engines have been buried alongside one of the runways. This system, known as 'Turboclair', is the only operational fog dispersal system for civil use.

Other schemes have been developed which 'dry' the air using chemical drying agents. Certain compounds, such as common salt (sodium chloride), calcium chloride, sodium alginate and urea have an affinity for water and, when sprayed into a fog, will absorb the water droplets. To achieve clearance in a well defined area such as a runway is, however, a difficult operation because of cross winds – it is a myth that there is no wind with fog. Also, the rate of spraying and particle size must be carefully calculated on the type of fog (that is, the size and density of the droplets).

More attention is now being paid to the dynamics of fog and the physical principles involved. To evaluate these, artificial fog chambers have been built where conditions such as temperature, pressure and humidity can be controlled. Experimental dispersal techniques have been tested under these conditions but have proved difficult to repeat under real conditions.

A recent development is a laser radar system which can measure fog densities at a distance up to 200 yds (180 m) away – something which was very difficult to achieve before, at any distance. Lasers have also been used as anemometers. These operate in the infra-red region and can see through fog and measure wind speeds between 100 and 200 m (328 to 656 ft) away.

A quantity more easily measured automatically is visual range in fog. This is achieved with a transmissometer, which measures how much light is transmitted over a certain distance through the fog by using brightly lit black and white strips and a pair of photoelectric cells to measure the contrast between them. Many airports have been equipped with these to determine, for example, the distance at which a pilot should be able to see the runway lighting pattern.

INDEX

Pictures supplied by:
Air France: 116/117
Alphabet & Image/BAC: 15T
British Aircraft Corporation, Preston: 53; 83TR; 89
British Airways: 82/83c
Colorific: 11r
Colorific/Diana Hunt: 10c
Colorific/John Moss: 101
Cranfield Institute of Technology/Photo: John Goldblatt: 109t
Decca Navigator Co Ltd: 106/107
EMI: 89
Ferranti: 108
Flight: 44L
Giraudon: 23b
John Goldblatt: 52r
Tim Graham/Transworld: 10b
Susan Griggs/Adam Woolfitt: 98
Imperial War Museum: 22; 28/29; 30t & b; 31tl & tr; 33; 35b; 38t; 42t; 43t & b; 52l; 60l
Israeli Government Press Office: 88/89
Japan Air Lines: 112/113
Keystone: 105t; 105bl & 105br
Lockheed: 76t
The Mansell Collection: 18/19; 20t
John McClancy: 55; 81b; 84l; 94
McDonnell Douglas: 110
Photo Researchers/Russ Kinne: 90r
Photri: 75t; 81c; 86; 87b; 100; 115tr; 115b
Popperfoto: 12
Port Authority of New York and New Jersey: 114/115
Rolls Royce Ltd: 95
Royal Aeronautical Society: 6/7; 21; 23t; 59t
RHL: 47
RTHL: 74l; 90tl & 90tr
SAS: 111
Science Museum: 16/17; 19t (24L and 26t: photo Hoffman); 74r
Shorts: 54t; 56t
Smiths Industries Ltd: 107
Snark International: 8/9
Staatsbibliothek: 54b
John Taylor: 70/71
US Navy: 93b
US Signal Corps.: 34t
USAF Official Photo: 26b; 64t
Roger Viollet: 20b
Zefa: 115tl; 115cl; 115cr